THE LIFE OF A GYM SCREW

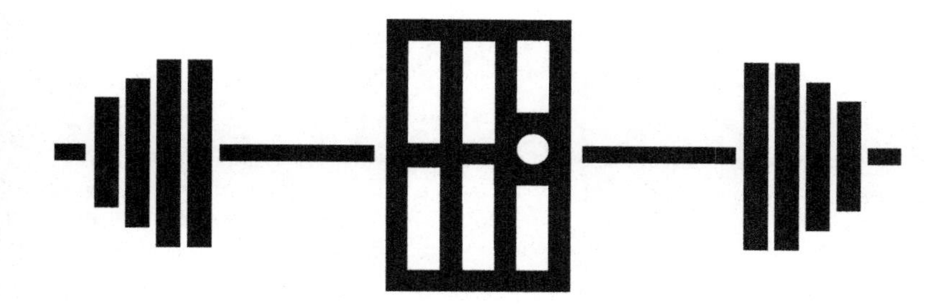

Phil Currie

Cover design by Emma Saunders

Editing, typesetting and publishing by UK Book Publishing

www.ukbookpublishing.com

ISBN: 978-1-916572-33-1

THE LIFE OF A GYM SCREW

CONTENTS

Prologue	*1*
The early years	*3*
HMP Hindley May 1991, the start of Training	*13*
Parkhurst Prison and Moving to the Isle of Wight	*18*
PE COURSE Pre-selection	*41*
Back down to earth with a bang	*49*
The Evil in their eyes 1	*53*
Charlie Bronson and the unfinished fishpond	*58*
PE Course	*65*
Back to the big house	*80*
The SSU (special secure unit)	*81*
Shadowing on my first course	*92*
The great escape	*106*
Long Lartin, starting again	*132*
Football at Long Lartin	*148*
The funerals	*157*
Midway message	*163*
The Hitman Victor Castigador	*180*
The magic room	*184*
Kick off in the Gym	*192*
The Evil in their eyes 2	*198*
The orderlies	*210*
Standing up to cancer	*233*
First ARM meeting with Governor Cartwright (Mr Angry)	*257*
ARM meeting number two	*269*
Dive, dive, dive	*272*
Mont Ventoux and the return	*282*
Calm waters	*285*
I predict a Riot	*300*
Whistleblower	*322*
The Hard Men	*347*

Comboshot.com

PROLOGUE

Radcliffe

Before we get into the early years, let's clear up why I wrote this book. Many people I've worked with over the years often say, 'Phil, you should write a book.' My response was always to laugh it off. After I recently received a cancer diagnosis for the second time, my good friend and ex-colleague Tom Hill, who recently published his book 'Life In The Max', again suggested it to me, and once more, I laughed it off.

Having received a stage four incurable diagnosis, I faced my own mortality, making me contemplate writing a book. Not to make any money, win any friends or create enemies. I thought it might be something nice for my children, grandchild, and future grandchildren as a keepsake. It's an accurate account of numerous first-hand experiences I had working in three prisons over a span of nearly thirty years. HMP Parkhurst and HMP Long Lartin were, at the time, both high-security prisons that housed some of the most notorious prisoners ever to be held within the prison system in England.

Many people who have known me over the years and who decide to read this book may wonder why I have mostly left my personal life out of the story. In short, that would be a book in its own right. As I said, I'm not out to make any enemies. I would say I've hurt many people along the way, including myself at times. I want to apologise if you're one of those people and if your memory of me isn't fond.

I want to dedicate this book to my long-suffering wife, Sarah. She's put up with me for all these years. We got there in the end. And to all my wonderful children, of whom I'm incredibly proud. Emma and my grandson Morgan, Sheri, Jack, Henry, and Dolly. My lovely mum, Brenda, lovely sister Julie, and brothers Les and, in particular Mark, who has been a tower of strength and support during my battle with cancer. My dearly missed friend Jay Shoker (RIP), Bealey and all the fantastic staff I've worked with and met over the years. Finally, Nick Dyer for all his help getting these memories out of my head and into a book. Now, let's get on.

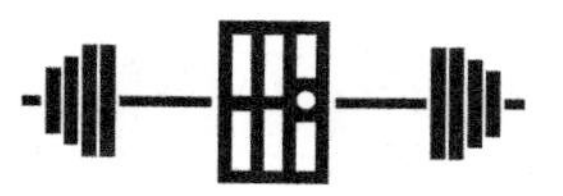

THE EARLY YEARS

I was born in 1965 in Radcliffe, a suburb of Bury famous for black puddings. It was an industrial town with plenty of pubs for a small place and large mills, one of which was a big cotton mill named Setacrapes, where my dad, Les Currie (God rest his soul), worked for most of his life. Setacrapes and a large paper mill provided most of the employment for the town. In Thatcher's Britain, this for many meant surviving on a two-day week. Radcliffe, at a later date, became part of Greater Manchester.

Later, when I was eighteen or nineteen, I would join my dad in working in the noisy hot mill. No wonder Dad's hearing wasn't very good!

My mum worked in a bakery and the local paper shop, which was handy when we were younger and seeking pocket money.

My lovely sister Julie didn't hold down the job of 'paperboy' too long. She had a fear of dogs borne from one day when a relatively large greyhound tried to mount her whilst playing outside. I recall my dad running out of the house after hearing her screams and seeing the horrified owner looking on. Dad shouted, "Get the fucking thing off her; she'll be having puppies."

Julie never had puppies, but there were other consequences from that day. When delivering the papers, if there was any sign of a dog, she'd immediately throw the paper over the gate into the garden. She was the fastest paper girl in the West. But not everyone was pleased with her work ethos. After a few complaints, she was laid off – after a short spell of paying me to do her round for her. We lived and grew up on a council estate with lots of roaming dogs; I can't believe Julie didn't grow up to be an Olympic sprinter!

We had a fairly strict upbringing, with my mum being the chief disciplinarian. We never had a great deal of money as a family. But then nobody did on our estate.

I spent most of my childhood playing football on any bit of spare grass my mates and I could find. We would organise football matches against neighbouring estates. Or in the enclosed yard at the local youth club. If we weren't playing a sport, we would build bogies, homemade go-karts made from wood and pram wheels.

My life revolved around sports though. I would walk to school early to play football in the schoolyard, where a form of murder ball would take place. Everyone went into the yard. Children of all ages would aimlessly kick a football into the air, and then everyone just kicked the shit out of each other to get a touch. If it weren't a football, it would be a tennis ball. My legs were battered and bruised, all for just a couple of kicks of a ball. There weren't any goals, winners, or losers, although you felt like a loser if you got lots of kicks by the end of the play but not a single touch of a ball.

We would also regularly play football with a tin can.

It wasn't Clarks shoes

As I said, we weren't well off as a family. Looking back, one fond memory we all have was going to Bury Market for new shoes. The shoe stall was piled high with random shoes and a bit of cardboard on the floor to try them on. All the shoes were tied together in pairs by a piece of string. It was very different from going to Clarks.

One day we were at the stall with my mum, sister Julie, my older brother Les, and myself. Julie and Les had chosen their shoes. It took me a while to find some I thought I could play football in. As I'd been told to try a hideous pair of multi-coloured platform-heeled ones, my mum decided to call time on the proceedings. Our old shoes were left on the stall, and we were marched off around the corner, where Mum produced a pair of scissors and cut the string.

I won a few headers in the playground but only a few kicks of the ball. I tried my best to kick my way out of those shoes dragging them along the floor to scuff them, but the things were bloody bombproof.

Growing up we had one bike between us, so we would take turns going around the block. My brother and sister would go for a bike stroll around the estate. I, on the other hand, rode around the block, pedalling like crazy to go faster than the last time. I was always looking to compete in anything and everything I did. I hated losing at anything. Board games, marbles, football, or just a bike ride around the block. It improved a little with age but stayed in my mindset totally. Unbeknown to me then, I would be grateful for it in my future dream job. When we were playing any game, my mum often secretly said, "just let him win," to keep the peace.

The first jobs

On leaving school at the age of just turned fifteen, like most boys that age, I wasn't sure what I would do with my life.

Unfortunately, opportunities were slim; many of my friends and the boys I'd played football with and against had started to disappear to Borstal and young offender prisons. They would talk briefly about their experiences; many complained about being 'inside,' and others saw it as a bragging right. One close friend from school was convicted and serving a life sentence for murder.

Borstal, in those days, was designed to be a cold sharp shock that supposedly stopped people from wanting to get into trouble. It's still debated today whether it worked or not. My thoughts on the subject are brief. It may have worked for some, but not for many.

After a few trips to the job centre, I found a youth training scheme (YTS) at a local lampshade factory. I was one of only a few men working there, along with a chap called Wozza, who remains a great friend today. The job placed me on a deep learning curve. I was working and associating with grown women who flirted with you at every opportunity, especially me. They found it hilarious watching as I went red with embarrassment every time. It was part of the job I grew into though. I started to enjoy the experience and found myself at home chatting to ladies about anything and everything,

I progressed from working in quality control with a lovely older lady, Val, to working in the warehouse, riding around on a forklift truck for much of the day. After just over a year, at twenty-three pounds a week, I was taken on full-time, only to be made redundant six months later.

In the mill

My dad managed to get me a job in the cotton mill where he worked. When I was younger, I would go to the door and ring the bell to speak to Dad. He'd take me in a couple of times to get a drink out of the machine. I always thought I'd hate to work there, yet here I was. You couldn't hear anything; voices were all drowned out by the overpowering noise of the machinery.

I soon learnt the ropes, and in no time, I was doffing (taking bobbins off) machines and getting them back loaded up and running quicker than anyone who worked there, including my dad. That competitive edge again, I saw everything as a race or competition. I started doing regular nights after two years, which suited me. I could get to the gym during the day and night-time in my breaks; I found a giant water pipe where I could do chin-ups on and off for most of the shift.

I was still playing football for a local team and training all week. The team I was playing for had reached the semi-final of the cup. It was a midweek fixture, and I was working nights so I couldn't play. After a few pleas from my teammates, I agreed to sneak out of work. I rushed to get all my machines up and running and ran off to play the game, scoring the winning goal to secure a place in the final. I returned to work, and everything was running smoothly. Phew!

Bang to rights

The following week I was called into work by the boss. I was quick and good at my job, 'but surely, they're not making me a foreman already'. I entered his office and on invite took a seat, and he asked me how the job was going. He was also a keen sportsman and into his rugby. I'd spoken to him a few times about it. He asked me if I was still playing football. At first, I wondered where he was going with this, and then he asked about last Tuesday and if my shift had gone ok. The penny dropped, and I said, "yeah, fine". He produced a local paper from under the desk, asked how I'd scored the winning goal and completed my shift. I put my hands up, bang to rights. But he was brilliant about it to be fair and made sure I got off for the final, which we won.

One thing I missed from working in the lampshade factory was the daily interaction with females and the flirting; quite a few ladies worked in the mill, but most worked day shifts.

A hundred yards down the road was what had become my local pub. On our breaks, we would stand at the front door of the mill to escape the noise and heat for a bit. On nights I soon learned that taking my break around 11:30 pm would coincide with throwing out time at the pub—an excellent opportunity to chat with the girls and ladies on their way home. I often had a lot of work to catch up on at the end of my break.

Married in a flash

In what seemed like a blink of an eye, I'd met a girl from Burnley on a lads' trip to Rhyl in Wales. Before long, we were expecting our first child, Emma, and were moving to Burnley.

Burnley was only 26 miles away, but it was like another world where everyone spoke an alternative language. I got a job in another mill; a weaving shed called Perseverance (the clue was in the name), where we wove Parachutes. If anyone out there jumped out of a plane with anything I wove, you have my sincere apologies. I wouldn't have risked jumping off the kerb.

"Has tha seen thoil?"

The weaving job could have gotten off to a better start. The guy showing me the ropes asked me to bend under the loom and tell him when I could see thoil. He turned the handle of the loom for what seemed like an age; he just looked at me, going red in the face.

"Has tha seen thoil?" he asked in an angry tone. He turned red when I replied, "There's no oil coming out of here, mate." Anyone from Burnley will know that thoil means hole. As in the saying, 'put wood in thoil,' for close the door. It wasn't the only occasion I suffered from the language barrier. As the song goes, 'communication let me down'.

At the time, I had a boxer dog, and one lad with three boxers often stopped me asking if my dog liked to 'farrrt'. I had him down as a weirdo until weeks later; he asked me if I ever wanted to 'toughen' my dog up a bit they could 'farrt' together. The penny dropped; he was saying fighting with the Burnley accent.

The job wasn't for me. I hated every minute and discovered what waking up and dreading work was like each day. All I can liken it to is seeing a magician on TV keeping those plates spinning; that was me; one loom would be sorted, I'd move on to the next one, and before I knew it, the red light was back on… which usually indicated a massive fray at the rear of the loom. My plates never got spinning.

Becoming a dad

My first daughter Emma was born in Burnley, and soon after, my second daughter, Sheri. I knew I couldn't hold down the weaving job much longer. In truth, only flirting with my female boss had kept me in the position for so long. Now with a young family to support, I needed to find something else.

Thankfully my mate Wozza from the lampshade factory came up trumps and got me a job delivering cars nationwide. I loved it.

It was a relief to be back enjoying a job and working with some great people. We travelled everywhere, delivering cars. It was also a great experience working in customer service, delivering to directors of large businesses etc.

I'd often drop a car off in places like Aberdeen, London, Wales, and if there wasn't a return car to bring home, or if Wozza or the other lads didn't have a drop near me, I'd catch a train back. I soon found that an excellent opportunity to talk to numerous different people.

Admittedly, I would always have a scan of the carriage to see if there was an attractive lady I could sit and chat with. I often arrived home with a phone number in my pocket.

On one trip back from London, I got talking to a Jewish lad who told me he was a trainee magician. I spent the whole journey letting him hone his skills with various card and coin tricks. Whilst I loved the job, I still wanted to play sports for a living, So I kept looking for something in the sports industry and also toyed with joining the armed forces.

Stumbling upon the Prison Service

One day, on my day off, I visited the local Jobcentre to again look for something sporty; on the side was a booklet for joining the Prison Service. I picked it up with no real intention of joining or applying, I skipped to the back of the book, and there was a full page on the specialist roles within the Service; physical education instructors (PEI) and dog handlers… on completion of reading about the PE role, I'd made up my mind. That was the job for me.

I approached the lady at the desk and asked her how I got an application form; I swiftly made it clear I wanted to work in the gym as a PEI. She laughed and said, "steady on, you have to become a prison officer first," or a 'screw' as I recall my friends referring to them. I duly applied and awaited a reply.

The interview

I received a letter in 1989 and had to attend an aptitude test; nothing too demanding, even with my limited education. On completion, half the room exited after having their names called out, and half stayed. I was left hoping for a few minutes, unsure whether I'd passed or failed. It turned out I'd passed and awaited a date to attend an interview.

I attended the interview with my shaved head, which I'd had since fifteen. It was all going quite well till a lady on the panel of three asked why I had a shaved head and did I think it could be intimidating. It threw me for a minute before I replied, "I don't think the people I will be working with or the prisoners will be intimidated by a choice of haircut, would they?"

I received my letter a few weeks later, and the bad news was that I had to wait two years to re-apply! Those two years flew by though. I carried on driving; I bought a few books on interview techniques for the next time I applied. It was all over the press what a mess the prison system was in, mainly caused by overcrowding and inhumane conditions. Two years later, I went through the same process. This time I was successful and was given a date to start my officer training course at Newbold Revell near Rugby.

I was also assigned a two-week induction period at Her Majesty's Prison (HMP) Hindley near Wigan. The induction period would have normally been at HMP Strangways, Manchester, but while I was waiting to join the Service, the prisoners had rioted and spent a month on the prison roof. A few years later, I met Alan Lord, the prisoner that started the riot, although only briefly. But that's for later in the book.

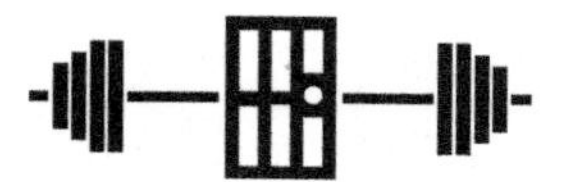

HMP HINDLEY MAY 1991, THE START OF TRAINING

In May 1991, I officially started my career. Every day of my first two weeks at Hindley would commence with a PE session in the gym. It consisted of circuit classes, games of football, gymnastics, weight training and bleep tests – what most in our group described as a 'beasting'. Everyone hated it. For me, it was the best part of the day, and I didn't want it to end. The gym staff were full of character; this is what I wanted. I didn't want the black and white uniform. I just wanted the tracksuit. On the third day, they asked if anyone aspired to be a PEI, and my hand was up in a shot. "Ok, son," said the PEI, an ageing man still in excellent shape. "Tomorrow, you're taking the warm-up."

I planned my warm-up the night before, and the next day had my first taste of being a PEI. It was only ten minutes, but I was in my element. We had to carry a log book and write down our experiences and observations throughout the day. I remember walking across the yard one day, and someone shouted, "Currie!" out of a cell window; to this day, I don't know who that was. I didn't enter it into my log either, just in case.

Newbold Revel officer training course

My two weeks at Hindley passed in a flash, much in the same way at Newbold. To my delight, the first thing every morning was

PE, which consisted again of circuit training and a weekly run in which you had to hit a specific time. The PE staff asked again if anyone aspired to be a PEI, and my hand was up instantly. This time there was a couple of us who expressed an interest. We took warm-ups regularly before any activities, including control and restraint (C&R).

Never be a PEI as long as I've got a hole in my arse

In an interview with one of the PEIs off the training team – I never forgot his name, Reg Pow – he kindly informed me I'd never make a PEI as long as he had a hole in his arse! I remember another NEPO (new entrant prison officer) in my training section, Steve Hamilton (who I was re-acquainted with years later at Long Lartin), asking me how it had gone. I told him what he'd said. Stunned, he said, "He hasn't got a clue; you're made to be a PEI."

I often wonder if Reg believed it or if it was a kick up the arse. In later years, I'd met a few who got told the same, and it put them off going for it. I was never going to let anything or anyone stop me. Well, I'm proud to say the next time I saw Steve after we left training school, I was a PEI and had been for five years. One or two other NEPOs struggled with the daily exercise, and I chose to try and push them along.

Dick Tongue, which do you want first?

I became friendly with a lad from Bolton on my course called Dick Tongue; he was a brash northerner, but we hit it off from the start.

His line with the women was "my name's Dick Tongue; which do you want first"! Many years later, I heard he was dismissed for sexual harassment. I guess she didn't take kindly to his lines.

The course consisted of lots of role-play and interpersonal skills, which mainly meant being able to communicate with people. Dick and I used to share a lift with a female NEPO from Blackburn, a lovely girl who would pick us up every Sunday on the way before heading off back to Newbold. She was posted to Risley. Dick said that you could see Risley from the motorway. But she was adamant you can't! This argument went on for a couple of weeks between them. Dick, as brash as ever, said, "I'll bet ya a fuck." To my surprise, she said yes, being certain she was right. The following week travelling home, Dick looked at me and said, "Phil, what's that over there?" pointing out the window at what looked like a giant factory lit up at night.

"No way," I said. "That's Risley."

She tried to argue, but the vote was two to one, so we were right. And to her credit, she paid up her debt in full!

Training complete; where am I going?

With Training almost complete, we had to put down three preferences. I was told there was no chance of getting any North West Prisons due to Strangeways staff being redeployed on detached duty in those prisons. And it would be a long time before it was back up and running.

This poor picture is the only one I have from the training school. Taken at the passing out parade it gives an idea of what I looked like with hair.

I decided if we were going to move, it might as well be to a nice area to bring the kids up. There were at the time, three prisons on the Isle of Wight. I put in for all of them. Parkhurst, Camp Hill and Albany. Each NEPO was given the slip of paper; I got Parkhurst, and Dick got Long Lartin, as did Steve Hamilton and a couple more from other sections. There were only two of us heading for Parkhurst, me and a Welsh lad called John Harvey.

HMP Parkhurst was a prison that held some of the UK's most notorious criminals.

Parkhurst began in 1778 as a military hospital and children's asylum. And, as I discovered, there were still tell-tale signs of that period. For instance, C wing which housed some of the most mentally disturbed prisoners at the time. Prisoners that Broadmoor, one of England's high-security hospitals, had assessed and deemed incurable.

C wing had tiny cell door entrances, at six feet two; I had to stoop quite a bit to enter. Even with my limited knowledge of prisons, I had heard of Parkhurst before joining and was aware it had held some of the most notorious and dangerous men in the system. On the last week of the course, we were visited by a principal officer (PO) and a senior officer (SO) from the training department, who gave us a brief outline of what to expect. We were told that 'you can forget most of what you've been taught at training college; the real world is different'. We were informed that we would be on a two-week induction for security and key training because it was a high-security prison.

The course finished with a passing-out parade where family members came down for the day to look around and see videos of us carrying out C&R training. We marched out on parade, my mum never really showed too much emotion, but I swear I saw her wipe a tear away.

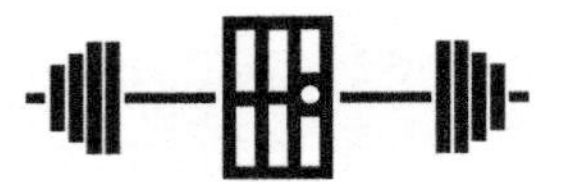

PARKHURST PRISON AND MOVING TO THE ISLE OF WIGHT

Parkhurst's B wing with its five landings.

I'd only ever been to the Isle of Wight once while delivering cars at my previous job. I did a drop-down there with my mate Wozza. From what I remembered, it was a nice place though. Had I been able to see into the future, I'd have taken time to go and check out the prison.

Moving your family with no assistance isn't easy. We stayed in a holiday park near Ryde for the first two weeks. My two girls were living the dream for those two weeks. We later moved in with a retired officer; the kids called him Grandad Don after being there for a while. He was a lovely man, and he helped us settle.

Green as grass

On one of our first days, Taff, John Harvey, and I were introduced to a few staff; the first being Officer Jim Boyce.

His first words were: "you look what you fucking are, green as fucking grass".

John and I just laughed. For years we would say those exact words to each other whenever we met.

Control room

We were put into the control room; I started getting into the gym whenever possible to meet all the staff. I wasted no time telling the PE Staff I wanted to be a PEI.

Being in the control room wasn't really suitable for a new officer; you didn't know the layout of the prison or the prison routine. And worse still, the timings there made it more awkward to get into the gym.

I made it known I wanted to move to a wing ASAP. I didn't have to wait too long for someone to snap my hands off for a swap.

My time in the control room wasn't wasted though; I was on a small team that included two men named Terry Ashdown (the SO), and Alan Randell, an officer with a great sense of humour. They both gave great advice for the future and taught me the layout of the prison and the basic understanding of the prison regime. Most shifts, it was like being on with a comedy duo, but between the laughter, I learned more than I realised.

Starting my log

On introducing myself to the PE staff and informing them of my desire to be a PEI, I was told to start a logbook recording any training I did. Any duties I volunteered for, like refereeing football. I also booked a place on an FA referees' course and a lifeguard award, two prerequisites for going on a pre-selection course. First, I had to complete a year on probation before being allowed on a course. Pre-selection was a five-day course at Lilleshall National Sports Centre in the Midlands.

On a wing and a prayer

I got my move onto B-wing, the biggest dispersal prison wing in England at the time. A dispersal prison is one of a handful of jails holding the highest category of prisoners in the country. Those prisoners would be moved between only this type of prison. This coincided with expecting our third and final child, Jack, in 1992.

A smell you never forget

The first thing I noticed on the wing was the stench, even though all the cells at Parkhurst were single occupancy. I remembered seeing the Strangeways documentary about overcrowding. When you think of three grown men in such a small space, I can only imagine the smell there, all sharing a bucket for a loo.

Morning slop out was the worst; it was also when you had to have your wits about you for many reasons. One reason is that, like many people, prisoners are not the most amiable when they first wake up. You also sometimes get prisoners wound up overnight, whether because they've been kept awake by someone playing loud music or arguing through their cell windows after bang up. Quite often, fights or stabbings happened at slop out.

The smell each morning was one that I'd never be able to put into words; if you want to get anywhere near understanding, continue to use your toilet at home, but don't flush it for a week, then times that by one hundred, and it still won't match it. No cells at that time had in-cell sanitation, so all wings slopped out, defecating into a bucket where it remained until unlock in the morning. Numerous prisoners would wrap their number twos into a parcel and throw them out of their cell windows. The wing employed cleaners, which cleaned the wing and a yard party that would go out cleaning up the parcels; it was better paid than cleaning on the wing, but as you can imagine, there are better ways to earn a living. It wasn't pleasant for the officer in charge of the yard party either. He often had to dodge excrement being thrown at him from a window. All the cells were numbered on the outside, so if you did see it coming, at least you could nick them for it.

I'd rather take a punch

While at Parkhurst on the wing, I witnessed a few pottings (wearing the bucket's contents), and it's the most depraved thing

I've ever seen. Honestly, I'd rather take a smack in the face. Someone I spoke to who had been unfortunate to suffer this act, told me how he could smell it for days, no matter how much he'd washed. Sadly, I also witnessed it done to a few female officers over the years. It was seen as a preferable option to assaulting a lady physically.

Cleaning officer (dogsbody)

After a few weeks on the wing, I was made a cleaning officer. The cleaning officer ran the wing; well, actually, the SO did, but you completed pretty much all the shit jobs on the wing while it looked like everyone else was drinking tea.

Duties included preparing cells for prisoner arrivals and cleaning by an orderly when vacated. Some of the cells smelled worse than slop out. I sorted out the canteen and distributed it, which can also be another flash point.

Canteen day was also a time for many prisoners to settle their debts; some often taxed others. And some claimed protection payments. A prisoner's family would usually send monies into the protector's private savings account on the wing. This act was common; a prisoner paid an agreed amount to stay safe on the wing.

Prisoners had a savings account, and a spends account. Some ran their shops; you could go in their cells to carry out locks, bolts and bars (LBBs) inspection and would discover practically a shop stocked with tobacco, chocolate and phone cards, all used as currency and sold on for huge profit. A PIN eventually replaced the phone card system. I'll cover later in the book that smoking in prison was also finally stopped.

Double Bubble

In prison, if you borrowed an item, it was paid double every day you went over your date to pay it back. You can imagine how that spiralled out of control. I often saw people served up (beaten up) on canteen days. Some would run for cover, either to the segregation unit or go on the numbers. If you went on the numbers, your debt would follow you, occasionally to the next prison. Sometimes, someone on the numbers (the numbers are the VP wing, also known as 'nonces' or 'bacons' placed in the Seg or another wing under prison rule forty-three) bought the debt for a reduced fee, and on it goes.

The other job you had as a cleaning officer was to be in charge of the menu board and sorting the meals for the day; this was a nightmare. 'Where's my tracksuit?' I thought.

The meals were given a number; one might be a stew, two might be fish and chips, and three might be a veggie option. A doctor or a nurse prescribed a special diet for health reasons; often, that was steamed fish. Everyone always wanted the opposite of what they'd requested, especially if it came with chips.

One of my first jobs on the hot plate was to stand next to another officer on the meal board. As a prisoner came through and approached the hot plate, the officer would call 'Smith, number one,' and so on. It was chaos—everyone who came through wanted chips even when it wasn't part of their menu choice. One of the officers on chips made an excuse and left the hot plate, so I jumped on the job.

"When the chips are down"

It was not quite organised chaos; I was serving the chips out on being given the nod by the officer… which I presumed meant it was ok to give a scoop full. Rodger's name was called out—Andy Rodger, a name that will become more significant later in the book.

I was scooping chips up and placing them on plates repeatedly whenever I was given the nod. Andy approached me with his plate. I put a scoop on his plate and stooped to get my next one full. When I looked up, he was still looking at me. "Are you fucking counting them?" he asked. I replied, "I haven't got time to count 'em, mate."

You could hear a pin drop; it felt like everyone was holding their breath. Andy walked out, muttering in his soft Scottish accent; it was the only thing soft about Andy. As he left, an officer told me he couldn't believe I'd gotten away with it. It turned out Andy was notorious for smashing up the hot plate.

Years later, in the gym, I spoke to Andy about the incident and asked him why he hadn't reacted. He told me he didn't think I'd said it in malice; he didn't like what I'd said but knew I wasn't doing it to be a 'dog'. A dog is a term used for a 'screw' that prisoners perceived were bullies or not very nice people. If I'm honest, I worked with a few 'dogs' down the years. I tried to avoid working with them if I could, but it's not always possible. Don't get me wrong; prison officers are made up from all walks of life and backgrounds; I'm sure some didn't appreciate my more laid-back approach over the years.

I found over the years though, that there are many methods of getting someone to do what you want. My approach was always to try talking first. I also found out relatively early, men didn't want to destroy your face if they were laughing. It wasn't always the message that caused problems for staff, but due to how that message was delivered. I got far more satisfaction from getting the same result where nobody got hurt. It wasn't foolproof and didn't work all of the time.

Now retired, I recently listened to two YouTube interviews with James English on his channel, 'Anything Goes with James English'. An interview with Vic Dark, who was at Parkhurst and Long Lartin during my time, and one with Alan Lord, the infamous Rioter from Strangeways Prison; Alan had a short spell at Parkhurst in the SSU after the riot and a brief period at Long Lartin further into his sentence.

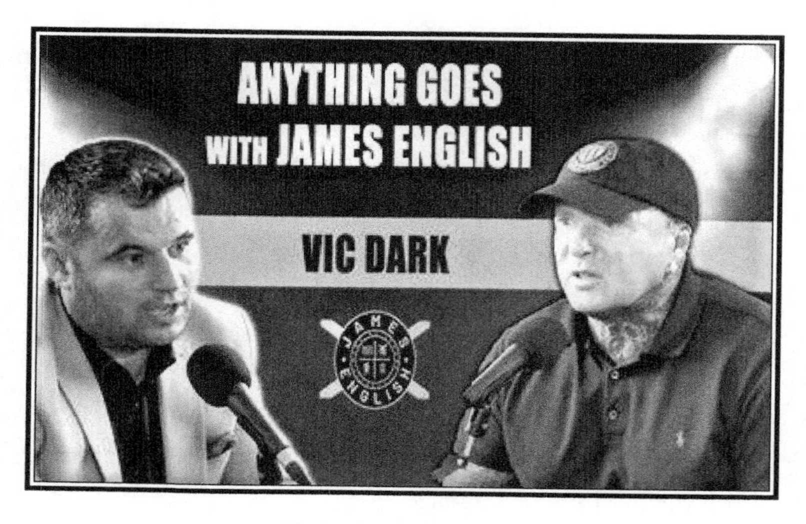

Vic Dark and Alan Lord.

Two things stood out for me when asked, 'What advice would you give to any gang member or villain now to stop them murdering someone?' Vic's answer was, "Always give someone a way out." Give them the opportunity for another way out without losing face. That is a really poignant answer. It mirrored my approach in my time as an officer and a PEI.

Alan was describing his very first day in prison when he was punched in the head by an officer and called a murdering black bastard. Forget about Alan and his history; ask yourself one question: if this was your first experience with a teacher or police officer when you were younger, how would it have affected and shaped your opinion of them?

The other style of prison officer I met many times was one who just said 'no' regardless of the question and regardless of whether the prisoner was entitled to something or not. The 'give 'em fuck all and lots of it' attitude and mentality. I met lots of those officer types. They could sit on a landing for an entire shift and not talk to a prisoner all day. No prisoner approached them or asked for anything because they knew the answer. It meant no real work for them or problems to solve. My mum always taught me if you can't do someone a good turn, don't do them a bad one, and treat people how you'd like to be treated. From day one, that was my approach.

The way I looked at it was – if two officers were gifted a wild dog in a cage to look after in their own way. The first officer treats his dog humanely, talking to it, building trust and understanding, showing empathy and rewarding good behaviour. The second officer shouts at his dog, poking it with a stick a lot; no quality time out of the cage, only let out to do its wee and poo and then puts it back into its cage. If that continued for five years, do you think those two dogs would be the same? The first officer might get bitten once or twice, but his time, effort and patience would be rewarded. I have to say I got my fair share of rewards, fulfilment, and job satisfaction over the years. I will go on to write about some of those experiences.

I can recall countless times in my career when I heard staff say they hated inmates (cons, prisoners, lags); many names have been given to them over the years, and my time ended with governors insisting on calling them simply men. I didn't understand how or why someone would work thirty years or more, hating prisoners. In truth, and in my experience, it didn't matter what title you gave them; it was how you treated people that mattered.

Luckily, being a PEI was a much better base to adopt my approach, although I had many shifts and experiences in the segregation unit environment in my career. It was completely the opposite end of the spectrum, but despite a few raised eyebrows, I kept the same approach.

Don't get me wrong. I admire plenty of staff working there daily; it wouldn't be my choice. Standing out like a sore thumb on the odd occasion was ok, but I don't think I'd have wanted it every day. It would have brought me problems with some staff. Just due to its very nature, the seg attracted staff with a more robust style. PE was the total opposite and generally drew characters that used being role models through sports and having a positive influence on prisoners through education in sports. Some officers found their dream job in the seg; I'd discovered mine in the gym; I discovered it that day in the job centre; I knew then it was the job for me.

Introduction to prison football

Prison football at Parkhurst was always feisty; they played regular inter-wing league games, a few games against outside teams, and the most intense games of all, staff v prisoners.

The pitch at Parkhurst was like no other you'll ever see. The touchline on one side was straight, and the other ran at an angle, which is why we generally played nine-a-side instead of the usual 11. The touchline was a two-foot drop off a brick wall. It would never happen in today's world of health and safety regulations.

As I've said, part of my preparation for pre-selection was keeping a running logbook. I attended the gym before unlock, getting in as early as possible, and at lunchtime, I would work on my weaknesses, gymnastics and Olympic lifting; I would then get the PE staff to sign it off each week with a short progress report. I would also take some staff for circuit classes at lunchtime.

Every Wednesday, the gym would have a 'special needs' group come in for an hour, where we'd do lots of minor games and fun activities and get the full-size trampoline out. It was an excellent opportunity for me to practise on the trampoline when they finished. I also took my young daughters to the prison on the weekend in the evenings and did gymnastics and trampoline practice with them. It allowed me to practise writing lesson plans and improve my teaching techniques for the course.

PEO Gary put in a lot of work with me, and I am forever grateful for that. They had great staff, including (SO) Mick Hind, Graham Wood and Roy Platts (the PO). It was just a different vibe in the gym. I was more confident than ever; that was the job for me. And, as part of my log, I had passed my life-saving and FA referee course.

I was coming in at weekends on my days off to referee football. The PE staff loved it. None of them particularly enjoyed refereeing but I loved it. Despite the grief you received, there was a real edge to games and no shortage of talented players either. I remember the first game where I'd get a few comments from some of the more prominent players, like Parker, a clever player, but mainly all left-footed. They'd say, "where the fuck have they got you from, Northern twat" and "Big useless fucker". Plus, a whole host of other expletives. But I've seen worse in local Sunday league games. I wasn't fazed by it at all. One thing's for sure: I'd rather be criticised out there than be coated (slagged) off for the number of chips I'd dished out.

Perri Terroni was usually a decent keeper and a very quick-witted lad. His team on the day was winning 4-2, but he'd uncharacteristically messed up for both goals conceded. I gave his opposing team a free kick just outside his penalty area. He immediately shouted, "ref, you're having a fucking mare," to which I replied, "maybe so, Perri, but I've still made fewer mistakes than you".

His teammates laughed, and Dennis Arif, who was on his side, and both captain, manager, penalty taker and throw-in taker shouted, "you're not fucking wrong there".

The game finished four-two for Dennis's team, so everyone was happy. The banter in the game and from the touchline was brilliant. The staff counted them back off the pitch, and I took the nets down. Gary had asked me how it went. "I enjoyed it," I said. "Brilliant," he replied. "You can do it every week!"

Staff v prisoners

I had started playing for the staff team and wasted no time organising a staff v prisoners match, the first of many. There was a real buzz all over the wings during the build-up. Many prisoners I hadn't spoken with talked about football, asking who was playing and what positions, and lots of banter.

Match day came, and the pitch was a mud bath, but considering the game was a decent standard, we got to half-time one goal down. Everyone who could be out there was watching. They were giving the cons grief for not being further ahead. They finished three-nil winners. I had been told it had been five years since the staff won a game. Fitness told in the end, but it was a great game.

I lost a few Mars Bars – common practice and a standard bet in those days, but frowned upon today and would be deemed corrupt. Suddenly, prisoners talked to me about the game and sport in general and asked when the next match was. Even prisoners I hadn't interacted much with were commenting and giving me the odd compliment on how I'd played. It gave me a great insight into how sports can break down barriers.

Parkhurst V Peacock Gym

Our SO Micky Hind had organised a Charity Football match against Peacock Gym, a well-known Boxing Gym in East London. Mick asked me if I fancied refereeing it, and I agreed; it was for charity and couldn't be any more fiercely contested than the North V South games we occasionally had. Governor John Marriott also talked about getting a burger van and an Ice Cream Van in for the event. This was leaked to the Press and was all over the national newspapers before the event. I had never met a single number-one Governor in the same mould as John. He'd also recently taken a Prisoner who was due to be released, into his family home, a beautiful big farmhouse I had occasionally visited socially. John took him in whilst they tried to find permanent accommodation for him. This just showed the measure of John; he truly was a remarkable man.

In the build-up to the event, we had a few feisty games that Dennis Arif picked the teams for, in view of selecting his team to play against the visitors, whose team would include Perry Groves of Arsenal Football Club, Terry Hurlock then of Scottish giants Rangers, and Terry Hurlock's brother who was also a decent player.

The day of the Game arrived, and I went down to the gate with Mick to collect the visitors; when we arrived, it was like a circus. There was one enormous man around 7 feet tall, a famous wrestler who had never been seen without his mask in public, so he refused to take it off to go through the search area. After a long-winded commotion, we made our way to the Gym. The week before this Game, Terry Hurlock had been declared injured and missed the Rangers fixture. He informed Mick and me that because of the terms of his contract, he wouldn't be able to play.

The large visiting Party, including the masked wrestler, was located in the Gym and the players started to get changed. Surprisingly, Terry Hurlock had the kit on and said he'd changed his mind and would play but added, no mentioning of him in any write-up. I figure it is now safe to do so.

The Match got underway; I remember thinking that Terry or Perry would never have played on a pitch quite like this one. Just five minutes in, Terry Hurlock, a well-known football hardman in those days, scythed a player down at waist height. I hadn't thought to bring out my cards, thinking it was just a Charity Match; it set the tone for the first 20 minutes until the visitors seemed to get used to the conditions of the pitch and the fact it was like no other. Just before half-time, Terry came off to generous applause from the massive crowd of prisoners watching. One thing is for sure, he wasn't intimidated by his surroundings. Perry knocked in a hat-trick before coming off, and Terry's brother showed he could also put in some meaty challenges of his own. The result finished 2-6 for the Visitors. But more importantly, a considerable amount of money was raised for a worthwhile cause.

Row, row, row, ya boat

I'd started going on the 'concept two' rower the gym had just purchased. It quickly became very popular for both staff and prisoners. Everyone was competing to get the best times. I created a leader board for various distances.

I held the record for the best times for several distances. Again, I discovered how this could give you kudos among your colleagues and prisoners.

I had prisoners approaching me and asking if I was the one who'd posted those times. Some even asked to witness it for themselves. I'd done a one-twenty for five hundred metres.

On one of my volunteer rest days in the gym, I was challenged by a prisoner to prove it, so I jumped on and pulled a one-eighteen. Just like football, it broke down barriers and created talking points.

My logbook was coming along nicely, and I completed my probation. I asked Gary about the chances of a pre-selection, and he put me through a mini-selection. To my great delight he said he was of the opinion I'd pass it. He continued, "We are proud of our record here, we've never had anyone fail!" No pressure then. I subsequently applied for a pre-selection but had to wait around five months.

My first escort

I was called to the SO's office on the wing with one other member of staff and an SO from security. I was informed that tomorrow, I was going out on escort. He said the prisoner's name and number; it was a name I recognised, but I had yet to have a lot of interaction with him. He had a reputation for being a bit of a druggy on the wing. He informed us it was to visit his seriously poorly Grandma. That morning we had the Security brief and paperwork, which included in red writing, 'prisoner to remain double cuffed at all times'. This means his wrists were cuffed and then cuffed to an officer, who was to be me.

Before leaving reception, the Prisoner remarked that the cuffs were too tight, which raised my suspicions. We arrived on a large rough council estate, similar to where I grew up.

Off the cuff

We arrived at the property, and he visited his Nan but didn't spend too long there; many visitors, neighbours etc were in and out of the house. He then started to ask the senior officer if he could have a few minutes alone with his Grandma. The SO told me, "We'll let him have five, then get off." I said, "Well, I'm not coming off the cuff." The prisoner started to throw numerous expletives my way, but I held firm and just said, "if you're going in, I'm coming with you". So I did, and we left soon after.

As we set off back in the van, he kept asking to see his sister quickly; I didn't give the SO) a chance to reply. I just said, "No, the next stop will be Parkhurst." We returned, and all was good. Three weeks later, he'd been out again, someone let him off the cuffs, and he did a runner. I was surprised he was allowed to go after the report I made following his first leave. My gut instinct had proven correct.

Bill The Bomb

Bill The Bomb Williams

I'm often asked who the most fearsome man I ever met in prison was.

Bill the Bomb from Canning Town is always the first name that springs to mind. He could floor someone with a quick flurry of punches or put them out with one. During my time on the wing and in the Gym I witnessed Bill knock out as many as five people at a time. For a big man he was exceptionally quick. Gary and I both got on well with Bill, and to be honest I think on more than the odd occasion it stopped him from putting us to sleep when intervening during his outbursts. You see a difference between a brawler and a trained boxer, although I think Bill was equally capable of both.

Bill had been in the ring with Muhammad Ali and other big names. Even before getting out of black and whites on the wing, I generally got on quite well with him. But you didn't want to be in his way if he was in a mood or had too much hooch (prison alcohol).

At teatime, the SO would pre-warn us: Bill the Bomb has a phone call booked tonight. If you were on the 1s landing, you were dreading the call; it could make or break your shift. One of Bill's trademarks on the wing was to rip the phone and the booth off the wall, especially if he'd had a bad call to his wife. I've seen him go a few times, and it's not a pretty sight. Bill sadly passed away in 2012. RIP.

The Arif Brothers

Dennis and Mehmet Arif, two of seven Turkish Cypriot brothers, were serving 22 and 18 years, respectively, for the armed robbery of a security van while wearing Ronald Reagan masks. The Arifs, from the Old Kent Road area, had reportedly taken over the void left by the Krays and were considered Britain's number one crime family. They were allegedly running the wing and the prison in general. Dennis used to manage the Prison football team then, so I had quite a good relationship with him. We often had Man Utd and Leeds banter. Dennis wasn't the best footballer but did ok, partly because nobody would tackle him.

Mehmet arrived at the prison and was made a gym orderly. Despite his role as Gym orderly, he was quieter than Dennis, and I didn't get to know him as well as the other two. Dennis was one of the three brothers I met at Parkhurst. Dogon was the third Arif Brother to arrive at Parkhurst. I found him to be more amiable and charismatic. I enjoyed many long chats about football, sport, training, etc., especially football. He started to run the prison football team, and you could see he had a way with players.

He owned and managed Fisher Athletic and built the club up, gaining four successive titles and numerous cups during the '80s. He also increased the ground's capacity to six thousand, enabling promotion to the Conference League. It was a trophy-ladened period over his ten years in charge.

Dogon introduced a far more professional manner to how the prison team was run. He would give out training exercises and talk to players about diet and their eating habits, all clues to his experience outside of running a football club. It wasn't just on the pitch that Dogon displayed his people skills. On the numerous occasions that Bill the Bomb ripped the phone off the wall or smashed the wing fish tank to pieces, it was Dogon or Dennis Arif that managed to calm him down. There were a few occasions when I'd been grateful for their intervention. These moments made me realise all prisons are run on the goodwill of prisoners. Some staff may never agree with that, but it's a fact. Strangeways and its Riot was a classic example.

Contract put out on me

I'd been to the Gym early before work but found a note on my keys to report to security before going to the wing. I completed my morning session, entered it into my log, and went to security. I was informed that a prisoner named Cyrus had put a contract on me. They told me it had come from a reliable source and must be taken seriously.

"Ok," I said, "so, has he been moved?"

"No, we're moving you off the wing."

I replied, "Sorry, but I disagree. If he's staying on the wing, then so am I."

I pointed out that putting me on another wing doesn't solve anything, as someone on that new wing could still carry out the contract. I refused to move and stayed on the wing. The only interaction I'd had with this prisoner was to decline his request for a new razor because he wasn't prepared to give me his old one in exchange; they were given out on a strict one-for-one basis. That's a classic example of how relatively small things can get blown out of all proportion in prison.

I was mindful of Cyrus' whereabouts on the wing and any of his known associates for a while. He would often walk towards me with a look of intent or follow me down the landing, despite constantly staring at me to intimidate me whenever I saw him. I just acted normally towards him. I was cautious at slop-out if I was on his landing; as I said, I'd rather take a punch. Thankfully, nothing happened.

A few months later, he returned to the seg after owing a debt.

Alarm bell Bravo

The bell sounded, and my radio went off, 'alarm bell Bravo,' my wing. I could hear the commotion on the landing above. The response is good in a Cat A prison when an alarm bell goes. We'd been having a spate of false alarms, where a prisoner would press the bell, often as a diversion or to mess the staff around. Or simply if someone was pissed off. On several other occasions recently, bells had been pressed or organised by one of the IRA prisoners we had at the time. Often when this was the case, John Kinsella who was convicted for his part in the Warrington Gasworks explosions, would be seen counting how many staff responded on certain days, testing the system for weaknesses.

Intelligence suggested they were plotting an escape or a serious disturbance. The IRA had previously attempted escapes at other maximum-security prisons, Long Lartin and Whitemoor. And, had a failed attempt at Parkhurst soon after I'd arrived.

It was a live bell on that occasion, and Mary McKee had been severely beaten and stabbed. I should point out that Mary is a male prisoner, not a female, but everyone referred to him as a female and by her prison name.

Mary was in a relationship with a man called Crusher on the wing. Crusher, however, always maintained that their relationship wasn't sexual; I think very few believe that. Mary was about five feet seven tall, petite, with flowing waist-length black hair and she minced everywhere she went. Mary was the best cleaner I had ever witnessed in prison, keeping the whole wing spotless. You could eat your dinner off her cell floor. You would need to look out for cockroaches; Parkhurst, at the time, was infested with them.

As the name suggests, Crusher was a large-framed man, powerful and physically fit. At the time, Parkhurst was the only high-security prison in the country capable of carrying out minor operations. Mary was quite dangerous in her own right with a weapon in her hand and had a record of stabbing other prisoners. Five prisoners had set about Mary, and she was severely injured but not critical; the five instigators were moved to nearby Albany Prison. Mary was taken to the prison hospital.

I will cover more about Crusher and Mary later in the book. But for now, to indicate the strength of their relationship, Crusher was released from prison but committed a further crime to be back with Mary. It wasn't unheard of; we had an Old Prisoner called Dickie at Parkhurst that kept the garden pristine, winning many awards. Upon his release, he clearly stated he didn't want to go. He committed another murder to be reunited with the garden.

The brighter news was the birth of our third child, Jack, born a caulk head. The term comes from the island folklore, which says the natives had caulk heads. They could float from Portsmouth to the Isle of Wight without drowning because their heads were full of caulk, so legend says. In truth, Jack will never really be classed as one; islanders believed you had to be the third generation born there to be a real caulk head.

Juliet 1

I wasn't on the chips much these days. More often than not, I carried out the duties of Juliet 1. This was the phonetic alphabet call sign given to the escorting and supervising officer for the gymnasium. Most staff didn't want to do the task for some reason, so I would swap duties to get down to the Gym and fill out my log book for my forthcoming pre-selection.

I still tried to help out the poor old NEPO that had been given the dogsbody job of cleaning officer; to this day, I don't understand why you wouldn't divide the job up a bit. Instead, everything was lumped into the role of cleaning officer, and this job was always given to the sprog (youngest, newest officer). As well as carrying out these duties, you also made the brews (cups of tea) for the other staff. I've never drunk tea, but I lost count of how many I made.

So, Juliet 1 would shout "gymnasium" at the top of his voice on all the wings, starting on B wing and then working around to the Gym, ensuring clearance from the control room beforehand. Another officer on the wing would put the names on the wing roll board to keep a running total on the wing. The reverse would happen on the way back, the officer on the roll board greeted you, and he'd wipe off the names. This had become my daily routine. Once in the Gym, you gave your numbers to the control room and locked yourself in the Juliet Box, a small central office where you could observe the weights area and sports hall.

The gym routine followed a structured weekly programme, so the prisoners knew what activity was on each daily session.

The sessions would last just over an hour; it's worth remembering this routine for what happens later when I write about the escape.

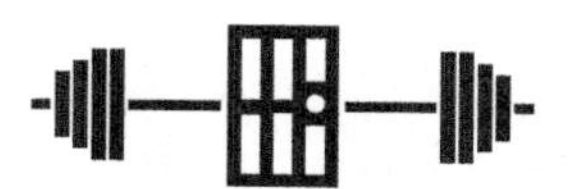

PE COURSE PRE-SELECTION

My big day finally arrived. The start of my pre-selection. Five days at Lilleshall National Sports Centre, near Newport, Shropshire. I had put in loads of hours of preparation, volunteering in my own time to carry out various PE tasks. I'd been given the last words of comfort and advice from the SO Mick Hind and the others: "Don't fucking let us down." I was determined not to let them or myself down.

I had a long journey off the Isle of Wight ahead of me, including an hour's ferry journey. I used this time to go over my fifteen-minute lecture on heavyweight champions of the world that I would have to give to the rest of my colleagues on pre-selection and to the training staff that included SOs, POs and Governor Roy Parkes RIP.

I finally arrived bright and early. The drive to the place went on forever. The building at the end of it was imposing, like a big stately home. As I entered the automatic gates, entering a code given out on the paperwork, I saw for the first time what I was hoping would be my home soon for twenty-six weeks. The course, if successful, is residential Mon-Fri.

You get the badge once you've earned it

I parked my car and went to reception, where I was greeted like a prisoner in a jail reception. Your name and the prison you worked in were requested.

The PEI looked me up and down. He threw me a few plain vests (not PE ones); in those days, they only got to wear the badge (a flaming torch) if they'd earned it. I was told to check in my room and report back to a lecture room downstairs in an hour. Back then, you could only really wear Dunlop Green-Flash trainers for the course; another thing that's changed. I got into my training gear, and Jim Boyce's words rang around in my head as I looked in the mirror; you are what you are, "green as fucking grass".

I had a smile to myself and got my notebook and pen ready.

Phil Hackney (legend)

We gathered in the room; from memory, there were around 20 of us, and we all started chatting. I seemed to be the only one who wasn't from a marine or ex-armed forces background of some kind. My nerves were jangling. This meant everything to me, I knew I didn't want to be an officer for the rest of my days, so I had to pass.

Passing wasn't enough though; I wanted to stand out as the best; Gary's words were, "go up there aiming to be the best," so that's what I was going to do.

Phil Hackney entered the room, and it fell silent. He got the domestics out of the way, fire procedures, and meal timings, and informed us that one of us would be the coordinator in the group. They were Gym orderly for the day.

Shut the door on ya way out

We were all given slips of paper to sign. Agreeing to go wherever posted if successful in completing a PE Course. I signed straight away, and so did nearly everyone else.

One Scouse lad raised his hand and said, "I'm not signing this." Phil Hackney just glared and said, "Fine, give me the form back and shut the door on your way out." The lad stood up red-faced and walked to the door.

Phil Hackney said as he left the room, "And leave my fucking wheel trims alone."

A few, including me, laughed. It was basically like starting the job all over again. At the end of the course, you would be allocated a prison, depending on vacancies.

The course tested various activities, including the following:

- *Gymnastics.*
- *Trampoline.*
- *Football.*
- *Volleyball.*
- *Badminton.*
- *Cricket.*
- *Circuit training (the dirty dozen).*
- *Weightlifting (clean and jerk and two-hand snatch).*
- *Basic anatomy and physiology.*
- *Teaching ability (taking a warm-up, cool down, minor activity, and stretching routine).*
- *And the fifteen-minute lecture.*

The course got underway; it was going well. It was midweek, and we had volleyball and a circuit. I was one of the biggest in the group, so I would have to go some to win a circuit that's all-body weight exercises.

We started the circuit, and I remembered Gary telling me to do it as fast as possible but not to miss a rep or perform any with poor technique. I looked around as I completed a run and saw a few dodgy exercises being performed. I just went as fast as I could, and if I lost count of reps, I made sure I did too many instead of not enough. I finished the circuit and then walked around encouraging the others to complete it, even quietly telling a few about their technique.

After the circuit, we met one-on-one with Governor Roy Parkes, an imposing figure; you could tell instantly he suffered no fools. He told me they were pleased with what they had seen so far, but it was essential to keep it up. At the end of the five days, we were interviewed by all the PE staff who had been assessing us throughout: Terry Standring, Stu McWilliam, John Thompson and last, but by no means least, Phil Hackney. We all delivered our lectures to the tutors and the group. Then we were given our results.

Get in; I've only gone and passed

I was given my final report on pre-selection. No fundamental weaknesses, and to my amazement Phil Hackney had written the following…

'It is of my opinion that this man was top of the crop. Having said that, it was a very poor selection. He will need to maintain the standards displayed; he will then achieve his aims of qualifying as a PEO. Recommended for further training.'

Many years later, I saw Phil at a reunion, and we laughed at his comments – if only he'd stopped at the cream of the crop. The statement meant so much to me because, before the course, everyone said he was the hardest to impress and had a reputation for being ruthless. Later in my PE course, I learned to respect him even more. I particularly enjoyed the teaching aspect of PE right from the start. And Phil Hackney taught me that you could take the most boring subject and make it enjoyable.

Stu McWilliam taught me how to come alive on the gym floor. Bubble, as he would say.

My Pre-Selection Report

NAME CURRIE Philip John

ESTABLISHMENT HMP PARKHURST

EIIR

FIT TO SERVE

PHYSICAL EDUCATION

Surname CURRIE

Forenames Philip John

Date of Birth 01. 06. 1965 Present Establishment HMP PARKHURST

Date to Service 13. 05. 1991 O.T.S. Course Number NR 25

Previous Occupation TEXTILE WORKER

H.M. Forces Experience

Married/~~Single~~

~~Quarters~~/Home Owner

Children

Boy	Age	Girl
1	9 MTHS	
	5 YRS	1
	6 YRS	1

Experience of Physical Activities

Played many sports, Referee Grade 3

Bronze medallion in Swimming.

Particular Interests in PE

Interested in the teaching aspect of the job.

Details of Involvement in Teaching/Coaching

Helped out in Parkhurst gym whenever possible.

Reasons for applying for PE Training

It appeals to me to work with inmates on sporting activities.

Any other relevant information

GENERAL ASSESSMENT

Ability to discuss PE Topics

Very much 'at home' in this situation, confident and knowledgeable.

General Practical Ability

Has displayed a good ability level at this stage in all areas with a 1st class attitude.

Strengths

All round ability, and the motivation, enthusiasm and willingness to succeed.

Weaknesses

No real weakness on this showing.

Acceptability as a Colleague

A very pleasant man, confident in his approach

General Course Staff Comments It is of my opinion that this man was "top of the crop", having said that it has been a poor selection. He will need to maintain the standards displayed, he will then achieve his aims of qualifying as a PEO

Signed [signature] Rank PEO 24.3.

End of Course Interview

Recommended P.E. Training

Signed [signature] Rank PEO 24.3.

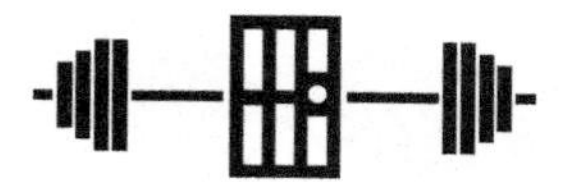

BACK DOWN TO EARTH WITH A BANG

The drive back to the Isle of Wight was just a daze. I was on my way to achieving my goal, but the hard work was just beginning. Anatomy and physiology are a big part of the course, so I needed to get studying.

I was back on shift on the wing the following Monday after my early morning session in the Gym. I was on unlock, and while doing a morning roll check, I heard an officer shouting, "Get health care!" I ran down and looked through the flap on the door, which was still open from my colleague's observation.

Boyle, a prisoner I didn't know much about or had many dealings with, had cut himself up badly, and blood was everywhere. We immediately unlocked him, and I began to administer first aid. Finding no pulse, I started CPR until the health care staff arrived.

We later got told that he'd passed away; it took a while to get those images out of my head, seeing him helpless and the blood splattered everywhere. Fortunately, once it was cleared to clean up, we had orderlies that carried out that job. The place was a very sombre area to work in for a few days. When there's a suicide on the wing, the mood is hugely affected.

A lucky twist of fate

Monday morning had begun like any other day. I was going in early to practise Olympic lifting. Gary was going to go through the snatch balance exercises. A sequence of movements that helped teach the complex dynamic actions. It's probably the most technical aspect of the course, along with gymnastics. Not many prisons still had gymnastics on the gym programme. Many people questioned the authenticity of it still being such a big part of the PE course. I thought it was a significant part of training, and if you could coach gymnastics with all its quick dynamic movements, it would help you in coaching numerous other sports. I'd say it trained your eyes.

I met Gary and we went through his planned sessions; he told me Mick would be in later and wanted to see me. Mick arrived and told me some surprising news: John Darwin, the most recent addition to the PE staff in the jail, had got a PEI job at a new private prison in Doncaster, where he was originally from. John was starting there in a few weeks. Mick asked me if I was interested in agreeing to fill his position. Gary was known for a wind-up, as was I, and I was looking for signs that I was being had. I asked Mick if it was a wind-up, and he produced some paperwork and showed me a letter from the governor agreeing for me to take up a position in the Gym with immediate effect. This news was a massive thing for me; not only did it mean I'd be in the Gym full-time, but it would also mean I wouldn't be on my PE course, not knowing where I would be posted. Mick said they'd all spoken, and they'd love to have me on board.

I had one more week to work on the wing then I was in the Gym. I was going to get my tracksuit, no badge, but I didn't care; I didn't want that 'till I'd earned it. The wing SO could put me on chips for the rest of the week for all I cared. Happily though, they didn't, and I spent most of that time as Juliet 1.

The week passed, and I was given my shift pattern working with Gary. I was happy with that, as he did most of the coaching with me. I also really liked his calm manner and how he communicated with prisoners.

Many of the most notorious prisoners gravitated to Gary in the Gym. He regularly played badminton against many big names like Bill the Bomb. I don't remember seeing Gary lose over the best of three games. Ironically, on the final weekend before I joined, Gary had been refereeing the inter-wing football match when he gave a decision against Bill the Bomb. Bill grabbed Gary by the throat and lifted him off the floor, Dennis Arif intervened, and the game continued. On my first day in the Gym, Gary told me how he was trying to reason with Bill with his hand around his neck. He was making light of it and laughing about it.

I'm in the Gym

I'm in the Gym in a tracksuit at last. I had no end of prisoners asking me for a game of short tennis or badminton all week. Apart from going over to the wings to collect classes, it was full-on sport. On the wing, after a while, those who knew me well would speak to me on first-name terms, and others would call me boss or guv. In the Gym, it was pretty much all first-name terms.

Gary filled me in on the weekend's events, mainly about the football match and the Bill the Bomb Incident. I remember my first thought being, Gary was lucky Bill liked and respected him – he would have been put to sleep with one of Bill's Bombs otherwise. High-profile prisoners would suddenly be happy to speak to you; a lot of that is down to simply wearing a tracksuit instead of the black and white uniform, which still included the peaked cap in those days. Many officers loved wearing the uniform and the cap; some even insisted on wearing their caps, years after they were no longer considered part of the uniform. I couldn't wait to wear mine no longer, except if I had to do escorts or failed my PE Course. But I didn't see failing as an option. I hated wearing a shirt and tie, even as a civvie, which remains true today.

Badminton and weights were on the second session. Gary had received a phone call from the wing to say Bill the Bomb wanted to come across to speak to him. Bill had been given and accepted a two-week ban from the Gym, but after being tipped off by Dogon Arif that Bill would apologise, Gary agreed for him to come over. Bill arrived, and I'd never seen him look the way he did, his head down and looking embarrassed. He duly apologised, and I believe it was a genuine apology.

They shook hands, and Gary accepted the apology. Before Bill left, Gary informed him he was lifting his ban and that he could return to the Gym tomorrow. We discussed the matter, and I agreed with his decision; it takes a big man to come down and apologise in front of all the other prisoners like that. The following day, Gary played and coached Bill in badminton like nothing had happened. I remember thinking this is a different world to working on the wing or anywhere else in the prison.

THE EVIL IN THEIR EYES 1

David Cheesman

Robert Maudsley together with his cellmate David Cheesman killed and tortured David Frances. They barricaded themselves inside a room with the tied-up the child molester. Cheesman was ironically also in Parkhurst on my arrival and was on C-wing, a small specialist wing that housed prisoners that Broadmoor, Rampton, etc., had deemed incurable.

Cheesman had taken a different route to Maudsley and claimed to have found God and repented his sins. He spent all day in his cell studying the Bible. Genuine or not, I don't know; I never really spoke with him. I saw the same coldness in his eyes as in Maudsley. I don't know if he'd found God as he claimed; we'll let God judge him.

In 2004, whilst in HMP Hollesley Bay open prison near Woodbridge, Suffolk, Cheesman, now renamed David Lant, had been arrested on a charge of rape and five sexual assaults on a sixteen-year-old girl. The attack was alleged to have taken place at the caravan he owned with his French wife in Thurston, near Bury St Edmunds, in October 2004. Lant was serving a life sentence at Hollesley Bay open prison near Woodbridge, Suffolk when he was accused of carrying out the alleged five-hour sex attack. He had been allowed out on licence as part of a pre-release scheme and returned to the jail each night after working at the Salvation

Army hostel in Ipswich. Lant / Cheesman got a not-guilty result. The last I heard of Cheesman was he'd absconded from the same prison just a year later and had been arrested in Cambridgeshire. I'm all for people having another chance at life, but you have to ask why he was still in open conditions., it poses the question, would the release of Charlie Bronson pose a more significant risk to the public?

The real Hannibal Lecter?

Robert Maudsley.

Robert Maudsley is one of the longest-serving prisoners in Britain. He has been nicknamed 'brain eater' and 'cannibal', although there is no evidence he ever ate any of his victims. Maudsley killed four men, three of them fellow prison inmates.

One night, while working as a prostitute, Maudsley was picked up by labourer John Farrell. Farrell reportedly showed him pictures of children he had abused, so Maudsley garrotted, stabbed, and smashed him over the head with a hammer. In 1977, at just 24, Maudsley and another Broadmoor inmate David Cheesman murdered prisoner David Francis as I said before. They held his body aloft so the staff could see him through the spyhole in the door.

Contrary to many reports, Maudsley did not eat any part of his victim's brains. Maudsley had made a makeshift weapon by splitting a plastic spoon in half to create a rough pointed weapon.

Maudsley then killed his fellow Broadmoor inmate by ramming it into his victim's ear, penetrating the brain. Inevitably, the plastic spoon blade was covered in gore, allegedly the victim's brains. It is a feature still used by many today, although knives aren't as difficult to come by as they were in those days (more on that later). It is understood the victim's autopsy report disproved the brain-eating rumours. But the nicknames which later arose, 'Hannibal the cannibal' and 'brain eater', have endured.

Within weeks of arriving at Wakefield Prison, Maudsley had killed again – twice. One Saturday morning in 1978, he lured fellow prisoner Salney Darwood, imprisoned for killing his wife, into his cell. Maudsley tied a garrotte around Darwood's neck and repeatedly smashed his head against the walls by swinging him around.

He hid the body under his bed and reportedly tried to get other inmates to come to his cell but was unsuccessful. Instead, Maudsley went out and made his way into the cell of Bill Roberts, whom he attacked with a homemade serrated knife – killing him within minutes.

After the two killings, Maudsley calmly walked into the prison wing office, placed the knife on the table and announced, "there will be two short when it comes to the next roll call".

During his murder trial in 1979, the court was told that throughout his violent rages, Maudsley believed that his victims were his parents. According to his lawyers, the killings resulted from pent-up aggression from a childhood of virtually constant abuse. Maudsley said, "When I kill, I think I have my parents in mind. If I had killed my parents in 1970, none of these people would have died. If I had killed them, I would be walking around as a free man without a care."

He was convicted of both murders and sentenced to life behind bars. However, this was not when he was given the whole life term. Home Secretary Michael Howard later decided Maudsley should never be released.

My first encounter with Maudsley at Parkhurst

From my time working in the control room, I'd witnessed on CCTV Maudsley being unlocked in the Hospital Wing, where he was housed in a special cell with a large lockable hatch that he was fed through three times a day to save having to unlock him. He was a six-man unlock whenever he was taken out of his cell. This meant six prison officers, in complete C&R kit, needed to go to the exercise yard—the kit comprised overalls, a stab-proof vest, boots, leg and arm guards, and a helmet. I would get to wear that gear regularly in the future.

When I was in the gym after my PE course, I briefly encountered Maudsley. He called me over to his door and asked if I was new. He went on to ask me if he could join my class; I informed him I was taking an aerobics class and I wasn't going to do it in C&R kit. I smiled and walked away, but not before recognising a cold look in his eyes that I was to witness a few more times before I retired.

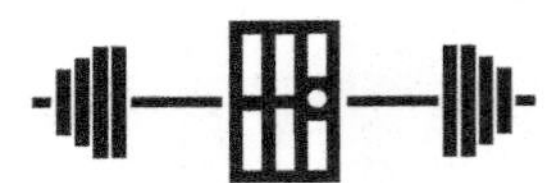

CHARLIE BRONSON AND THE UNFINISHED FISHPOND

Most people who know I was at Parkhurst ask me about Charlie Bronson; my automatic response is to say "I liked him". It always surprises people.

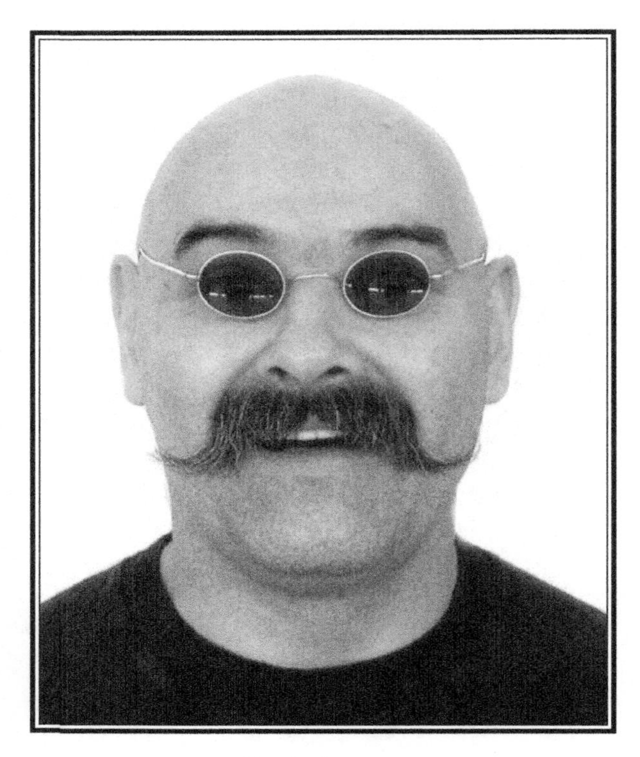

Charlie Bronson.

Charlie was born Michael Gordon Peterson on 6th December 1952. Bronson has also been known as Charlie, Charles and Salvador. After being involved in petty crime and trouble with the authorities for years, Bronson was convicted of armed robbery in 1974. At 22, he was sentenced to seven years in prison. Over his imprisonment, Bronson added more time to his sentence for attacking prisoners and prison officers, and destroying prison property. He was also continuously transferred to different prisons, including Parkhurst Prison in 1976, where he met and became friends with the notorious Kray twins. After his release, Bronson went on to have a short-lived career as a bare-knuckle boxer in the East End of London.

Bronson pleaded guilty to armed robbery in June 1988 and was sentenced to another seven years. It was during that sentence I got to know Charlie.

My first sighting of Charlie Bronson was on M wing. After I'd been called into work one night in response to an incident, it transpired that Charlie had asked the PO on nights to unlock him, complaining of being unwell. The PO got on quite well with Charlie, so he contacted health care to come and see him at the door. Once unlocked, Charlie went on a one-man rampage on the wing; it looked like a war zone when I arrived at the prison with other C&R staff. Eventually, the incident was brought under control; looking at the wing, you wouldn't believe only one man had done so much damage.

My experiences with Charlie after that incident may seem surprising to those that had never met him. I found the man to be intelligent and charismatic, with a quick wit. It helped that we shared a love of training. He used to attend weekly Art classes during his time at Parkhurst. Charlie also had numerous pieces of his artwork displayed in Newport on the Isle of Wight in the art gallery.

Peter Leath, a famous artist on the island, used to volunteer in his spare time to come in and take an art class. Charlie became friends with Peter. Before his release in November 1992, to keep him occupied, the then governor, John Marriott, had permitted Charlie to dig out a massive fishpond on the main yard. Charlie could be seen digging like mad with a pick axe and spade in a rush to get it done before his release.

I was on the yard one day playing tennis but spent more time watching Charlie digging. He had a young lad with a wheelbarrow ferrying the barrows to and fro stacked high with soil and rubble. Charlie was an extremely fit, powerful man and would have the wheelbarrows full in no time. You could hear Charlie shouting, "faster, boy". It was a warm day, and the lad looked exhausted. He was practically doing shuttle runs non-stop. Charlie was released, and the pond that was the size of a small swimming pool never did get finished. My last conversation with Charlie was short, out on the yard while he had a quick break from digging. He said, "Hey Guv, I'm out soon." I replied, "I know, Charlie; I hope all goes well for you."

Charlie, without delay, said, "I haven't decided whether to be a train driver or serial killer," followed by his unmistakable laugh and a slam on my back with his hand.

Sadly, one day when Charlie was out there on the yard before his release, there was an altercation. It was alleged that a prisoner named Dessy Cunningham (RIP) had stabbed Charlie in the quarrel. I knew Dessy quite well; he was always polite, reasonably quiet and highly respected within the prison. I remember being surprised that he had been linked with the stabbing. Charlie had lost a lot of blood and was still bleeding profusely but refusing to go to the outside Hospital.

I'm pleased to say Charlie did survive the stabbing. I've been informed many times that it was, in fact, Bill the Bomb that had initially helped stem the flow of blood from the wounds, helping to save Charlie's life. I recently had this confirmed when I viewed a letter written by Charlie stating those facts. The letter confirms that he went to the nearby St Mary's Hospital for blood transfusions. At the time, I wasn't sure whether he attended an outside Hospital or was just treated in the prison Hospital.

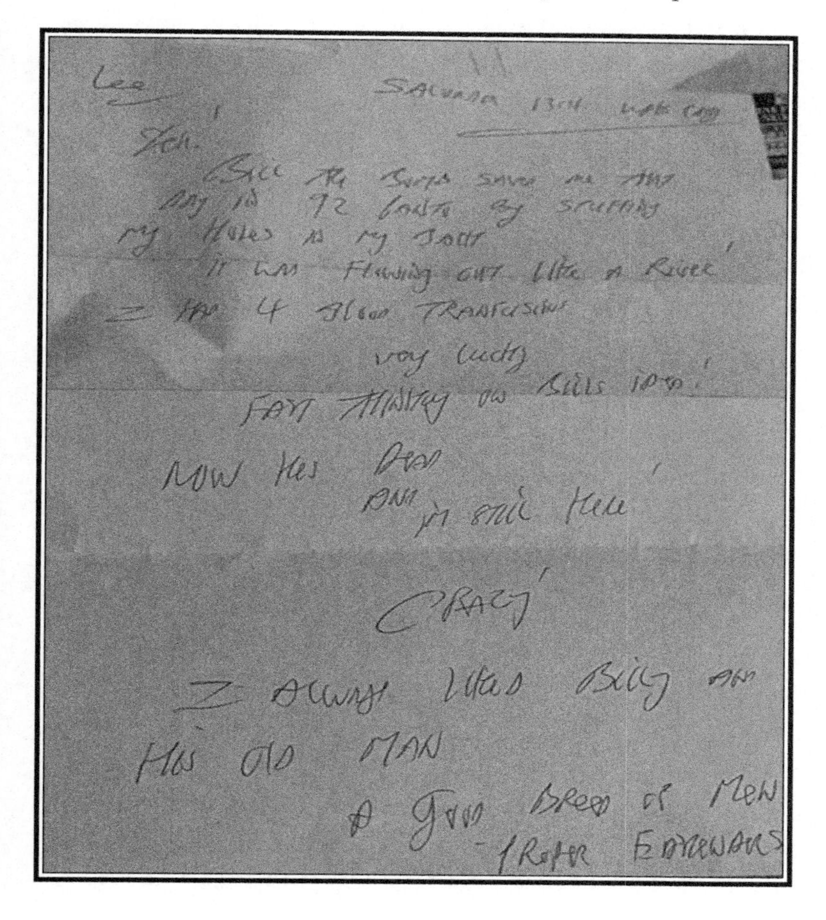

Lee

Salvador 1304 [illegible]

Yeh!

Bill the Bomb saved me that
day in 72 [illegible] by stuffing
my holes in my body
It was flowing out like a river!
I had 4 blood transfusions
very lucky
Fast thinking on Bill's part!

Now he's dead
and I'm still here!

Crazy!

I always liked Billy and
his old man
a good breed of men
– Respect [illegible]

Charlie spent just 50 days free before he was again arrested for conspiracy to rob. While these charges were dismissed in February 1993, he was arrested 16 days later for conspiracy to rob and possession of a sawn-off shotgun. In September 1993, he was found guilty of intent to rob and was given an eight-year sentence.

The rest is history, as they say. At the time of writing, Charlie is still in prison, and was recently refused his latest parole, which was only the second public hearing in UK history. I'm often asked my opinion about that; my honest answer is, if David Cheesman (Lant) is deemed to have reduced his risk and considered suitable for release, then indeed, Charlie should be given the same opportunity. When all is said and done, Charlie hasn't murdered anyone.

Getting Ready for My PE Course

I continued getting to work early, despite now working in the Gym. I aimed to be the best version of myself in time for my course. Anatomy and physiology was a large part of the course syllabus, so I started reading books that Gary kindly let me borrow. Gary, Mick and Woody were unwavering in their support. I was working on Gary's weekend, and he quickly became my mentor. He had an excellent teaching manner and seemed to know everything about PE. Gary also, like myself, loved a good wind-up. Together we would plot and carry out many wind-ups on staff and prisoners.

I remember Dave, my good friend and main training partner, was on Juliet 1 duty one day. Dave was a handsome lad who looked like the lead singer from Wet, Wet, Wet. Between Gym sessions, he told us about the problems with his then-girlfriend, Stella.

Stella was a beautiful girl from a mega-rich family on the island. Dave had aspirations of marrying into her family. He told us of Stella's lack of culinary skills and how she would never have food ready for him at the end of a shift. Dave also said that he didn't get much activity in the bedroom either.

I winked at Gary, and we both told him that that's 'just not on'. I said I would go home and give her an ultimatum: things either improve, or you're off. Dave argued her case a little, stating how well they got on other than these problems. He reminded us of how wealthy her family were. Me and Gary tag-teamed him into submission. He left the Gym, saying how he would give her the ultimatum.

The following day, Dave came down to the Gym, declaring that he'd done it, giving her the ultimatum. She wasn't happy, and they ended their relationship. When Dave told us, we both responded together: "What the hell have you done that for?" Dave's demeanour changed, saying, "You two fucking idiots talked me into it!"

Dave went home at lunchtime to tell Stella it had been a mistake, but she wouldn't take him back. He would talk about it for years, how we'd cost him his future and a big inheritance. We were rolling with laughter.

Dave eventually became a PEI some years later and married a PEI. So I like to think Gary and I did him a favour that day. I wasn't certain what the future held for Stella. For the book's sake though (this will be the only made-up or fabricated line) and for a happy ending, let's say she happily married a Chef with a low sex drive. Everyone's a winner.

Lilleshall National Sports Centre

PE COURSE

The day arrived to start my PE course, a residential course from Monday to Friday. My bag was packed with a few A&P books, a whistle and Dunlop Greenflash trainers to see me through the week. It was a journey I would get familiar with over the coming weeks and months. Arriving at Lilleshall didn't feel as daunting as the Pre-Selection because I knew what to expect. My other significant advantage over others commencing their course was knowing which establishment I was returning to.

As far as I knew, I didn't know any other potential PEIs starting the course with me. I was sent to get some lunch after signing in and being given my room number and key. The rooms at Lilleshall would be best described as small but functional; you had a single bed, a shared toilet and a shower with interlinking doors to the bedroom next door. I discovered that in the room next to me was Johnny Butler, whom we later nicknamed Doc for his knowledge of A&P. He seemed a lovely lad. Thankfully, we hit it off immediately. John was from a young offender's prison, HMP Feltham. After an ice-breaking introduction, we went over for some lunch.

We all entered the classroom for the first time and were given a programme for the next few weeks. I observed the group of 11 and noticed a diverse bunch, all shapes and sizes, but all looking physically fit in their way. That was a given, being we were all on a PE course. We were asked to briefly introduce ourselves to the rest of the course members.

We got all the domestics out of the way and outlined the Programme's first month. It consisted of many class teaching practices, related warm-ups, minor games, etc. We always got at least the night before to prepare a lesson plan. Each session would last around 20 minutes, so three of us was a good one-hour session. It also incorporated a bleep test.

The bleep test was a maximal effort sequence of shuttle runs over a 25-metre distance. We needed to reach a minimum of 11. I knew this was in the bag. At Parkhurst, I'd managed this comfortably each time I'd practised; in fact, I often did level 11 running backwards and still managing to talk comfortably.

The first month passed in no time at all. We'd completed many related activity warm-ups, cool-downs and minor games. I had to pinch myself that I was getting paid for doing it. When I thought about my weaving job (spinning plates), it was like I'd landed in heaven. I'd got through without any referrals, which meant you had to repeat your session after taking on board the constructive criticism of the tutors and the group. At first, most of us felt uncomfortable criticising one of our fellow course members, but as the weeks and sessions passed, we got more comfortable with having input. It was a strong group; I can only recall a handful of referrals throughout the course.

Sporting body awards – gymnastics

We were introduced to the national gymnastics centre at Lilleshall by being challenged to jump into the foam pit at one end and race to the other. I thought I'd got off to a good start, but it felt like attempting to run through quicksand. One body would catch you and then come over the top, followed by another. And then I'd find myself returning the favour. It was surprisingly exhausting but, at the same time, great fun.

In those days, gymnastics was a huge part of the course. Gary had diligently taught me many basics, including headstand, handstand, forward and backward roll, cartwheel and straddle and through vault. I had never done any gymnastics at school or as a child, so it was time-consuming but, at the same time, enjoyable. It was for me; I was unsure if Gary had the same opinion. One of the benefits of having Gary teach me, he not only concentrated on teaching but showed me how to break the moves down for coaching. This proved beneficial when it came to formulating my lesson plans.

The PE course though, was a whole new level. Having to perform and coach on multiple discipline apparatuses like pummel horse, parallel bars and high bar, which included getting strapped to the bar before swinging around. On my first attempt, I started going all the way over, thinking this was alright, then getting faster and faster before thinking, I can't remember them telling me how to stop. When I eventually came to a halt, assisted by Barry Beasley, the tutor, I felt like I'd just stepped out of a washing machine. Next were the rings. I watched on in admiration as our tutor Barry Beasley displayed a perfect crucifix position and watched the GB gymnastics team train. They trained for eight hours a day, every day. Their dedication was admirable, especially when comparing the rewards pampered footballers enjoyed. I'd suffered severe blisters on my hands from the various bars, bruised balls from the pummel horse, and almost broke my neck attempting back flips. But I'd passed. On to the next.

Plas y Brenin National Outdoor Centre (outward bounds)

Looking at the Programme that was part of the course, everyone, bar Paddy and me, was excited about it. We would leave Lilleshall behind for a few weeks and head to Capel Curig in Snowdonia, North Wales. We had all stocked up on Helly Hansen attire and other recommended articles for the trip.

Banksy, my mate from Camp Hill, was on the course before me. He had already excitedly told me what to expect. We all got loaded onto a van and headed for Wales. I had minimal experience in mountaineering or orienteering. Those who knew me would know I could get lost in a large shopping centre or in an attempt to find my way back to my car in a car park. When my brother and I shared a room as kids, I had the bottom bunk bed for a reason. The highest I'd ever climbed was Holcombe Hill, standing at 128 feet, near where I grew up as a child. I could only manage a few rungs of a ladder before freezing. I first discovered my lack of head for heights in my first job at Cascades all those years ago, when I had to go up on the forks of the forklift to get some flat-pack boxes.

Day one was enjoyable. We did a long hike and a river crossing, then camped out for the night. Thankfully, our instructor Trevor, for the duration, seemed a nice guy. Although, he did inform us that they call him VFM, short for value for money. It meant we would be getting the ultimate experience. Much to everyone's excitement the following day, but to my and Paddy's trepidation, we were heading for Mount Snowdon.

Snowdon (Crib Goch)

VFM wasn't just taking us up Snowdon; we were taking the route up Crib Goch. Crib Goch is described as a 'knife-edged' arête in the Snowdonia National Park in Gwynedd, Wales. The name means 'red ridge' in the Welsh language. The highest point on the arête is 920 metres above sea level. The Crib Goch scramble from Pen-y-pass is the toughest walk-up Snowdon and one of the best scrambling routes in the country. It's also one of the most exposed and challenging routes on a walk up Snowdon. VFM insisted it was the one you should do if you wanted to climb Snowdon.

The Crib Goch ridge is very exposed and similar to walking on the apex of a shallow roof. It is recommended for those with a head for heights only. This was a rough, tough and challenging route up Snowdon. Most would say, 'If you're unfamiliar with mountain walking, move along and find another more suitable route up the mountain.' Having completed my research, I discovered a train that takes you up it or a few other routes with a much wider path. I suggested these quicker safer routes to VFM, but he laughed it off, not taking me seriously.

Crib Goch is a Grade one scramble, meaning that the competent scrambler shouldn't need ropes, and only find technical sections within their capabilities. The operative word being, competent. It's still in a different league than Snowdon's other walks.

VFM had declined my idea of taking a somewhat easier path, so off we went. I recall Paddy starting to grumble only a few miles in. I was enjoying the initial walk, and in no time at all was higher than I'd ever been without getting on a plane. Then we arrived at what I can only describe as a wall of rock and some of the most enormous boulders I've ever seen.

It quickly became apparent that we would scramble up this rock wall to the top. As I said, what the more competent climber might describe as walking on the apex of a shallow roof, I'd describe it as a bloody knife edge. I looked along the ridge, and it just seemed never-ending. The view when I dared look was breathtaking. We had a beautiful sunny day, and VFM told us how lucky we were, informing us that sometimes up here, you can't see your hand in front of your face. For a moment, I contemplated whether this would be better for someone like me with a fear of heights. VFM told us that on some parts, we would have to have four points of contact to cross the path; I think I had five at some points!

It didn't take long to realise that my good friend Madgey was a mountain goat in disguise. He went over that ridge with his hands in his pockets whistling. On the other hand, I had four points of contact for the whole length of the ridge. I had worn a hole in both gloves in no time. Madgey was fantastic. He walked with me, encouraging me; I would say every step, but for me—every crawl.

At one particularly narrow point, a gentleman and his two children were walking along, stood up and walked past me while I was on all fours. The youngest child got a little scared and stopped at the narrow section; his dad told him to wait there and said he'd return for him. I shouted, "Me too." Madgey and a few others near us all laughed.

Eventually, we reached the summit. I must admit it was a fantastic feeling looking down. We finished the descent, mud sliding down the last part of the mountain on our backs, a great end to a memorable day. It was, to date, the hardest thing I've ever done; not so much physically, but emotionally and overcoming my fears. I say overcoming them; I still had a mountain called Tryfan to overcome. The walk down was terrific. It felt great to stand up on two feet again and take in the stunning views. It sparked something in me. I quite often now head for the hills whenever I can with my dog Freddy.

On my way home to the Island on Friday, the traffic was horrendous. It was so bad that by the time I'd got to Portsmouth, I'd missed the last ferry to the Island. Waste not want not; after my initial disappointment, I decided to get changed out of my PE kit into some clobber for heading to a pub/nightclub. I danced the night away until it was time for the early morning ferry. Despite being on my own, I had a great night. The DJ even played 'Ain't no mountain high enough'. It must have been fate. My wife Sarah, our children Henry and Dolly, and my older children Emma, Sheri, Jack and all our dogs are going to Snowdonia for a week's holiday in May 2023 and intend to climb Snowdon to build memories. I'll avoid taking them over Crib Goch and take one of the easier routes.

Tryfan Mountain

With Snowdon and Crib Goch ticked off, next up was Tryfan. Tryfan is a mountain in the Ogwen Valley, Snowdonia, Wales. It forms part of the Glyderau group and is one of the most recognisable peaks in Britain, having a classic pointed shape with rugged crags. Tryfan is the fifteenth-highest mountain in Wales.

Tryfan has two pillar stones on its summit; they are often referred to as Adam and Eve. The stones are two natural monoliths at the summit of Tryfan (three thousand feet above sea level) known locally as Sion a Sian. The rocks are approximately three metres high and nearly one and a half metres apart. People who jump from one rock to another are said to gain the Freedom of Tryfan.

VFM had informed us, 'there are two main routes up Tryfan; an easy one up the south ridge and a more difficult one up the north ridge'. And, of course, we were taking the most difficult one. We would all be claiming the freedom of Tryfan at the top. Yes, that meant jumping from one stone to the other. Paddy had a few words to say about that. He protested to the point that the leaders agreed to take him up the other way. As daunting as it was, I wasn't going to back out; I was doing everything the others did, even if it looked unorthodox. Honestly, if they'd said you have to walk barefoot across hot coals to get the badge, I'd have done it.

Tryfan soon had me scrambling on all fours. Even Madgey, the mountain goat, got his hands dirty. With incredibly high gusts of winds forecasted, after a quick discussion between the leaders, it was decided the jump from Adam to Eve was unsafe. My relief soon evaporated when VFM suggested we just briefly climb onto the rocks for the experience. As we finally approached the summit from the shelter of the scramble over the large boulders, from nowhere, a wind appeared as I'd never in all my life encountered, not even up Holcombe Hill. One by one, we scrambled on top of the enormous stones. The gale was getting stronger by this point. As I climbed the huge rock, I felt my balaclava lifting from my neck. With another colossal gust, it blew off my head entirely and was seen sailing over the top and down the mountain; I couldn't help but think, 'I could be following!'

I froze on the top with all four contact points on the rock. John Thompson, one of the instructors, had to physically move my limbs one at a time until I eventually got down. The instructors, including VFM, seemed to be getting concerned about the conditions. We made a hasty descent off the top of the mountain.

Orienteering

Next up in Wales was Orienteering, which consisted of the group set off independently at few-minute intervals. For the ex-forces lads, like Martin (Oxo) and Eddie, it was a walk in the park. Most of my family know that my navigation skills could be better, even with road signs to follow. When we travel somewhere new in the car, usually just before getting lost, I often joked to my wife Sarah, "Don't worry, sat nav Currie has got this."

Armed with my compass, a map and the experience of some night navigation and map reading coaching from VFM, we were off. I managed to get to the first checkpoint and felt quite pleased. Rather worryingly though, I hadn't seen or heard anyone else off the course. Now for the second checkpoint. After what seemed like an eternity and, actually, at one point, trying to ask people for directions, I found it. I approached it again, feeling like I was 'getting the hang of this,' only to discover I'd gone around in circles and was back at the first checkpoint.

By this time, I was getting quite worried. 'I can't fail the course; it's not an option.' After 15 minutes of running around like a headless chicken, I ran into Madgey. I don't know how I restrained myself from kissing him. We (he) completed a few more checkpoints and decided to stop and have lunch. We could now see the van in the far distance, with the other ten course members. Oxo had been back ages and was asleep in the van by the time we returned.

But, thanks to Madgey, I'd got back in one piece without having to call out the chopper to look for me. To celebrate we went out that evening to a local pub. Paddy, Madgey and I decided to go to the nearest nightclub. Madgey, who had got talking to a young lady outside, chose to remain in the extremely long queue while Paddy and I thought about going on somewhere else. A couple of ladies offered to come with us and show us another club they knew. Madgey gave me his car keys as I tend not to drink. I was always the designated driver.

After what seemed like hours around dark narrow lanes, we arrived in Rhyl, over 30 miles from the club where Madgey had gone. To say the place where we ended up was rough was an understatement. Paddy and I stood watching the two ladies' drink for them, while they danced. We feared they'd beat us up if we didn't. When we finally picked Madgey up from the club he'd gone to, his petrol tank was running on fumes. He immediately clocked it and asked where we'd been. "Rhyl," I declared. "Fucking Rhyl?" Madgey replied, with a look of astonishment.

Kayaking at Holme Pierrepoint, home of the National Water Sports Centre

As a warm-up for Holme Pierrepoint, we went to Jack Field Rapids near Ironbridge, Shropshire, for a week of Kayaking. I'd done very little Kayaking before, besides having a few sessions with an officer on the Isle of Wight. He'd mainly concentrated on me being able to roll myself back upright if I capsized. That turned out to be very handy because capsizing was all I ever did for the first few days. It didn't help that the water was shallow, and every time I went over I felt my helmet hitting the rocks on the bottom.

We partnered up. Paddy was my partner. When one of us was in the canoe, the other would stand on the side with a rescue line to pull us back into the side. Poor Paddy would hardly get a chance to fold the line back in a loop before I was over again. I may as well have been given a submarine.

Training complete, we headed for Holme Pierrepoint. We had a quick recce of the course. It started with a huge weir, followed by minor stoppers and eddies. Towards the end, there was a giant stopper.

The first exercise was to paddle into the stopper and sit there. I managed to get into the stopper for a few seconds before being flipped around and back upright. They all cheered as if I'd got myself back up; in truth, the force of the water had just flipped me around. Trying to get out of the stopper, I was over again, and Paddy was once more throwing me the rescue line. At that point, I was grateful to be returning to a maximum-security prison, where outward bounds wouldn't be an option, even with John Marriott in charge.

The day was nearing completion. We had one last task: to have one final attempt at completing the whole course. Mitch, Wiggy and quite a few others had managed it, even stopping in the eddies on the way down and doing a transverse across the river. My turn came, and I just decided I wouldn't be clever. I just hit it hard and straight from top to bottom. At the top of the weir, I sat with the nose of my canoe tilting over the edge. It seemed like a huge drop. I paddled like mad and got to the bottom of the weir in one piece. In no time, I'd been through some stoppers and was approaching the big stopper; I got stuck in it, and like before, it spun me round, only this time it spat me out, but upside down. My race was run, but I enjoyed it. Maybe a bit of that coaching had paid off.

BWLA (British Weightlifting Association)

This part of the course carried a vast amount of pressure. You couldn't become a PEI without attaining this qualification. Barry Beasley took this section of the course.

Barry was small in stature but powerful, pound for pound. We, as a course, had already witnessed his flexibility and strength during the gymnastics part of the Programme – when he had jumped up on the rings and performed a perfect crucifix position; trust me, that's not an easy feat.

We would also be expected to perform the two Olympic lifts showing sound technique. The lifts are the two-hand snatch, and the clean and jerk. Both are very technical, with fast dynamic movements. That made it challenging to coach; you had to train your eye to break down the movements. The theory exam was intense, and the practical exam was even more so. The course culminated in having to perform the two lifts in front of the late great John Lear, who sadly passed away recently after a long illness. John would sit analysing your every move over the spectacles on the end of his nose.

Photo of myself and the Legend John Lear. A fascinating man with an absolute wealth of Knowledge. RIP John.

John Lear RIP was the national coach for 40 years

John served on performance and team-management committees at the British Olympic Association. His foresight, wisdom and experience were constantly in demand during the transition from amateur to professional sport.

Lear also helped to coach his friend, Dave Prowse, the actor, bodybuilder and weightlifter who gained global fame by playing Darth Vader in the original Star Wars trilogy. Prowse was a national champion who represented England at the 1962 Commonwealth Games in Perth, Australia before he took up acting. He became a lifelong friend of Lear after training with him at Bisham Abbey, the former national training centre for several British sports in the 1960s. Prowse mentioned him several times in his 2011 autobiography.

I had the pleasure of completing the coaches award a few years later. A course that John was heavily involved in delivering. I also attended a PEI reunion a few years ago. I spent considerable time talking to John about all his fascinating stories regarding the numerous Olympic games in which he was involved. Those games included his first-hand account of the tragedy in the 1972 Olympics in Munich when eight Palestinian terrorists invaded the Olympic village on September 5th and killed two members of the Israeli team. Nine other Israelis were held hostage as the terrorists bargained to release 200 Palestinian prisoners in Israel. John was lucky to survive this siege.

It was an intense but enjoyable part of the PE course and provided us with an excellent platform for going forwards and delivering courses for prisoners.

Dreaded scheme of work

It was a massive file you compiled on a fictional prison PE department. If one part of the course weren't enjoyable, that would be it; I don't know a single PEI who would disagree. A few got lucky and were given similar amounts of staff to their home establishments. I had kindly been handed my friend Banksey's to work from, but only to be given a different setup. I got there eventually, but it took me some painstakingly long, boring evenings to complete.

Swimming teachers

A significant part of the PE course was where your teaching skills were tested by schoolchildren attending swimming lessons, at the local pool. A challenging course to pass, but I did pass. It's also an award that, over the years, I'd put to good use with my children.

End of course

The PE course was ending; it would end with an evening meal and a presentation of awards for all of us. I've heard many PEIs say they wouldn't want to do it again; I never understood that. I'd had the time of my life. All our partners came up for the meal and started to mingle and chat. After a while, Alison, my then-wife, approached me, looking perturbed, before asking me about the subs. Subs being short for subsistence, petrol money and expenses we could claim throughout the course. I replied, "Oh, don't worry; I've paid them."

Paddy and a few other lads restrained themselves from laughing and giving me away. With the course concluding, I looked forward to returning to work wearing my PE course tee shirt with the badge I'd wanted all those years. I also couldn't wait to run my own courses and start putting into practice all my newfound skills and qualifications.

The awards included the following: manual handling instructor, first aid instructor, level two award in understanding substance misuse, first aid treatment and management of injuries, BWLA instructor, FA football prelim coach, volleyball level one coach, badminton leaders, BAGA general gymnastics and men's artistic level four coach, rugby league level one coach, British canoe union; coaching award supervisor, two-star coach and lifeguard union award, rugby union coach. ASA swimming teachers Award. a City & Guilds award and BTEC award. Over the years, I went on to complete various development coaching awards as well.

I recently received the tremendous honour of being invited to Lilleshall to present the end-of-course certificates and badges. And give a speech about PE in the Prison Service.

A recent photo of myself on my return to Lilleshall.

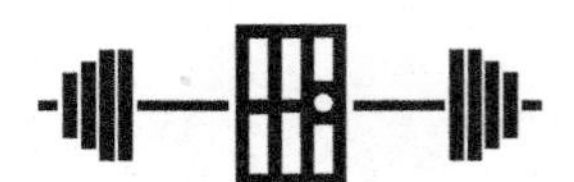

BACK TO THE BIG HOUSE

With the course all completed and passed, I had a week off, then went back to work. I would be staying on the same weekend with Gary. It was a win-win for both of us. Gary would pass on his wealth of knowledge and experience, and I would referee all the football. After his recent experience on the pitch with Bill, he was also pretty happy.

I soon settled back into my surroundings in the gym. My day would often consist of a workout before work, a game of tennis or badminton, and sometimes doubles with Gary against two prisoners, usually Bill the Bomb or Charlie McGee RIP. McGee was someone who rarely spoke to officers at all but made a begrudging exception for PE staff; you could tell he wasn't entirely comfortable with it. Kevin Brown fell into the same category but would play tennis or badminton against us.

Kevin was an armed robber who had come to Parkhurst after an escape attempt on a bulldozer at his previous jail. In those days, Kev was notorious for having a short fuse, even with us down the gym. He would, from time to time, fly off the handle. I remember on one occasion, he just turned on the PO and threatened to rip his face off. I will write more about Kev later in the book, where he has mellowed a little.

On other days, it could be a coached session of Volleyball, a game of five-a-side football, weight training or a circuit; every day was different. However, one general theme that stayed the same was the interaction with prisoners. It was different to the relationship I had with them on a wing.

THE SSU (SPECIAL SECURE UNIT)

The Colonel Brian Robinson (Brink's-Mat)

One of the PE staff had to go to the SSU (Special Secure Unit) located near the Gym; you weren't allowed to enter with your keys, and Security here was at the highest level. It had a small Gym, so prisoners here never left the unit; even visits took place within the complex.

The SSU was effectively a Prison within a Prison that at the time held some of the highest profile Prisoners in the system, people like Brian Robinson, often referred to as the Colonel. Over the weeks and months, I usually had a workout with Brian. He was probably my first real close-up experience with an old-school criminal, a bit of a dying breed in prison today. He was always polite, with a moral code. I was to experience this on numerous occasions throughout my career. I enjoyed these sessions, training and having a chat.

Many years later, I wasn't too surprised to hear that Brian went on to go straight and was running a wine bar the last I heard, before years later hearing of his death in a nursing home in 2021.

Brian was said to be the mastermind behind the £26 million Brink's-Mat heist.

Robinson had assembled the premier division team of six South London robbers for the Brink's-Mat heist.

Micky McAvoy wanted the Arif crime family members, specialists in armed robbery, on the job.

Robinson, however, vetoed them, as an Arif associate was involved in the earlier murder of his close friend Peter Hennessy.

At that time, Robinson was a 40-year-old career criminal who had served several prison sentences and was on a Flying Squad list of London's 20 most prolific armed robbers.

So too, was childhood friend Tony White, who had just served a 12-year sentence for a heist, and the younger man McAvoy.

Their £26 million haul is worth more than £100 million in today's currency.

One of the guards picked out Robinson in an identity parade as the robber referred to in court as the "Cool Boss". McAvoy, known as "The Bully" by guards, was also picked out, but White was not.

Robinson claimed he was visiting his mum in Kent on the morning of the robbery. And to this day, friends insist the robbery's mastermind was not on the job itself.

In December 1984, an Old Bailey jury acquitted White but convicted Robinson and McAvoy of conspiracy to rob.

Police estimate that 15 people were involved in planning the Brink's-Mat robbery, but only three of the gang members were ever convicted.

Robinson, whose nickname was 'The Colonel', was already well known to the police, while McAvoy was one of South London's most prolific armed robbers. Quickly realising that the sheer knowledge available to the gang, pointed to an insider participant, the police soon came across Anthony Black, who had been late to work on the day of the robbery and had missed the entire heist. The connection to Robinson's sister led to a swift confession by Black, who gave up the names of the newly wealthy McAvoy and Robinson. Neither McAvoy nor Robinson helped themselves by 'laying low'. Within weeks of the heist, both moved from humble South London council houses to a grand estate in

Kent, paid for in cash. Rumours are that McAvoy had bought two Rottweiler dogs to protect his mansion and named them 'Brinks' and 'Mat'.

Micky McAvoy (Brink's-Mat)

A little while later, I also met Micky McAvoy in the Gym; I found Micky to be a completely different character to Brian, but no less interesting and engaging. Again, I trained with Micky a few times at Parkhurst. Sadly at the time of writing, Micky passed away soon after losing his wife; Micky, I believe, had also had a battle with Cancer.

Micky was dubbed 'The Nutter'.

Micky was a career criminal, and one of the country's most prolific and violent armed robbers; he'd played a significant role in one of the largest bullion heists in British history.

In more recent years, Micky's nephew John was imprisoned after allegedly carrying out a robbery with the very same Kevin Brown I mentioned earlier. Micky's nephew used his time in Prison and the Gym to good effect, and he became an Ironman champion. He was also writing his book Redemption, from iron bars to Ironman. Again, this is an excellent story of how PE can turn a life around. I will go on to present many more examples throughout my book.

Micky was a straight talker with an air about him. But something drew you to like him. Colleagues throughout my career said you like a quirky character; even my family throughout the years would say, "you don't half attract them". I found people and their ways fascinating, always have. I also learned to take people as I found them regardless of reputation. Micky came across as a straight talker that didn't suffer fools, but I never saw the side of him that presented him as a Nutter.

Micky McAvoy. RIP

Valerio Viccei

Some days, I'd turn up at the SSU and nobody would want to train; other times I might just have one taker. I'd either supervise or join in a workout. I always try to join in, never one to waste a training opportunity.

On one occasion, I arrived for an SSU gym session. Viccei who I'd trained with a few times, asked if I played chess. After telling him, "yes, but badly," we agreed to exercise the brain that day. Having no sooner agreed, Viccei was walking back into the gym with a chess set. I hadn't played since school, so I didn't prove to be much of a match. We shook hands at the end though and I told him my name. "You can call me Gi Gi," he replied.

At that time, Viccei was being held in the SSU with Brian Robinson. Valerio was often referred to as the playboy gangster. He was jailed for the 62 million pounds Knightsbridge safe deposit robbery in London.

Gi Gi was machine-gunned to death while in Italy. It is believed the 45-year-old was planning his next hit when he was shot on a lonely dirt track.

Viccei, who was technically still serving his 22-year sentence for the 1987 robbery, was killed as he struggled with a police officer. He spent just five years behind bars in Parkhurst SSU (special secure unit) before being extradited to Pescara prison where, since 1996, he had lived a high life of fast cars and loose women. Thanks to an Italian policy of semi-liberty, on his return to Italy he was allowed to do as he pleased, as long as he returned to his cell at night.

I remember the escort going out. Helicopters and armed police guard all the way to the airport. Big Andy was the SO in charge of the escort. From what I recall, the staff got a bit too inebriated on the way back and the prison received complaints of raucous prison officers at the airport on their return home. The Staff all got a slap on the wrist from the then-governor, John Marriott.

Terrence Perkins

Terry would be more famous for his recent role in the Hatton Garden raid. However, I knew him from an earlier stint in Prison. Perkins has a long history of criminal activity and was jailed for 22 years for robbing the vaults of Securicor, also known as Security Express. On Easter Monday 1983, a gang broke into the Security Express depot in Shoreditch, east London, and escaped with £6 million. John Knight, the brother of Ronnie Knight, the former husband of actress Dame Barbara Windsor, masterminded the robbery.

Terry was also in the SSU in Parkhurst. Terry was very much in the mould of Brian Robinson, reasonably quiet on first meeting him. Though he was a classic old villain, he had charisma and a great sense of humour. Perkins had celebrated his birthday during the Hatton Garden raid and was involved in all stages of the operation, including disposing of the stolen goods. He drove a blue Citroen Saxo that police placed recording devices on after the raid.

He was inside the Hatton Garden building posing as a builder and "working" inside the lift on March 31. Diabetic Perkins claimed to have taken enough insulin to last him three days in the vault. When his address in Heene Road, Enfield, was searched, police found jewellery, cash, blue overalls, five pairs of white fabric gloves and many euros. After the raid, it was decided that on May 19, the loot would be taken back to an address linked to Perkins in Sterling Road, Enfield, and then divvied up.

Over forties gym (remedial gym)

One of the best sessions of the day was the first session of remedial gym. We used to get all the older prisoners attending, mostly armed robbers. People like Johnny Hilton, who at the time, was one of only a handful in the British system told they would serve natural life (never to be released). However, I understand John is now in his 90s and has been released.

Johnny was the fittest old boy I'd ever met. Every day without fail, he'd run to the gym to reserve his equipment, ready for his workout. I always thought I'd like to be in his shape when I'm his age; he would have been well into his late 60s then. I always remember Johnny telling me the story of one of his robberies, or 'a bit of work,' as he said. He'd been casing a job where the security guard walked up the steps. He watched him a few times, thinking, 'how can I be on those steps without raising suspicion?'.

One day when Johnny was casing the job, he noticed a tramp on the steps; the security guard walked straight past him every time without giving it a second thought. John got rid of that tramp and replaced him himself a few days later. "Give me the bag." The rest is history.

You couldn't help but like Johnny. He's one very physically and mentally strong man. Everyone in the jail respected him. I'm pleased to see him out, and I've no doubt he'll be around for years to come.

Billy G

Billy Gentry, or Billy G, as he was known to many including staff. History had revealed that Billy was the reason behind a plot to kill the Kray twins before they got arrested. What sparked the plot against the Krays was Freddie Foreman being summoned by psychotic Ronnie to be ready to dispose of the body of Billy Gentry, who was about to be lured into an ambush.

"Billy Gentry was a good fellah," Foreman recalled. "I've done loads of bird with Gentry, so I told Ron to forget about it and calm down. I thought he was raving mad." My view on Billy Gentry is the same as Foreman's—a sound guy with a great sense of humour.

Ronnie Easterbrook

Ronnie Easterbrook was another who attended remedial Gym regularly in the early days of his sentence. Ronnie was another old-school armed robber who at the time, was the first to have been given a whole-life tariff. Ronnie always protested against his conviction, and after I'd left Parkhurst in 1996, Ronnie decided to go on hunger strike in 1997 and 1999. Sadly, Ronnie passed away in 2009 after a third hunger strike. RIP.

1,2,3 down

Once a week, we would have a local special needs group attending the gymnasium. We had various levels of disabilities visiting the Gym. We would also have some prisoner volunteers to help out with the sessions. Many of the prisoners that helped would talk about how it made them realise how lucky they were and realise that their lives weren't so bad.

We also ran a PE course with prisoners called the Community Sports Leaders Award (CSLA). The course covered taking warm-ups, stretching, cool-downs, and organising competitions; and prisoners had to complete a minimum of ten hours of working with the community. Prisoners couldn't be allowed out to fulfil that criteria at Parkhurst and other secure jails. So we covered it with the special needs group.

Many prisoners who completed the CSLA and the community hours would choose to carry on as helpers beyond completing the course. The sessions consisted of various activities, like getting a huge parachute out and playing cat-and-mouse games where the prisoner would go under the lowered parachute. Everyone would hold and shake it, hiding the prisoner's whereabouts, scrambling around on all fours. Then, I'd select one of the visiting group to go hunt them down. If they were struggling, I'd choose someone else to help them. Much to our amusement, apart from the mouse, one or two of the group would get overexcited when they caught the prisoner (mouse) jumping all over them.

Often, we would get the full-size Trampoline out. We had one lad called Stephen who would come to life on it; over a few months I'd taught him to perform a seat drop, where you bounce down onto your backside and back to your feet in one movement. The group loved this activity.

One week I got out the Trampoline and Stephen was in the waiting group; they all had a go one by one. Once I'd assisted Stephen up on to the Trampoline I would call, "one, two, three down," and Stephen would drop and spring right back up. His face would light up, clapping his hands with excitement and a massive smile every time. The group leader told me they'd never seen him like that.

The following week I once again helped Stephen up on the Trampoline and got him to do a few bounces. I said, "Ready?" And his eyes lit up. I said, "One, two, three." As usual, Stephen went down and back up. His face lit up as it always did. "Again," I said but this time to my amazement, Stephen started to count with me and shouted just as I was finishing my count, "Down." Just as he performed his seat drop.

The guy from the centre looked like he'd seen a ghost. He came round to me and said, "Phil, I can't believe it. Stephen has never spoken to my knowledge at home or at the centre."

Over the coming weeks, it continued. Stephen's counting and shouts of 'down' got louder and more enthusiastic. I was approached by the leader and asked if Stephen's parents could come in to witness it. I got them security cleared to attend a couple of weeks later. The session started, and we got Stephen on the Trampoline. His parents looked nervous. So was I, thinking, 'imagine if he doesn't do it; imagine their disappointment; they wouldn't believe it happened'.

I started to get Stephen bouncing, but before I said ready, Stephen called out. "Ready, one, two, three, down." His face lit up. I looked over at his parents, who were embracing each other in floods of tears. They thanked us for giving them an experience they never thought they would have.

Looking back, that was the moment I realised: you can never underestimate the power of sports and physical education. To this day, it's one of my proudest moments regarding PE, and I've had more than a few.

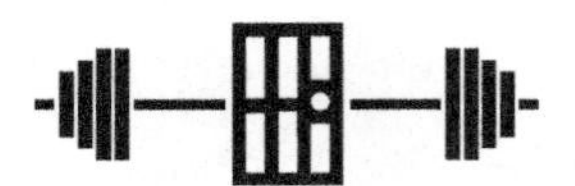

SHADOWING ON MY FIRST COURSE

Gary was advertising a Community Sports Leader's Award (CSLA) course and had asked me to be his second in charge. The courses at Parkhurst were advertised on the wings, and in the gymnasium, it would take on 16 suitable applicants. They last ran a course a while ago, being short-staffed with me being away on my PE course.

We had plenty of applications. All the applicants were called down for interviews. We wrote to all the selected ones. The PE course programme was written by Gary, who discussed with me what aspects of the course each of us would cover, depending on our detail. The CSLA course was an ideal first course for me to be involved in, having just qualified.

Excited to at last be involved and deliver a course, I was determined again to learn from Gary's wealth of experience and knowledge. But, I was also mindful of being my own person and developing my own teaching style. Gary played it relatively safe when selecting prisoners for his course. Although all the prisoners had to be security cleared before we did our sift, some applications never got past the first base. There was a couple I'd have given an opportunity that he didn't.

The course started, and I enjoyed watching some prisoners develop throughout. Some were surprisingly nervous when delivering their first warm-up to the group. But by the end of the course, their confidence had risen beyond recognition. They would all be proficient in refereeing various sports and organising minor games, like crab football.

The six weeks passed quickly; we got a hundred per cent pass rate. Quite often during any Course, the number of successful passes could be taken out of our hands if someone was suddenly transferred from the prison.

We had an external moderator come in for a day, to assess the course and check if their logbooks were adequate. The prisoners gained high praise for the standards they displayed on the day. The Prisoners felt proud of what they'd achieved. I had served my apprenticeship now and couldn't wait to be in charge of my own course.

My first course in charge

The next time was my first chance to be in charge. I used Gary's previous course as a template but changed the order of the programme to suit my shifts. As usual, I advertised the course and had many more applicants than we had spaces for. I selected my 16, picking a couple that raised Gary's eyebrows, Though he said it was my call. I decided to give a couple an opportunity; if they took it, great; if they didn't, I'd just run the course two people light. As I said, you can lose Prisoners off a course for other reasons.

One thing I've always tried to do, not just at work but in life, is to take people as I find them, regardless of what I may have been told or heard about them. I've met many members of staff and prisoners over the years that I've liked, despite others' personal opinions of them. From my first course to the last course I ran, I always looked to give a couple of inmates with bad reputations an opportunity. More often than not, I'm pleased to say I wasn't let down.

One of the risks for my first course was a lad named Mack, who was due out soon. It was rare that a prisoner, especially in those days, was released straight from a Cat A prison. But, having talked to Mack, this was indeed what would happen to him. He'd had a chequered past at Parkhurst but only had a year left of his fixed sentence. I spoke to him about his plans when he got out; he would return to Australia, where his dad resided. He said he would probably do his last six months in the segregation unit. I mentioned I was running a CSLA course soon and invited him to apply. At first, he was dubious, but I said, "You'll be down the gym full time, and surely that's got to be better than the seg." He applied, as did my other risky prisoner.

Mack completed the course and was probably the pick of the bunch when taking a warm-up. He possessed an excellent teaching manner; he was even picked out for individual praise by the external moderator at the end of the course. For balance here, my other gamble wasn't so successful; that prisoner was moved to the seg in the first week of the course. My thinking was, a significant achievement would be attained if I hit a fifty per cent success rate. That's pretty decent; if they don't get an opportunity, any success rate for those guys is zero.

Even Gary was amazed at how Mack had developed. Mack went on to complete various other courses in the Gym before he was released, and he finished his last three months as a gym orderly.

A few months after his release, I received a postcard from Australia thanking me for giving him a chance. Mack went on to say he was helping out at a local sports centre. It was the first of this type of correspondence I was to receive as a PEI, but not the last.

A few people have asked me, 'If both of them had let you down, would you still adopt this risk method throughout your career?' Without any doubt, my answer always was an emphatic 'yes'. If a girlfriend or two let you down, you wouldn't just not give another one a chance, would you? I pointed this out to Gary, who smiled and said, "I think there's more chance of you letting the girlfriend down." He had a point.

Gary mentioned my other gamble not paying off. I never beat myself up over the prisoners over the years that didn't grasp an opportunity. I considered likening it to my PE course in that canoe when I'd capsized, in the fast rapids. The water was often too choppy for me to catch the rescue line Paddy so frequently had to throw me, but when I got to calmer waters, I could grasp the rope. The waters may be too choppy for some prisoners, and I may have thrown the line too early.

My First BWLA Course

I was honoured when Micky, the SO, asked me if I'd like to run a British Weightlifting Association Course (BWLA course). The syllabus included prisoners being able to write a weight training programme for a beginner, some basic A&P, and the two Olympic lifts, clean and jerk and the two-hand snatch. I would run the course over four weeks. I decided to run the course entirely without assistance, so I came to work even on my rest days. I had run numerous courses over my years in the Gym by this stage, but only Micky had run this course previously.

We always went over and above the required syllabus, which would impress the external verifier when they came to assess a course. I'd already planned to go deeper into the A&P. I advertised, looking for 12 candidates; ten that I had confidence in and two risks. The first of my risk was Fowzi Nejad (Fozzy). I had recently talked to Fozzy and trained with him regularly. At the time, I hadn't a clue who he was or anything about his crime. Over a period of time whilst chatting, he told me about himself. Fowzi Nejad was the only surviving Iranian Embassy siege gunman.

Fowzi Nejad

The Iranian Embassy siege took place from 30th April to 5th May 1980; Nejad and five other terrorists forced their way into the Embassy in West London in April 1980, demanding independence for part of Southern Iran and taking 26 hostages. They killed a hostage after six days, which led the then Prime Minister, Margaret Thatcher, to order the SAS to storm the building.

Fozzy told me he was the only survivor when the SAS took the building. He said he had hidden amongst the hostages; the other five gunmen were shot down.

The SAS handcuffed all the hostages together and led them down the stairs. They discovered Fozzy and immediately went to uncuff him to drag him back and shoot him. Then, one of the hostages said, "no," and pulled Fozzy back in line, saying he'd been kind to them during the siege.

Fowzi Badavi Nejad was later convicted of conspiracy to murder, false imprisonment, and two charges of manslaughter. He was released from prison in 2008 after completing his 28-year sentence. He cannot be sent back to Iran because of human rights laws, so instead lives in Peckham, South London. Fozzy could speak good English by the time of my course but couldn't write or read so well. By chance, there was a very well-travelled hospital officer who could speak very good Arabic and numerous other languages. I approached him and asked if he'd be willing to sit alongside Fozzy in the exam and translate the test paper for him.

My second risk was a lad called Stu. He was an armed robber from a well-connected family in London. Stu hadn't been back on the wing and recently did his induction. I told him if he kept his head down, I'd give him a chance; he was a keen weight trainer, and the incentive was enough for him to behave himself.

The course ran like a dream. I didn't lose anyone. I ran a mock exam, and everyone passed the practical, but Fozzy narrowly failed his theory. The questions he mainly got wrong were A&P questions, so I concentrated on this aspect of the course for a few days before their final exam. I'm pleased to say everyone passed what would be the last course I ran at Parkhurst.

Gary wrote a letter to the head of PE praising me for my initiative to enable Fozzy to participate in the course. I received high praise in his reply, and John Marriott mentioned it in his full staff briefing, praising the gymnasium department for our work.

Hospital wing

Roy Platts (RIP), our old PO, had retired, and we'd sadly heard his health had deteriorated. Roy's health was never quite the same after going into a smoky wing and cell to save a prisoner from a fire. Roy was held in the highest esteem by all who knew him. Before my time on the PE course, Roy was the national trainer for anatomy and physiology. I thought Gary had lots of knowledge on this subject till I spoke with Roy.

Roy sadly passed away not too long into his retirement. As you can imagine, he would be a hard act to follow, especially in the eyes of the older staff at Parkhurst like Micky, Gary and Woody. Mike, the new PO, would also be the first to admit adapting to life in a cat A prison after arriving on promotion from a cat C, wasn't easy for him either. He struggled with being on first-name terms with prisoners. And the more senior staff struggled when comparing him to Roy.

Once a week, we would go over to the hospital wing. For those of you who've ever watched the film *One flew over the cuckoo's nest*, you can get a good feel for the place. The hospital wing was a standalone building on the other side of the prison. It had fantastic staff and some of the country's most notoriously mentally ill patients.

Governor John Marriott had asked if we could deliver some form of PE for the patients once a week as they couldn't attend the gym. We only had a large empty room to work in, and limited resources, so we would usually do stretching or yoga. Mick, who ran an aerobics class in visits once a week with staff, families, and people from the local community, decided to carry out an aerobics class. It went down a storm with the patients and became the mainstay of what we delivered there.

I remember going to the hospital with our jukebox one afternoon to take the session. As always, Tommy Mulligan (RIP) was the first to arrive. He would normally ask what music we had got to play. I had many takers that day, around eight in the group, which was pretty decent. It depended on how patients felt with their medications, etc. Sometimes, it would be only two or three patients.

I noticed that day Tommy had a Walkman and headphones on. I pointed out to him that if he wore them, he wouldn't be able to hear me counting him in to change the moves or listen to the same beat of the music as the rest of us. Tommy was adamant; he wanted to listen to his headphones, I didn't have time to stand discussing it, so I started the class. Starting nice and slow, with some mobilisation exercises, arm circles small to big etc. I observed the group and saw Tommy line dancing at the far side of the room.

I tried to ignore it, but in the end, after he'd crashed into a few people, I went and took his headphones off. Thankfully, he agreed to listen to my music. As part of the class, I always liked to get them involved and would call one of them out one at a time to give the course a move. It was entertaining at times; everyone would be pogo dancing to a warm-up track, and I would keep trying to steer them in the right direction, but it didn't always go to plan.

The following week I took Mike, our new PO, for his first introduction to the hospital class. Tommy was again the first to arrive. The hospital officer had rung the gym in the morning and informed me that loads were asking about the session and wanted to do aerobics.

I had 12 patients turn up. I got ready and noticed Tommy with his Walkman and headphones again. This time though, he wanted to go further and asked me if he could start the class. I agreed to let him. We all spread out facing Tommy; Mike's face was a picture.

Tommy started making a few warm-up moves to the music he could only hear. I went up to Tommy, took his headphones off and pointed out that it might be better for the class if we could all hear the music; he agreed to let me put his tape in our jukebox. I could see Mick shaking his head. I could imagine him saying, 'this doesn't happen in a cat C'. We started the class again with Tommy's tape now playing for all to hear. The first song up was 'You picked a fine time to leave me, Lucille'. I couldn't stop laughing; eventually, I took back charge of the class, but I spent a lot of the day laughing about it. Not sure Mike found it funny; he wasn't a regular attendee of the hospital class after that day.

NEPO training

NEPOs (new entrant prison officers under training) better known to more senior staff as sprogs; this abbreviation was at a later date to be known as POELT (prison officer entry level training) but still referred to as sprogs or NEPOs.

We had an influx of new staff starting, and I was tasked with training them in the mornings. They had to complete the bleep test first and show a marked improvement when they completed it the second time. After discussing it with the other PE staff, we shifted slightly from the norm of a beasting session. I'd talked about my NEPO course and how, for many, not including me, it put them off coming to the gym after completing their training course. I suggested we make it fun and attractive so they might consider coming here on their lunch break instead of the staff club for a few pints. Yes, that did happen in those days. Only a few prisons now still have a staff club, if any. Very few even have a staff mess as they did back then. The staff mess at Parkhurst was run by Daryl, a big chap who always looked after the gym staff when we had lunch there.

We had 15 NEPOs. So, after a brief introduction and a health and safety chat, I got them on the line in the morning and invariably gave them press-ups for failing to get there quickly enough. We hadn't gone completely soft on them. Circuit day as well, so they would be working hard. At the end of the session, I got them back on the line. I explained the weekly programme and told them they were lucky compared to previous courses. We would be playing far more sports to make it more enjoyable. I told them how staff could use the gym facilities over lunch and how it was essential to keep themselves physically fit to respond to alarm bells and do the job to the best of their abilities. They must have looked at many staff in those days and thought, 'well, not many are using the gym'. I also said what a great governor we'd got in John Marriott and, "he's aware that PE might be hard for many of you, so he's given me a weekly pass for you to get a free lunch each day from the mess".

After completing their final bleep test, the NEPOs were off to complete other training. On Tuesday, I received a letter from John Marriott asking me to make an appointment to see him. I hadn't got a clue why. I arrived at his office; he invited me in.

John had his custom red tie on, being well-known as a Labour man. He handed me a bill from Daryl in the mess for two weeks' worth of lunches. A bit like back in the mill, I was bang to rights. John thankfully laughed when I did and followed with, "I can't believe Daryl didn't question it, thick bugger!"

First development course and meeting Joanna Lumley

Gary and I were going to a development course in the South East, with an overnight stay in a hotel. The course was just a short distance from an old acquaintance of Gary's. Despite not having seen each other for years, they remained in contact.

Gary used to call her Joanna as she looked like Purdey, the character from the '70s TV series, The New Avengers, played by Joanna Lumley. So, Gary excitedly contacted her and arranged to meet in the evening. She would bring a friend along, and we would have a meal and then take it from there. Gary was a little nervous, having not seen her for years. He showed me an old photo, and I reassured him that she couldn't have changed that much.

Off we went for the day's course, which was a bit of a jolly. Then we got back to the hotel and got ready for the evening. As we waited, Gary said, "If I say ring the prison, it's a signal for you to use the excuse of having to go back to the jail because there's a problem."

We sat waiting. At the same time we were expecting Joanna Lumley to appear, in walked a very large lady that didn't remotely look like Purdey, or Joanna Lumley, apart from still having the '70s bob hairstyle. On the other hand, her friend was quite pleasing to the eye. Over she walked, recognising Gary immediately, and greeted him with a hug. I quickly told her how well she'd aged and looked better than in the photos Gary always showed me. Gary just agreed and backed up what I'd said.

He couldn't hide his disappointment from me, though. I could see his jaw hit the floor when he first saw Purdey. I offered to get us all a drink, and Gary said, "Phil, get the ladies whatever they fancy, but before we have one, you'd better ring Mick at the prison just to check we are good for staying over." He turned to Joanna Glumly (in my head, I'd renamed her) to explain how the prison had problems and we were unlikely to be able to stay overnight.

I went to the reception and asked if I could borrow the phone. The lady at the desk stayed around, so I pretended to dial out and then had a made-up conversation with Mick. I got us all a drink on the way back.

Gary said, "Did you speak to Mick?" I replied, "Yes, mate; he said all was good and for us to have a nice evening." Gary went a little red in the face and then a little redder as I went on to say, "Isn't it great news? After all these years, we don't have to rush off anywhere, and you and Purdey have got all night to catch up."

At breakfast, Gary came into the self-service with Purdey holding his hand. When she went for her big plate of full English breakfast, he looked at me and said, "you fucking wanker".

He didn't swear very often. When Purdey returned, I made a point of saying how pleased it made me to see Gary so happy again. I added, "I know he was a little nervous about meeting you after all these years, Purdey, but you haven't changed much from the photos Gary was always showing us."

When we got back to the prison, Gary ripped up his photo and apart from me reliving that night with him on a few occasions, he never mentioned her again.

A win at last (almost)

Back in the swing of things, and Gary was ignoring all calls and contact from Purdey, I had arranged a staff v prisoners football match. At the time, we had a strong team, with me and Dave,

Stella's ex, forming a good partnership up front. I'd planned it for my weekend off, so I would just come in on my rest day to play. John Marriott, who was very supportive of these events, agreed to let staff on duty play.

I was out on the field the weekend before the match, having put up the nets before an inter-wing fixture. It was a big game between the two leading wing teams, with many big hitters participating. I was there as the two teams came out. Gerry Parker, the captain of one side, began shouting, "Where's Scouse?"

Scouse was one of their best players and probably the best player in the prison at the time. Scouse had yet to appear for the match. He had had his throat cut on the walkway to the pitch. Thankfully, after a trip to outside hospital, he survived. The odds for the game had been balanced up. The other team won, so someone had done their homework. Bets always took place on the football, and the games were always feisty. The following week would be the same.

At the time, Dogon Arif was our gym orderly. So, we had a week of banter leading up to the game. I jokingly asked if he would be dropping his brother Dennis for the match. The game day arrived, and Dogon and I shook hands on a bet for a Mars Bar. He confidently gave me the draw after I pointed out we were the away team.

The game kicked off, and Dave put us into a quick lead. Everyone in the prison who could be, was out watching the match. There was anger aimed at the prison team from the touchline. Staff beating prisoners didn't happen. The whole yard felt on the verge of rioting when we went two-nil up. Prisoners were on the sidelines arguing, and players had also started to argue with each other, and you could see this could turn nasty. With ten minutes to go, the prisoners pulled one back.

Having refereed the games regularly, I knew it was standard practice to play until the gates were opened for the prisoners to return to their wings. The PO in charge of the movement always called time. As the game neared the end, I noticed quite a crowd had worked its way over to the gate. I've witnessed Fergie time before, but this was ridiculous. We had been playing for over 15 minutes past the end of the association. Gerry Parker struck a well-taken goal; the gate immediately opened. The whistle was blown; we had drawn two-two in what was one hell of a hard-fought game.

You could see the relief on Dogon and Dennis's faces. A draw was a fair result on the balance of play, but I couldn't help but feel gutted when I was later told that the crowd at the gate had threatened the PO into not opening the gate.

THE GREAT ESCAPE

When I arrived at Parkhurst in 1991, it was a building site. I was amazed at how much building work was going on in a high-security prison, home to some of the most notorious and dangerous men in the prison system. It's also worth noting that Parkhurst wasn't built or designed to be a high-security prison. The continual building work at the Victorian jail, which began in 1988 and should have finished in 1993, took over a decade to complete.

I remember having numerous full staff meetings where John Marriott would address the ongoing work. On several occasions, he informed staff how he'd put business cases forward for more security cameras and higher-grade ones than were currently in use at the Victorian jail. He'd also requested an upgrade on the current geophone system, an alarm mechanism for fences, to alert of any attempted escape.

One of the major concerns at that time was to get dumper trucks, cranes, bulldozers, numerous other vehicles, and contract workers in and out of prison. They effectively put a hole in the wall on the section running towards HMP Camp Hill to put in a second gate.

I know John Marriott had asked the then national head of security, Richard Tilt, to consider removing all category A prisoners from Parkhurst whilst this work was being carried out.

To get a clear indication of just how deprived of funding Parkhurst and the prison system was, you only needed to look in the visits hall at Parkhurst. At the time, it didn't even have any substantial CCTV, this being an area where prisoners and their visitors assembled in large numbers. As you can imagine, drugs would enter prison with considerable ease. It's no wonder that the go-to jail for long-term prisoners was Parkhurst.

Since retiring, after talking to some ex-prisoners of that era, I've discovered how some convicts had successfully bribed the tactical management officer at their previous jail to arrive at Parkhurst – paying substantial amounts of money.

In 1992-93, a prisoner named Pewter escaped from Parkhurst. Unlike what is considered 'the great escape' a few years later, Pewter got off the island and was re-arrested in London a few days later. The escape was kept out of the headlines by what is referred to as a 'D' notice. That stopped the press from revealing the facts to the public.

Pewter, who worked in the prison laundry, was believed to have hidden in the back of a bin wagon, which used to enter the jail and, at the time, before the roll was declared correct on the wings. Some practices changed afterwards, but the place was still a building site with antiquated security systems.

January 3rd, 1995. The day that changed Parkhurst and the Prison Service forever.

The day started with me on an A shift, meaning I was in all day, from 7.30 till 8.30 in the evening. But I went in early for a workout on the rowing machine and a quick weight training session. Later, I took an aerobics class in the hospital wing, where I had quite a surreal experience, recognising a prisoner called Dave.

I recalled chatting with Dave on numerous occasions whilst banging him up on B wing. He had many photos on his pin board of him at the side of a rally car and various snaps of other vehicles. I am not interested in that sport or cars, but I would engage in conversation, especially if I carried out LBB checks in a cell. Many prisoners didn't like what they perceived as an intrusion, so I used that as a distraction, so Dave didn't mind me doing my job. It was my way of making the job easier.

I set up my jukebox and got my music ready to play, then in walked Dave, or at least I thought it was him. He used to have what could be best described as a biker look with long, thinning, greasy hair. Today, Dave had washed his hair, applied makeup, and wore a long flowery dress. "Hi Gov," he said as I looked him over, still trying to confirm that it was him. "Dave, isn't it"? I replied.

We went on to talk about his journey and how he was now living in role for 12 months before he would be moved to a female prison. To this day, I don't know whether that materialised. I know it's still debated whether it's right or wrong.

The lesson ran smoothly; even Tommy joined the group without his Walkman or headphones.

Dave danced around in his dress with his now washed, thinning, long hair trying its best to flow with him. I can honestly remember thinking, 'I Love my job.' At the end of the session, I began rubbing (searching)everyone down and then got to Dave. He extended his arms to the side at shoulder height; I asked him to empty any pockets, then remembered he was wearing a dress. He ran his fingers through his hair, showing that he wasn't concealing anything, and then I rubbed him down. "Watch my tits," he said. I replied, "Why? Do they do tricks?" He laughed, and I commented on liking his dress.

The rest of the day, up until the evening, was like most days, made up of playing or refereeing sports. It was Micky and me on evening duty. We also had a designated Juliet 1 officer who was I/C of the gym party off the wings. He had a radio and would seek clearance.

Mick and I walked around to the furthest wing, the wing that also supplied the Juliet officer. Mick or I would call 'gymnasium', then the prisoners who wanted to go would come down. The cleaning officer marked them off his roll, usually by simply writing a G on a board in chinagraph (every Officer carried a red and black one in his shirt pocket).

Juliet 1 would count the prisoners off the wing and confirm the figure with the Officer on the roll board. When we left, the Officer would report those numbers to the control room, keeping a running roll.

We walked to the next wing, the Juliet or a PEI would enter the wing whilst the other two stayed outside, supervising the prisoners. The same roll procedure occurred before leaving and adding to the gym party. We walked all the way around to the rear of the wings to collect from the front of the final wing, the smaller one of the three wings. With all the prisoners in one group, one PE staff member walked at the front, one in the middle, and the Juliet took up the rear. On arrival at the gym, the PEI counted the prisoners through the gate and confirmed the numbers with Juliet 1.

On that particular evening, we had five-a-side football and weights going on in the gym. Micky was in the weights room, and I was refereeing the five-a-side. I had three teams, so it was quite a busy session. I ran a round-robin competition, a mini-league. The games were, as usual, feisty affairs but nothing out of the ordinary. Mick went around with a book, writing the names of everyone in the gym. Three prisoners, Rodger, Rose and Williams, were among those names.

With the system that was in place, Mick had to come to the sports hall to get the names of everyone in there. He then gave the list to Juliet 1, who would lock himself in his office between the two areas, with windows all around, so he could supervise and press the alarm bell if needed. He would again ring the control room and confirm his roll.

At the far end of the weights room was a smaller room with a door leading to a storeroom and yet another exit out of the weights room that led to a small sterile area, which we occasionally used for gym equipment deliveries. It was also where the special needs van parked on their weekly visits. There were gates leading out to the exercise area, football pitches, and some old workshops that included a metalwork shop known as the engineering shop, where, unbeknown to me at the time, Rodger worked.

I was aware Williams worked in a workshop as he had previously built an exercise bike, which, when pedalled, produced an electrical current that ran through the handlebars. The prisoners held competitions on who could handle the biggest current.

Having spoken to both Rodger and Rose years later, I was told that when Micky had taken their names, they made good their escape through that door. I was also told the key they had made was manufactured over a period of time after they had picked up on the fact that a governor grade would point his key at them as he talked.

Many stated the key was tested on several occasions; just a few days before the escape, they had allegedly tried and the first gate, a wooden gate, opened but wouldn't lock behind them. So, they aborted that attempt.

One significant security lapse was that one key got them out of the gym and gained access to the exercise yard and the workshop, where they had manufactured and concealed a ladder. Over a few months, Williams had tested for camera black spots by approaching various parts of the fence on the association field to see if it was noticed. As far as we were concerned back in the gym, everything was normal. The five-a-side got feisty, but that wasn't unusual. The first time I noticed something untoward was at the end of the session.

Bear in mind that Rodger, Rose and Williams had made good their escape. We called time at the end of the session. I cleared the sports hall, collecting all the shin pads and putting the other equipment away. Mick cleared the weights room. The Juliet got permission to move back to the wings where the procedure of coming to the gym would be reversed, with the cleaning officer on each wing ready to receive their prisoners back and rub them off the roll board.

In the gym, the practice was for the Juliet to count the prisoners into a holding area just outside the entrance to the gym. The Juliet usually waited for us to give the all-clear, and then he would count them out of the holding area with one of us going ahead to supervise. Me and Micky, as always, did a sweep of the place and shower areas to check we were empty of prisoners.

There was a lot of shouting going on. I came out of the shower area to find the Juliet and the prisoners starting to leave. I called to Micky that they were going. I caught up with the Juliet. The prisoners had shouted and were complaining about getting cold after their workout, so the Juliet had let them out and failed to do a proper count; in his mind, I guess he thought if we had done our job correctly behind, he'd have everyone he should have. Whilst the alarm could have been raised sooner, it's worth noting, it wouldn't have prevented the escape.

In truth, the whole evening was a catalogue of errors. I dropped prisoners back onto the first wing while Mick and the Juliet would carry on to the other two wings. I confirmed numbers with the cleaning officer and walked around to meet Micky in preparation for our second evening gym class. Mick had dropped his party off on a wing and confirmed numbers. Juliet continued to his wing and was met by the cleaning officer. All three escaping prisoners were on the same wing. We'd had 35 prisoners that night but only returned 32 to the wings. All I can imagine is that the cleaning officer had presumed he'd missed them and scrubbed the names off without thinking or that he thought he'd made a mistake marking them off in the first place.

We called for a second gym and repeated the whole process. The second gym was always much quieter because prisoners wanted to get on the phones or into the TV room.

Just as we were ending the second gym, the alarm was raised. A dog handler doing his perimeter check had found a hole in the fence and the makeshift ladder; a fake gun was later also discovered.

As you can imagine, all hell broke loose. The wings were ordered to lock up and complete a full prison roll check. After helping with the roll check, I was told to go to the gate and await further orders. With the roll check complete, it was discovered that Andrew Rodger, Keith Rose and Matthew Williams were missing and now believed to have escaped.

It soon became clear that the three had been in the gym on that first session. The escapees had almost a two-hour head start on the police, who began a major manhunt. Unlike the previous escape, this one couldn't be covered up. I remember thinking of the three prisoners who had escaped, you just wouldn't put the three of them together; to say it was a strange mix would be an understatement.

I had been told Rose's primary intention to escape was to plead his innocence again. My only logic was that Andy had been the muscle, someone who could easily cut through a fence and bend it back with his bare hands. After all, I'd witnessed Andy almost break through a cell door after he folded his bed in half. I can only imagine Williams was the brains to make the key. Rose had told the other two he could fly a plane; Rose had always protested his innocence and, if you cared to listen, would often talk to me about the lack of ballistics evidence surrounding the gun in his case. I knew him primarily for his time on the rowing machine, wearing his customary headband.

The three men on the run were all considered extremely dangerous. Keith Rose, a computer company director, had been jailed for life in 1991 for murdering Juliet Rowe, the wife of a supermarket owner, at her home in Budleigh Salterton, Devon, in 1981. He allegedly shot her dead in a bungled kidnapping attempt but remained at large for eight years until he was caught in 1989 for kidnapping and holding the son of a food tycoon, Victor Cracknell, for ransom.

Cracknell had been kidnapped at gunpoint in his home near Guildford and tied up. But he managed to free himself after five days, and Surrey police arrested Rose. Detectives in Devon reopened the investigation into Mrs Rowe's murder.

Rose was jailed for the murder in 1991 while already serving 15 years for kidnapping. I recall when I worked on the wing, Rose's crime was going out on 'Crimewatch' – they all made their way to the TV room to watch it. Keith was only expecting the programme to cover his latest offence. Much to his and other prisoners' surprise, it also covered the link to the earlier hostage attempt and murder for which he ultimately got convicted. He kept a low profile for a little while afterwards because the alleged first offence was against a female, which can sometimes cause problems in prison under the 'prisoner moral code', which existed more then than it appears to today.

Matthew Williams, who studied microbiology and genetics at Leeds University, was detained for life after admitting 11 charges, including arson, theft, and conspiracy to cause explosions. Williams was described as 'a gifted student who so hated the human race that he set out to destroy it'. At his trial in 1989, a jury was told he placed a nail bomb in a crowded street in Liverpool. He also tried to poison the North-west water supply by injecting a fly with poison.

A PEI, who became one of my best friends when I went to Long Lartin, was taken hostage when Williams had previously tried to escape on escort from Long Lartin to Parkhurst. Williams had made it clear he didn't want to be transferred to Parkhurst. Williams suddenly produced a needle on the escort and held it to my friend's neck. He claimed to have AIDS and had cut himself with the needle. He demanded that the driver stop and for them to let him out. The driver got on the radio to the police. As they exited the van, the police used batons to disarm Williams.

I'm guessing Williams, on arrival at Parkhurst, must have been located in the segregation unit and should have spent some time in patches, yellow and blue overalls worn at all times by a prisoner deemed an escape risk or had recently attempted to escape. I can't recall ever seeing him as an E-list prisoner, but that's not to say he wasn't. If he was, someone made the decision to take him off it.

Andrew Rodger had been jailed for life in 1987 after he told the Old Bailey, "I went berserk," when he attacked John Garrett, a nightwatchman, with a crowbar, after being caught trying to steal from vending machines in Ilford, East London. He was very stocky and spoke with a soft Scottish accent – even when asking if you were counting the chips. The escape triggered an extensive manhunt that lasted for five days.

After getting over the wall, the three of them didn't know they had a good head start. Had they realised and got a taxi straight to the ferry, they would have had an excellent chance of making the mainland. Instead, they stuck to their plan, catching a cab to Sandown Airport. Rose had told the other two that he could fly a plane on the night; however, he couldn't get one started, let alone fly it.

They went to the local Tesco not far from the airport and got some food, and it's believed they had smuggled money into the prison through visits. They went to Ryde, where they hid in a garden shed. Five days later, they were spotted on Lushington Hill, literally a mile from where I lived. They were planning to try and steal a boat when the off-duty officer from Parkhurst spotted them. Rodger and Rose surrendered immediately; Williams briefly got away by diving through a hedge. He was finally cornered on a mud flat as he attempted to swim across the River Medina.

Even though, at the time, the police seemed adamant they were still on the island, I was surprised that they were only really a stone's throw from the prison five days later. When the three were back in custody, amazingly and to everyone's astonishment, they pleaded not guilty for the escape.

A trial was held in Woolwich Crown Court, Belmarsh. Micky and I had to attend the court each day in case we were called to give evidence. I was told early in the second week that I wasn't being called, so I went to the public gallery to watch the proceedings. Keith Rose objected to this through his solicitor. Still, the Judge overruled and said if I wasn't giving evidence, he saw no reason to remove me from what is a public gallery. I gave Keith a little smile.

Exclusive Interview with Keith Rose. 02/04/2023

I met with Keith currently at HMP Leyhill Open Prison and awaiting his parole hearing, for an exclusive interview to establish the facts about the escape from Parkhurst that night on 03 Jan 1995. Keith described the build-up and the planning of the escape. Keith told me how his main reason for the escape attempt was to highlight his murder case, for which he still protests his innocence. The plan was first hatched whilst the three of them, Keith, Matthew and Andy, were watching the London Gangsters playing football out on the exercise field/yard. They told each other that if prisoners could escape from the SSU in Whitemoor, they could get out of Parkhurst.

There were many discrepancies between Keith's version of events to those widely reported by the media, and even according to the reports relayed to me on the evening of the event. Keith has nothing to gain by disclosing anything and was happy to record an accurate account of the night that changed the Prison Service forever. Andy Rodger was key to the escape in that he was employed in the metal workshop, where the ladder and the key were made. Many, including myself, had previously believed the key was made by either Keith or Matthew.

Keith told me that the plan that started in October 1994 only took six weeks to be ready to carry out. They held back on the escape attempt because they knew the repercussions the escape would have on the prisoners left behind. With Christmas looming, it would significantly impact the jail at an important time for many.

Keith and Matthew had discovered that there were two primary keys to the gates in Parkhurst, and both were marked with a piece of coloured plastic, one red and one blue; they had also noticed that one key opened all the gates from the rear of the Gym to and including the metal workshop where the key and a ladder made up of 12-foot steel poles, that Andy had made brackets for to piece together to make a 24ft ladder; he also made rungs and bracketed them on. These were stored around the workshop in pieces till the night of the escape.

At the time, a Governor at Parkhurst, Alistair Munroe, would always get his key out and wave it in front of the prisoners as he spoke to them. Matthew would engage the Governor in conversation whilst Keith memorised the key markings. These details were then passed to Andy for him to make a key that he would keep testing in the workshop gates; once it finally worked in the workshop, it was taken to the Gym and tried on the door and gate at the rear of the Gym.

Keith also confirmed that he was indeed a qualified pilot, and the plan was to go to the Airport near Lake/ Sandown and take a plane to fly to Bournemouth. Keith, a pilot, knew the frequency to call a mayday and then to subsequently make a landing. Keith had then planned to take another plane. Keith would fly the three escapees to Belgium, where Keith claims the air space isn't as well manned as it is in France.

I also discovered that Keith had tried to give Ronnie Easterbrook, a prisoner I mentioned previously in the book, who later died on a hunger strike, the opportunity to jump on the escape. Informing him that if he could manage to switch his Gym class to an evening class, it could benefit him.

Keith told me they had been given a substantial amount of money, all in fifty-pound notes, by a high-profile IRA prisoner, one of only a few prisoners that knew about the plan.

When the three of them had reached the workshops to get the ladder, a dog handler had appeared and went into the spectacles workshop to carry out a security check. The three of them lay frozen on the ground, believing the game could be up. The dog stared at them momentarily then the dog handler called his dog away.

The money accumulated from the IRA prisoner was used to pay for a taxi which they cheekily flagged down outside Newport Police Station on the Island to take them to the Airport.

I pointed out to Keith that unbeknown to them at the time, but had they gone straight for the ferry, they would have gotten off the Island before the alarm had been raised. Keith said yes, if they had been aware, they would have headed straight for the Hovercraft, which only takes 15 minutes to cross the Solent.

When they arrived at the Airport, the first plane they tried had no battery, and the second was proving problematic to start. Whilst trying to get it started, an Air-sea rescue Helicopter flew over, spooking Matthew and Andy, them believing it to be the police searching for them. They ran off in opposite directions before returning to the plane.

A decision was made to abort the plan to take the plane; they went to Tesco just up the road and bought some provisions to get them through the night. They planned to lay low for a while before trying to steal a boat to cross the Solent. They went towards Ryde, where they stayed in a summerhouse they found unlocked in the back of a garden.

Five days after escaping, they were spotted by an off-duty Prison Officer and subsequently arrested. Andy and Keith both gave themselves up immediately. Still, Matthew managed to escape through a hedge momentarily and tried wading through water to escape.

All three pleaded not guilty to the escape but were given three years added to their sentences in the subsequent trial. Michael Howard later extended Keith's sentence to life that on appeal was later reduced by David Blunkett to 24 years.

Keith openly admits to the kidnapping that he was convicted of, but still protests his innocence of the murder that he was found guilty of despite numerous ballistic specialists claiming that Keith's gun wasn't the gun that carried out the murder. Markings on the cartridges were alleged to be the same or similar in both cases by the prosecution.

I know that Keith's version of events has stayed consistent, having had many conversations with him over the years regarding his case. If indeed he is innocent, I hope he manages to eventually clear his name; with recent discoveries of historical corruption in the Police forces, one cannot help but have reservations about his conviction on the murder charge. Especially when you consider if he had admitted the offence, he would likely have been out many years ago.

As far as the outside was concerned, the ordeal was over; but for all the staff in prison, it was only the beginning.

It sparked an extensive inquiry into Parkhurst and the whole prison system coming on the back of a large escape from HMP Whitemoor in 1994, where six prisoners had escaped. The investigation was to be carried out by Sir John Learmont and Sir John Woodcock and was referred to as the Learmont Woodcock Report. For balance, I've provided a summary of the report.

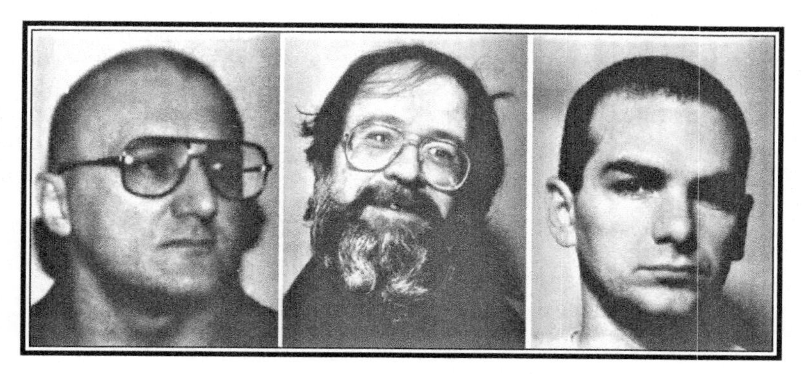

Left to right: Rodger, Rose and Williams.

The Woodcock Learmont report (feel free to skip)

"I am today publishing the report by General Sir John Learmont into prison security. I am extremely grateful to Sir John and to his two fellow assessors, Sir John Woodcock and Mr Gary Dadds, for their comprehensive and authoritative report. Let me begin by reminding the House of the circumstances which led me to ask Sir John to conduct his inquiry.

In September 1994 six exceptional risk Category A prisoners escaped from Whitemoor Prison. I asked Sir John Woodcock to conduct an inquiry into the escape and I presented his findings to the House on 19th December last year. I also asked General Sir John Learmont to conduct a comprehensive and independent review of physical and procedural security in the Prison Service in England and Wales and to make recommendations.

On 3rd January this year two Category A prisoners and one Category B prisoner escaped from Parkhurst. All three were recaptured on 8th January. I pay tribute again to the police for that successful operation.

An immediate inquiry was carried out by the Prison Service Director of Security. As I told the House on 10th January, this immediate inquiry highlighted very serious deficiencies in procedural and physical security at Parkhurst. I asked Sir John Learmont to extend his inquiry to include an independent assessment of the events surrounding the escape.

The report makes the most serious criticisms of Parkhurst and its management. On security procedures, Sir John found that the Prison Service's own security manual was disregarded and that the most basic security procedures were not observed. Sir John also makes a number of criticisms of the physical security of Parkhurst, including the failure of the Prison Service to provide the prison with the full benefits of technology.

I am also publishing today the report of the inspection of Parkhurst by HM Chief Inspector of Prisons, Judge Stephen Tumim. The inspection took place in October last year and the report was submitted at the end of February.

Judge Tumim also makes a number of severe criticisms of the situation at Parkhurst, including weak and inadequate security, unacceptable conditions in health care and drug dealing which pervaded the whole sub-culture of the prison. There was a reluctance by staff to assert proper control in areas such as searching and accounting for inmates. The judge considered the problems were so serious that he wrote to the director general before he even left the prison, with a copy to me, drawing attention to the serious shortcomings he had found. As I told the House on 10th January, I immediately spoke to the director general and asked for a full report. He assured me that all Judge Tumim's recommendations had been implemented.

Sir John Learmont recommends that Parkhurst should be taken out of the dispersal system as soon as possible and consideration given to its replacement by a more appropriate establishment (paragraph 2.179). I accept this recommendation. Parkhurst has not in practice operated as a dispersal prison since April when all Category A prisoners were removed from normal location. I have asked the Prison Service to identify another prison in the south-east of England to take Parkhurst's place in the dispersal system as soon as possible.

Sir John's inquiry was not a disciplinary inquiry. Sir John has recommended to me that no disciplinary inquiry should be undertaken into the escape from Parkhurst. He is of the view that such an inquiry could finally break the resolve and commitment of many of the staff at Parkhurst, with the very real possibility that the secure running of the establishment could be severely compromised. He is also of the view that it is difficult to see what a disciplinary inquiry would achieve. In considering this recommendation I have been influenced by the fact that more than one of those concerned will not be staying in the Prison Service. I have therefore decided to accept this recommendation.

The Learmont report makes it clear that responsibility for the Parkhurst escape was not confined to management and staff at Parkhurst. On the contrary: the report says that, 'alarm bells should have been ringing throughout the Prison Service' (paragraph 2.255), and that many of the ingredients, can be traced along the lines of communication to Prison Service headquarters. In his covering letter Sir John Learmont makes it perfectly clear that responsibilities ultimately reach the level of the Prisons Board and that is where criticism stops. Sir John has not found that any policy decision of mine, directly or indirectly, caused the escape.

I turn next to the organisation of the Prison Service and its relationship with the central Home Office. It is now some two-and-a-half years since the Prison Service became a next steps executive agency. The decision to make the service an agency was taken on the recommendation of an independent inquiry conducted by Admiral Sir Raymond Lygo. Sir John Learmont does not recommend that there should be any change in the agency status of the Prison Service. He does recommend that someone with wide experience of the workings of agencies should undertake an in-depth study of the relationship between the Prison Service and the Home Office. This work is underway and I shall report on it to the House when it is complete.

Sir John's report makes 127 detailed and wide-ranging recommendations. I accept the broad thrust of Sir John's analysis. About half of the recommendations endorse actions that have already been completed, are under way or are already planned. I will deal today with Sir John's key recommendations, and I will come back to the House with a full response in due course.

A key recommendation of the report is that there should be one maximum security prison to house the most dangerous prisoners in the system. This was a recommendation first made by the Mountbatten Inquiry in 1966 and accepted by the then Home Secretary (who is now the noble Lord, Lord Jenkins of Hillhead). But the Radzinowicz Report in March 1968 recommended against it and it was not implemented. Since then, the policy has been to disperse such prisoners among a small number of high security prisons. Sir John concludes that, 'the continuous development of explosives and weapons and their availability to criminals and their associates pose a much greater threat to the security of our maximum-security prisons than the Service has previously encountered'. He believes therefore that the most dangerous prisoners should now be housed in a purpose designed and built maximum security prison. This is a very far-reaching proposal which would represent a major departure in penal policy. The report makes a strong case for it. I have already asked the Prison Service to consider the feasibility, costs and benefits of building such an establishment and report to me in six months' time. The Prison Service will also consider Sir John Learmont's proposal for a single control prison to hold the most unruly and disruptive prisoners. I should welcome comments on these proposals.

Sir John also recommends a fundamental review of the system under which prisoners are allocated to different security categories according to the threat to the community and the likelihood of escape. I accept that a review of this system should take place.

Sir John also recommends that minimum physical security standards should be set for each category of prison. Work is well underway on bringing the dispersal estate up to the standards of security recommended by Sir John Woodcock. National standards exist for all new prisons. Decisions on the appropriate security standards for non-dispersal prisons will be based on the outcome of the review of categorisation.

One particular aspect which I asked Sir John to consider was the extent to which visits should be closed. He recommends that there should be closed visits for exceptional risk Category A prisoners other than in exceptional circumstances. This coincides with the policy I introduced in June this year.

I turn finally to Sir John's recommendations on the ways in which physical security is enhanced by activities and incentives. I told the House in December last year that the Prison Service would introduce a national framework of privileges and incentives. That framework is already in place and implementation has begun. Sir John recommends that a system requiring early release to be earned, not granted automatically as at present, would be a significant additional inducement to good behaviour. Last week I set out proposals for ending automatic early release and for introducing a system of earned remission.

But there are two issues on which Sir John and I must agree to differ. I reject his proposal that in-cell TV should be made widely available. This would not be consistent with my view that prison conditions should be decent but austere. Nor can I accept Sir John's proposal that home leave should be more widely available. In my view, the restrictions introduced earlier this year have an important role in protecting the public; and I have no plans to relax them.

Sir John Learmont has found a great deal that needs to be put right within the Prison Service, spanning leadership, structure, the management chain and the ethos of the service. He says that responsibilities ultimately reach Prisons Board level—and the criticism stops there.

These comments, coming so soon after the Woodcock Report on Whitemoor, cause me great concern. I must be able to assure this House, and through it the public, that the grave weaknesses in the service which have been disclosed will be put right. I have come to the conclusion, with some sadness, that this requires a change of leadership at the top of the Prison Service. The present director general has served in his post for nearly three years. I pay tribute to him for what he has achieved.

But I cannot overlook the serious criticisms in the report. I believe the service requires a change of leadership to carry forward the programme of reforms which is needed and to increase public confidence in the security of our prisons. The director general has accordingly ceased to hold his post with effect from today. The director of security will take over temporarily until a successor is appointed.

I believe that this report will be seen as a major milestone in the evolution of the Prison Service. I heartily endorse Sir John's conclusion that there is an abundance of excellent people within the Prison Service whose most fervent wish is to do a good and worthwhile job.

The changes that I have announced today will help them to achieve that goal. My Lords, that concludes the Statement."

Well done to any of you who read all of that.

The main gist was that Parkhurst would immediately be removed from the high-security estate. That had already effectively occurred by removing all category A prisoners by April 1995. That meant a massive reduction in staff with lots of uncertainty about how it would be achieved.

It touched on the failure of the Prison Service to provide the prison with the full benefits of technology. It was also a recommendation that they build one big supermax prison, then rumoured to be on the Isle of Wight. Mentioned many times since, but it has yet to happen. The report should have mentioned the number of times John Marriott had requested this and much more. Sadly, John was one of the first scapegoats for the escape.

Ironically, and of no surprise to those who worked for the Prison Service, Richard Tilt, who John had requested these upgrades from, was promoted temporarily to the director general of the Prison Service. John was also widely believed to be the scapegoat for saving Michael Howard's skin.

On the back of the report, prisons would introduce a national framework of privileges and incentives. This was probably one of the real successes of the report going forward and had a substantial positive impact on the smooth running of Britain's prisons.

Woodcock and Learmont disagreed on a couple of points, one being Learmont's proposal that in-cell TV should be made widely available. That happened, and many staff disagreed with it at the time. It was a great decision to impact prisons positively.

For one, it removed the TV rooms prisoners would try to make no-go areas. It also significantly impacted the IEP (incentive and earned privileges) scheme introduced in prisons. In some prisons, it was a place where tempers often flared over who watched what. In the Service, there's a saying, 'shit rolls downhill to the lowest possible level'. I witnessed that for the first time at Parkhurst. John Marriott left to work in mental health but sadly passed away in 1998 after a heart attack.

Governor John Marriott.

I was fortunate to know John, both socially and professionally. No one who met John Marriott, whether staff member or prisoner, ever felt they were taken lightly or dismissively. The capacity to engage with people of all backgrounds and to make them think they were fundamentally important was a great skill and no artifice. John loved people and related emotionally and instinctively to them. Prisoners and staff recognised the integrity of the man they dealt with. Perhaps it is a weakness in such as John that they assume that those above them in the hierarchy will display similar qualities.

I've never forgotten John Marriott, one of the best I ever had the pleasure of working for. RIP John.

The aftermath

With John Marriott having left and now head of mental health for the Isle of Wight, a few officers went to work both part-time and full-time for him.

Parkhurst was in a period of absolute uncertainty. Ricky Highmoor, an SO that had come over from Albany and was one of the best discipline SOs I'd ever worked with, was working the night of the escape. Ricky was moved back to Albany; that's how far the 'shit rolled'. He was a massive loss, he and PO Brooksy were a great team, and the staff all loved them.

Some staff moved to Kingston, over in Portsmouth. Later I would see some of them again when I did a brief three-year stint there. The prison football pitch and the big exercise yard containing the tennis courts were closed. The morale of staff was at rock bottom. The gym, by comparison, was still a very good place to work with the same great team. It felt different though.

Something had changed. It felt like the place had lost more than three prisoners that night; it had lost its soul.

Stick or twist!

Out of the blue, Stu McWilliam, the PE course director at Lilleshall, contacted me. He was ringing to see if I'd be interested in a vacancy that had become available at HM Brinsford Young Offenders Prison, near Cannock, in the Midlands. It was a huge honour for me to be the first PEI on Stu's list with all the PE staff he had trained. I gave it lots of consideration. Stu tried to secure a paid move, meaning I'd get some relocation assistance. Unfortunately, that didn't materialise, despite Stu's best efforts. The conversations had sparked my interest in a move though, and the Midlands would place me back nearer to visiting my mum and family in Manchester.

I looked through the vacancies, and a place for a PEI at Long Lartin was advertised. I already knew of Long Lartin from my initial training course when Steve Hamilton and Dick Tongue had been posted there. Dick had since been dismissed, but Steve and Adam Rodgers from my training course were still there. Unbeknownst to me, Madgey the Mountain Goat off my PE Course was also in the gym at Long Lartin. I wanted to continue in the high-security setting, so I duly applied.

I attended an interview. The interview went quite well. I also knew a couple of the other PE staff that had applied. Jayne, the lady on the panel, said she had to look twice at my sick record; I never realised, but I hadn't had a single day off sick since starting the job.

To my surprise, they told me at the end of the interview that I would be offered the job but to keep it to myself until I had written confirmation.

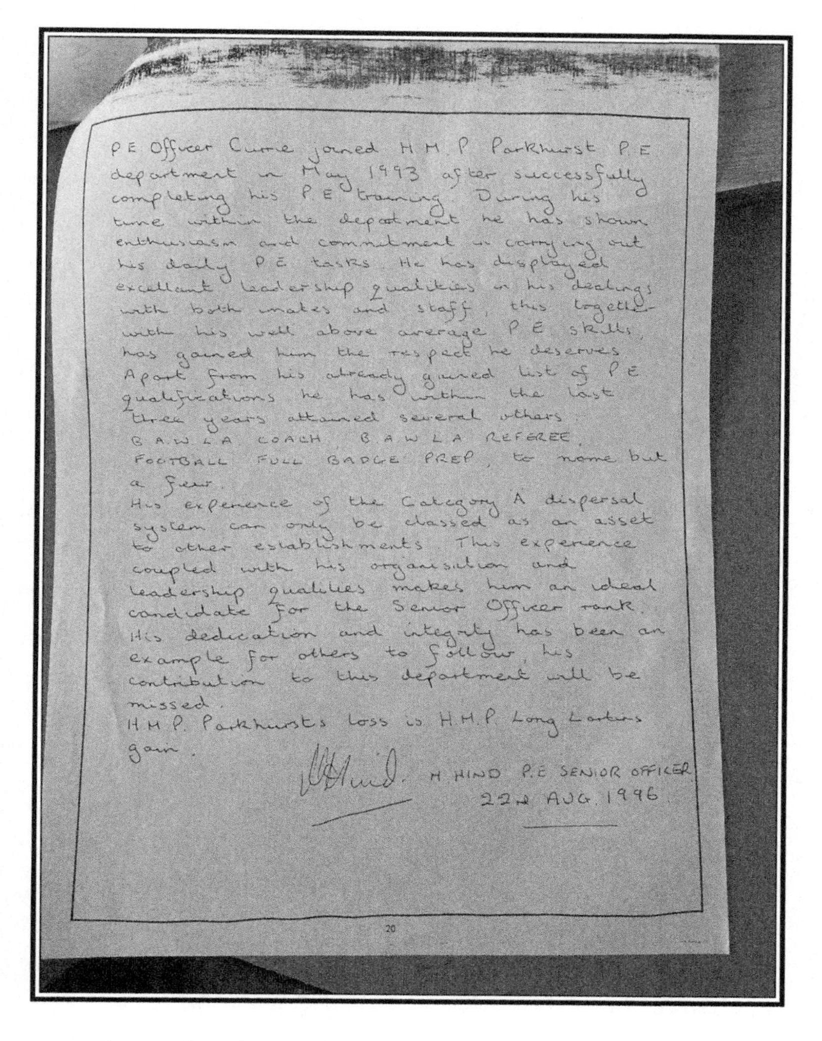

P E Officer Currie joined H M P Parkhurst P E department in May 1993 after successfully completing his P E training. During his time within the department he has shown enthusiasm and commitment in carrying out his daily P E tasks. He has displayed excellent leadership qualities in his dealings with both inmates and staff, this together with his well above average P E skills, has gained him the respect he deserves.
Apart from his already gained list of P E qualifications he has within the last three years attained several others.
B.A.W.L.A COACH, B.A.W.L.A REFEREE, FOOTBALL FULL BADGE PREP, to name but a few.
His experience of the Category A dispersal system can only be classed as an asset to other establishments. This experience coupled with his organisation and leadership qualities makes him an ideal candidate for the Senior Officer rank.
His dedication and integrity has been an example for others to follow, his contribution to this department will be missed.
H M P Parkhursts loss is H.M.P. Long Lartins gain.

H. HIND P.E SENIOR OFFICER
22nd AUG. 1996

20

A copy of a reference from my PESO Micky Hind at Parkhurst.

After the interview, I went to look around Long Lartin's Gym, where I caught up with Madgey and the others. It was a new gymnasium that hadn't been opened for very long. The Gym was a decent size and had an adequately equipped weights room with an outside area with a football and rugby pitch.

All the lads were welcoming and spoke quite positively about the place. Then I met John, who said, you don't want to come here. I later discovered John is a great lad, but even by his own admission, he's very much a glass half empty guy. I went home with a big decision to make. I'd secured the job if I wanted it, but now I had to decide whether to stick or twist.

Decision time

I went back to the Island and weighed up the pros and cons. The most significant pull was that I didn't want to serve my entire career in just one prison. The easy decision would be to stay at Parkhurst in my comfort zone. Many prisoners at Parkhurst had gone to Long Lartin or would at some stage. Moving to Long Lartin would be like starting again, maybe less so with prisoners than staff.

The downside was, as far as I could ascertain from my look around and talking to half-glass John and the others, little quality PE was going on at the place. I didn't want just to be supervising. I deliberated on it long and hard, chopping and changing my mind. My marriage to Alison, my then-wife, had hit difficulties, mainly down to the person I was then. I'd like to blame it on my youth, but sadly, I maintained my ways for way too long. hurting many people along the way. Not least of those, my three older children, Emma, Sheri and in particular Jack who was still very young. My decision to move hundreds of miles away and a ferry ride had obvious repercussions, and looking back I didn't realise the impact it would have on my three children or on how much contact I had with my older children over the years. Luckily despite the distance and my selfishness at the time, I still have a very close relationship with all three. My infrequent visits to the Island, and subsequent lack of contact in their early years still weigh heavily on my conscience. Some of my proudest moments were giving my eldest daughter Emma away at her wedding and attending her passing out parade when she joined the Navy. Both of these were surpassed by the birth of my amazing grandson Morgan.

I spoke with Gary, Mick and Woody, and they all wanted me to stay, or at least said they did. My confirmation letter arrived, and even if I accepted, I wouldn't start for 12 weeks because Parkhurst would hold me until they got a replacement. I made up my mind; I accepted the position.

I managed to find a room to rent in the area, lodging with a lady called Netty. Time passed quickly, and I was on my last shift before I knew it. The gym orderlies and numerous other prisoners I got along with came down on my last working session. They presented me with a goody bag full of prison soap, a prison vest signed by them all, and a pair of prison work boots with a 'Nike Tick' painted on the side with Tippex and 'Nice Hair' instead of 'Nike Air'.

It was a very emotional farewell. In the evening I went for a drink with the staff. The PE Staff gave me a card and presented me with a sports watch. I couldn't help but think, 'I hope I've made the right decision.' Before we said our goodbyes, Gary said an old friend was one of the governor grades there; his name was Ferdy. "Make sure you pass on my regards. And if you need anything, he'll look after you." I told him I'd make sure Ferdy got the message.

LONG LARTIN, STARTING AGAIN

I travelled up on Sunday and arranged to spend the first week at my friend's place, Paddy, from my PE course. I played five-a-side football on Sunday with Paddy's football team, and Monday, they were all going to Bridgenorth for a drink, so I went along. I wasn't a big drinker but had more than I should have, starting my new job the next day. Monday was a bank holiday, so I was starting on the Tuesday.

I was in an induction week with the training SO Tony Taylor, RIP (who sadly passed away recently; I later learned his nickname was BIFFO (big ignorant fucker from Oldham)). Tony greeted me at the gate; I couldn't draw keys until I had completed key training.

In the morning, I was a bit delicate, to say the least; in fact, I had to pull over to be sick on my hour-long journey to the prison.

"Follow me, daft lad," he said. I liked Tony from the word go. He reminded me a little bit of Dick Tongue, a little brash. We got to the training centre, and he said to a lady there, "get the kettle on, wench". She smiled and asked if I wanted a cuppa. I informed her I don't drink tea or coffee. "Some fuckin' northerner you are, Currie," he said. The day went on the same. Bob, the SO from the Gym, rang to check how it was going and when I'd be over there. So, I went at lunchtime to train and say 'hi' to the lads.

Tony did my key training the following day and told me to return to my department. He said, "You're going to the gym; it's not like you're doing a proper job, right?" The training was over, and I was off to start my new job, PEI, HMP Long Lartin.

I started to get to know more people and all the PE staff. For the first few days, it was like starting all over again, getting to know the routine, observing how people worked, and how they interacted with prisoners. After a week or two, I was invited to a night out, and many staff were going.

As I said, I don't drink much, but I like to hit the dance floor all night; most people think I'm drunk as a skunk, but I'm sober. It was a great night and a friendly atmosphere; it would appear the whole club was full of prison staff or firefighters from a nearby training college, and many ladies were there for that reason.

A few weeks passed quickly, and I was getting my feet under the table at work and socially. Chris (Gucci), John, Ralph, Kev and Bealey had all, at some point, been around before a night out and met my landlady Netty. She was a lovely woman and even offered the lads who lived further away to crash for the night if they wanted.

Since working 12-hour nights in the mill, six to six, I've never needed much sleep; four to five hours is plenty. So, when Chris stayed and wanted to go to sleep by three, I was more than happy to stay awake and wind him up. After arriving back in the early hours one night, Chris pleaded with me to let him sleep. I'd sit talking to him; I'd drip drops of water off my fingers onto his face as he closed his eyes, I tried anything. He was, as always, downstairs near the kitchen on a put-you-up bed that Netty had made for him. "You Love it," I said." Chris was now getting annoyed. "What makes you think that, you knob."

I replied, "Well, if you didn't, you'd have got in Netty's bed."

"What?"

"You'd have got in her bed upstairs; she's out at her boyfriend's tonight."

Chris got up, marched upstairs, and pulled back the sheets on Netty and her startled boyfriend. I heard Chris scampering down the stairs. "You absolute tool," he said.

I was rolling with laughter. Even more so when he angrily described the look on their faces. Chris had given her a swift apology and fled.

Surprisingly, I stayed at Netty's for a good few months until I moved into the then governor's secretary's place, Mary, again renting a room. I landed lucky there. Mary and her friend Jules became lifelong friends of mine.

Payback

I'd started to feel more at home in the Gym, getting used to the routine and getting to know quite a few prisoners. They'd always ask where I came from; once I said Parkhurst, they accepted me.

One morning, on my way into the prison, I was walking across to the Gym, among a group of staff and what I presumed to be a governor in a suit. As we walked through a gate en route, one of the officers called him by the name of Ferdy. I suddenly remembered Gary's message for his friend. I approached him and asked if he was Ferdy Parker. "Yes," he replied, looking intrigued. I delivered Gary's message, passing on his regards. Ferdy didn't speak. He just looked through me, stone-faced. I made a hasty exit from the group.

The first chance I got, I rang Gary and told him of that morning's events. All I could hear was him crying with laughter. He then said to me that Ferdy had joined the job on the Isle of Wight, and the PEIs there, including Gary, had made his life hell during training, dangling him over the railings at one point. I'd innocently made a high-ranking enemy; my woes had just begun.

A couple of days later, I was called up to Ferdy's office, where he and another Scottish governor, who I also didn't know at the time, sat. "Come in, Currie," he demanded and told me to take a seat. "Listen carefully; one step out of line, and I'll have your job."

I replied, "That sounds like a threat."

"It's a promise." He added: "And close the door on your way out."

Only a couple of days later, after going to lunch in the staff mess with Chris and sitting with the admin ladies having a laugh, I was called into Bob, the SO's office. He told me Ferdy had just rung and heard me talking to the women in the staff mess. Ferdy claimed, what he'd heard could be classed as sexual harassment. Gary had certainly paid me back for my Purdey prank. I left in shock, wondering, 'what the hell have I done coming here?'.

I had a week or so respite before I was summoned to Ferdy's office. I sat down to a tape-recorded interview, going through all my claims to date for subsistence. Being on a paid move, I was entitled to claim overnight allowance for my lodgings etc. Thankfully, to my relief and Ferdy's annoyance, nothing was untoward.

Seeing an old face in the Gym

Back in the weights room at work, I bumped into a prisoner I'd known from the Gym at Parkhurst. He was a little stocky Turkish lad who was quite strong, especially doing a bench press, most prisoners' favourite exercise. I briefly spoke to him about how long he'd been at Lartin and what wing he was on etc. I was in the weights room and was having a workout as well. I was walking past him towards the end of the session when he stopped me and said he'd lost a lot of strength since Parkhurst; I said I'd noticed but wasn't going to say anything. I asked him about his diet and then invited him into the office for a chat. I ran through a series of questions, including "how's your sleep pattern?".

I then asked him how often he masturbated. He looked shocked but said, "Phil, I'm in prison man." He told me it was probably five times a day. Well, there's your problem. I informed him, "you're sapping your energy levels".

I told him not to worry, that I had a nurse friend in health care, and if he wants, I'll ring her to arrange a prescription for Bromide. He agreed. I proceeded to pretend to ring health care and asked to speak to Ruth. I continued the pretence, asking Ruth if she could prescribe the Bromide, but I would collect it from health care and administer it from down in the Gym. I left relevant pauses so he believed Ruth was on the other end of the conversation. I ended by thanking her and saying, "I'll pick it up later today." He thanked me and shook my hand; I said I'll see you tomorrow, and then hopefully, after a couple of weeks of taking it regularly, "your strength will return".

I told the other PE staff, then made my way into our back office to mix a concoction of milk coffee and a few other bits and pieces we had out there. Turkish lad turned up the next day excited to get started. I gave him some fluid, and he downed it in one. The other PE staff watched in disbelief. This process continued for the next week before I called him into the office and asked him how his training was going. He said a little better. So, I then enquired how many times he was now masturbating. He sheepishly told me still three or four times a day. "Ok, I'll ring Ruth again and ask her to prescribe a little stronger." I again pretended to have the conversation stating it had helped but that he was still masturbating three to four times, so I requested that she prescribe a stronger dose. I pretended she'd agreed and said I would administer it from the Gym again.

When I hung up, I said, "The Nurse told me this next dose is the maximum, and it's the equivalent of what they use for gorillas in the zoo to stop them from being over amorous." He smiled and looked quite proud. I said, "You Turkish boys have one hell of a libido."

He walked out with his head held high.

When I returned, I asked Andy how Turkish was doing on the Bromide; he confessed he couldn't keep a straight face, and he'd sussed him out. When Turkish came down, we had a good laugh about it – fair play, he may have been a big wanker, but he could take a joke.

Weeks passed, and I'd managed to stay out of Ferdy's way, and then someone broke the news that he'd gone for promotion at HMP Hewell, which isn't too far away but far enough for me to breathe a little easier. One morning, a full staff briefing was called where the governor, Jim Mullen, announced Ferdy was moving on. What a result; I clapped the loudest. It would be a few months before he left, but there was light at the end of the tunnel.

We did have one last exchange of words just before he departed. I arrived at the gate at the same time as Ferdy and joined the queue behind him. Ferdy used to wear a Stetson Cowboy Hat, and on this day, he was carrying a huge fruit cake in a see-through box. As we proceeded through the search area, he placed the Stetson on top of the cake box. I couldn't help myself. "Ah, morning, Ferdy, now that clears something up."

"What, Currie?" he replied.

"Staff have been wondering for years what you kept under your hat." I pointed and said, "Fruitcake." He scowled and went through the search.

Stomper

I said I wouldn't cover my personal life in this book, but Stomps was also a large part of my prison story, so I couldn't avoid it. So please be patient. I promise you; it won't turn into a Mills and Boon paperback.

I developed a good relationship with many of the ladies in the administration block. None more so than the typist department, where I frequently visited to get booklets made up for courses. I was preparing to implement a full-time PE course in the gym where we would employ 12 to 15 prisoners for a year on a roll on, roll off basis. Whenever I saw them, I usually rewarded Sandra, Andra and Vega's hard work with a box of broken biscuits from a local store. Even to this day, they'll joke about it.

This one day, I'd dropped more work off and a box of biscuits, then proceeded along the corridor to go see Carol in finance to sort a cheque out for me. I'd checked to see if Ferdy was in that day, so I knew I was in the clear.

En route, I walked past the switchboard office and saw Cazza talking to a young lady I hadn't recognised. I looked in and called good morning. Cazza and the new lady both said 'morning' and smiled. I caught the smile of the young lady; her whole face and eyes lit up; I did a double take and took a step back, then entered the office. I introduced myself to the new lady, and Cazza remarked about ignoring the charmer.

Sarah was the young lady's name; she was a local girl who had just started that week. I also gleaned from our brief conversation that it was her twenty-first birthday that week, and all her friends from work were going out on Thursday night. On my return to the gym, I told them about the girl I'd just met and said she looked like Courteney Cox from the sitcom Friends. I arranged for us all to go out on Sarah's party night without ulterior motives.

I saw Sarah a couple of times that week and rang to see how her new job was and to check where they were going for their night out. Kev, who had recently joined us in the gym and worked my weekend, was also coming out. He had recently split up with his wife. When we had a phone call in the gym, I'd often pretend to be one of the other lads, usually either Chris or Kev; it used to annoy Chris if the caller believed I was him as I would answer with a put on, Brummie twang. On one occasion that week, I pretended to be Kev. He was a youthful good-looking lad with rosy cheeks and a flat-top haircut. The phone call was from a not particularly attractive lady. I kept her on the phone, chatting her up for a while. After putting it down, she called back, and I again answered, "Gymnasium Kev speaking, can I help?" It was her again. She asked if I (Kev) was going on the night out. I said yes and flirted big time, saying, "make sure you save me the slow dance".

The night out arrived; I was excited to see Sarah and to watch how things unfolded with Kev and the not-so-attractive lady from work. The pub was rammed, prison staff and fire brigade galore. I spotted Sarah with friends: Becky, Clare, Cazza and others from the admin block. Not to be overly obvious, I started talking to Becky. She's a lovely girl, attractive, with long golden curly locks. I asked about the new girl Sarah and made it clear I fancied her. Becky being Becky questioned whether I was a little old for her; I was 11 years Sarah's senior. "That's not too bad, right?"

Becky gave me the lowdown on the new girl. Sarah already knew many of the girls at the prison from school, being a local. Becky then hit me with the blow of revealing Sarah had a boyfriend; he was in Spain but due to return home soon. "Ok," I said. "That gives me a little time," and I gave her a wink.

On that note, I went to wish Sarah a happy birthday and tell her how gorgeous she looked. Despite a few attempts from Cazza and others trying to rescue her, we had quite a long chat. I asked about her boyfriend, telling her I couldn't believe he'd let such a stunning lady come back from Spain without being with her.

We hit it off, and we laughed and joked; making her smile was a great feeling. She had those eyes that smiled with her; I was hooked.

We agreed to chat later and dance; I loved to hit the dance floor where I could stay all night. As luck would have it, Sarah was the same; she loved a boogie. I think most of our PE department had come out on the night. Chris (Gucci), Kev, Ralph, Madgey and John (half-glass empty). To my delight, I also spotted the not-so-attractive lady who believed she'd been chatted up by Kev all week. I remember smiling to myself as I kept catching her staring at him.

We stood at a raised bar, looking down at the busy dance floor. I could see Sarah and her friends dancing. Kev's admirer had finally plucked up the courage to go and talk with him. I watched, both intrigued and interested in how it might develop. At that point, it wasn't going anywhere.

A little while later, I saw Kev's admirer talking to her friend; I went over and made general conversation. During that chat, she asked me what was happening with Kev; I acted confused. She told me he'd chatted her up all week and asked her to save the last dance, "but now he doesn't seem interested". I pointed out that she'd got it all wrong: Kev had told me how he really liked her. I also said Kev had recently broken up with his wife, had had his confidence knocked with women, and was quite shy. "Easy to be brave on the phone," I added.

I convinced her to give it another go but told her she needed to be more assertive with him. I left it there and went over to chat with Kev and Chris. A few minutes later, 'not so attractive' was approaching Kev. She started to talk, needing to get close, with the music playing so loud. As she closed in for what Kev thought was to speak into his ear, she grabbed his head and pulled him in for a full-on snog. Kev gently pushed her off and shouted, "What are you doing?"

The poor girl looked confused and replied, "Well, you've been flirting all week." And stormed off. I was literally on my knees laughing. I filled him in on the story. Now to go and find Sarah.

I was throwing Sarah around, picking her up and having a great time. We were all on the dance floor, even ones like Chris, Kev and Madgey, who didn't dance too much. Kev had recovered and was now enjoying dancing with Clare, a massive flirt herself; she was flirting with Kev, and he was buying into it. I knew Clare from other nights out; she would have a good tease but nothing more.

Slow dance time came around all too soon. Not sure it's still a thing in the clubs anymore. I grabbed Sarah, and we chatted and laughed some more. She really did have the most fantastic smile. Clare had done her usual disappearing act, and Kev stood on the side looking glum. I told Sarah I'd walk her home and arranged to meet her outside. I asked Kev what had happened to Clare, subtly reminding him that his other admirer was still there. He didn't find it funny. I remembered that Clare shared a place with Becky and said, "Never mind, mate, I'll take you back to their place and sort it for you to stay." Kev perked up a little.

Outside, I met up with Sarah and said Kev has nowhere to stay, so we will just go to Becky's and ask if he can have the sofa for the night.

We walked to Becky's, and I knocked on the door; the light was still on, Becky answered, and I explained Kev had nowhere to stay, so was it ok if he had the sofa? I saw Kev inside, and Becky went off to bed. I went to tell Clare that Kev was staying; she was half asleep though, and, in no uncertain terms, told me to do one.

I went to Kev and whispered, Clare said to give it half an hour for Becky to get to sleep and go get in with her. His little face lit up. I walked Sarah back home to her parents' house, where she lived. I couldn't help but notice that with a few drinks inside her, she walked with a kind of stomp; this continued on the way home, even after she'd stopped to sit on a wall to remove her shoes, almost falling backwards in the process.

The next day we were at work. Chris had stayed with me, and I'd kept him awake as usual. When we caught up with Kev, he told us how his night had unfolded. He gave it ten minutes before snuggling in at Clare's side; after a few failed attempts to wake her, he fell asleep.

In the early morning hours, Clare started to pad her toes against Kev, and he thought it might be the start of something. It was, but not what he imagined; Clare Donkey kicked Kev out of bed and ran into Becky, screaming, "There's a man in my bed!"

Kev, by now, was panicking, not knowing what to do. After contemplating jumping out of the window before they returned, he explained what had happened. It was a standing joke for a long time. A year or so later, Clare was on a first aid course that Kev was running for staff. You can just imagine the jokes with Kev whilst teaching unresponsive with a pulse. And placing Clare in the recovery position.

Sarah had now been christened Stomper or, often shortened to Stomps. She's still known by that even today; it was a name that stuck. All my older children know her as Stomps. Whenever the gym lads rang her office, they'd ask to speak to Stomps. My lad Jack asked as a teenager, "What is Stomps' real name?"

Sarah and Mary, my Landlady, were good friends, so I would see her and chat when she visited. Sarah and I went out for a drink several times, and she clarified that we were just friends. Her boyfriend was coming back from Spain. Stomp's boyfriend, Lee, returned, and I saw them together several times.

I worked a few doors at the clubs in Evesham, not very often, but to help out. This one night, I was working on the door with Kev; Sarah and her friends arrived around 10.30. I chatted briefly and asked where Lee was; I was gutted when she replied, "He's with his mate and will be here soon."

The club had a policy where nobody was allowed entry after eleven. Just before then, I noticed Lee and his friend walking down towards the club, I checked my watch, and it was ten minutes before eleven. I quickly put my watch forward and told Kev to do the same. As they arrived, I said, "Evening, lads; sorry, but I'm afraid you're too late." I added, "I would let you in, but we are full." Lee pointed to his watch and said it was not eleven yet; Kev and I showed him our watches. They walked away. Once everyone was in, and it had gone eleven, I chatted to Stomps and casually asked where Lee was. It gave me another opportunity to spend some time to try and work my charm.

The break-up

A few months later, Stomps and Lee broke up, and we moved from friendship to seeing each other. Ferdy and probably a few others weren't happy. Ferdy told Stomps on more than one occasion she could do better; to be honest, he had a point. It was anything but plain sailing; if I hadn't been such a big idiot, it might have been.

We briefly broke up when I told Sarah I didn't want more children. We remained friends though, and I hated not being with her; it broke my heart every time I saw her. We got back together, and I was happy to plan a future with her. That should have been the start of where we lived happily ever after.

I should have heeded my words; I was in calm waters but still chose not to grasp the rope I'd been thrown.

After a short stint in Portsmouth, when I was at HMP Kingston with Geordie Foster and Mick, Stomps worked at Haslar Detainee Unit. At this point, I started to look back and saw myself living my dad's life; my father loved my mum but messed up. My mum could never forget though, even when she had forgiven him. He lived the rest of his life without the lady he really and truly loved. He went on to marry again, and gladly didn't die a lonely old man, but I think he regretted his actions for many years. Our son Henry was born when we moved back to Evesham, where we broke up for two years.

The make-up

I'm forever grateful Stomps gave me a second chance, despite the understandably voiced concerns from her friends. Before we got back together, I promised to never let it be thrown back in her face. She would never hear the words, 'I told you so,' from her friends. We married in Cyprus in 2010 and had our little girl Dolly in 2012. For better or worse, we will spend the rest of our days together. No matter what the future holds, I'd rather have a shorter life with Stomps than have lived for a century without her. Now let's get back to prison.

Early bird's gym

At the time, we used to run an early bird's gym session. A circuit class that ran for around 40 minutes before prisoners moved to work. Despite being a short session, it was very popular. I trained with a gym orderly from the Black Country called Chambers (Mooney). He was a real character. It all started with him saying, "You might be alright at football and ya weights, but I'd take you on a circuit any day."

So, I set up the circuit, and we went full tilt from the off. Pushing each other to the limit. I beat Mooney most days, taunting him as we went along and doing the run backwards. But he would always be back the next day to go again. This went on for years; it was a great start to the day and saved me from coming in early to train. I was gutted to hear a few years later that he'd been shot dead when chased out of the rear of a pub. Shot as he tried to escape. What made it sadder was that Mooney had his young daughter with him. This is one of those moments that Vic Dark's words on the James English interview really resonates. "Always give someone a way out." RIP Chambers; whoever you're doing circuits in the sky with, you'll give them a good run for their money.

Mooney's sidekick in the gym was a lad from the same area named Pittsy. He was a real character; he was a convicted armed robber who used to turn over a lot of post offices. He told me once how he owed a bag of money to a local gangster. The guy came round to Paul Pittsy's house to put it on him; he either paid up or was getting 'it'. Paul told him to wait ten minutes, and he left the house. He went to a post office a hundred yards down the road and held it up. Pittsy made off with two bags. He arrived back at the house and gave the gangster a bag. By now, the police were swarming the area; sirens going off everywhere.

"What have you done?" the gangster asked Paul.

"I got you your money; now do one."

The man left, leaving the two bags for Paul.

Paul took his own life a few years later in Stafford Prison. RIP, Paul. Hopefully, there are no post offices up there.

An alarm bell on a wing interrupted one early bird's session. We had an orderly from Wolverhampton called Denton Pearce. He was ripped and had washboard abs, even though he never completed a single sit-up. He had been pressuring a few lads on his wing to pay their debts, but they decided to take their opportunity when they made an early bird attack of their own. They rushed his cell at unlock and stabbed him up. The hospital said he was lucky to survive, and only his muscle mass had saved his life.

FOOTBALL AT LONG LARTIN

Football at Long Lartin was very similar to the feisty affairs at Parkhurst, just played out on a far better pitch. When I first arrived, football played second fiddle to rugby. It was more down to the fact that a few PE staff, like Madgey and John, were from rugby backgrounds. I remember trying to organise a game on one of my first days when out on association. One of the prisoners I didn't know then, Pat Timlin, approached me and said, "Gov, you're not another fucking egg chaser, are you?"

I replied, "No, I'm out to get some names together for a decent football game." He was excited and said put my name down and introduced himself. He said he'd boot the ball over the fence if he saw another game of rugby without a game of football. I pointed out that I was into football more than rugby, but the idea is to kick it between the sticks, not over the fence. Pat smiled and, again told me to put his name down. Timlin was a decent fullback when sober; I later discovered he was among the prominent Hooch brewers on the wing.

In one of the early football games, Eddie Levy, a London bank robber, played in an inter-wing game. On the opposing team was the son of John McVicar, Russell Grant, also in for armed robbery. The game, as always, was a bit feisty, with no doubt a few quid on the outcome. A large crowd was watching, which was always a sign there would be an edge to it. Kev was running the line for me, and I was refereeing.

Grant didn't take kindly to a heavy challenge by Eddie Levy. In the blink of an eye, Eddie had stuck the nut on him and was starting to pummel Grant to the floor. For a moment, I thought both teams and spectators would get involved. To my surprise, none of the officers in the boxes observing or the SO in charge of the association hit the alarm bell.

Between us, Kev and I calmed it down. At the end of the game, we escorted the teams back through to the gym to change, keeping Levy and Grant apart. I told the SO that it was a bit feisty and thought it would kick off. The SO was oblivious to it; I told Kev "it's a good job, it wasn't us getting a kicking".

Years later, Eddie became a gym orderly, and Eddie was a big West Ham fan. His family used to attend 'family visits'. I would spend some time coaching his kids on the trampoline, which he appreciated. When he moved on from Long Lartin, he came down to the gym to thank me and gave me some bits of West Ham stuff like a pen etc. I always remember having to go and do a C&R move on him. The wing staff thought he would kick off; we chatted at his door, and he calmed down. We walked him to the seg; he checked our trainers to know who we were. We all laughed as we walked, and he turned to say, "you saucy cunts".

He had a great character, Eddie. He carried a lot of body fat, and had an operation whilst at Long Lartin to remove excess skin after losing a lot of weight; after the procedure, he had more scars than Denton Pearce. You underestimated him at your peril though; he was a real game lad.

Staff v inmates

I hadn't been at Lartin too long before we had a staff v inmates game. Parkhurst had a half-decent team, but the inmate team here would wipe the floor with them, in my opinion. They had a powerful team from front to back. Two players though, really stood out: Ranko Zikovic and Vinnie Cockovic, the latter man in particular.

Vinnie Cockovic had played professionally for Red Star Belgrade and appeared in the old European Cup Final in 1991. The final was held at the Stadia San Nicola, in Bari, Italy, on 29th May. That saw Red Star Belgrade of Yugoslavia defeat Marseille of France in a penalty shoot-out.

Cockovic was the best footballer I ever saw grace a prison football pitch or five-a-side pitch. In all my time watching Leeds since the 1970s, I'd put him up with the most skilful. On the five-a-side pitch, he would be boxed in by two or three players in the corner. Next thing you knew, the ball had been flicked through their legs, and he was off. Players tried everything to stop him, kicking him to shreds, but he'd still mesmerize them. He didn't even go down when kicked, and he never moaned.

Remember me telling you about the scouse lad at Parkhurst who had his throat slashed to even the odds? I reckon you could cut this lad's throat, and he'd still bag a couple of goals before going to the hospital. His skills were ridiculous. If he was on your team, you won.

I almost felt sorry for Ranko Zikovic. If I hadn't seen Vinnie play, I'd probably have been saying he was the best I'd seen. Two very different players; Ranko would sit in the middle and dictate play, spraying balls left and right. But the only tactic you needed as a team was to give it to Vinnie. I saw him dribble past almost every opponent before rounding the keeper; he was unbelievable. He was also an excellent soft tennis player; he and Ronnie O'Sullivan, senior father of the snooker player, would have some great tennis games and epic rallies.

Vinnie escaped from the Verne after moving on from Long Lartin.

The Staff team wasn't bad, but you can probably guess the outcome. I'll maybe remember the game for two things: The intense atmosphere, Prisoners gathered right up to the touchline all around the pitch baying for blood, and meeting mad Brian – AKA psycho Davis (The General) for the first time; he was an ex-Para and one that must have jumped out of a plane with a parachute that I'd woven at Perseverance. I'll go on to cover more about mad Brian later in the book when he became a PEI and a great, great friend. Brian was no Messi or Vinnie, but in his head, he was. When anyone else got the ball, he'd demand it, saying, 'just give it to me, and I'll score.' Even Vinnie didn't say that. After a few minutes of coming on, he clattered one of the prisoners on the touchline. The whole of the crowd gave him abuse.

Despite getting well and truly beaten, it was a great game, and, just like in Parkhurst, it gave the whole place a lift. We managed to get into the local football league for a couple of seasons until, I think, the league got tired of us winning every week and stopped us taking part because we couldn't play away games.

Another outstanding player at the time was a centre-half called Terry St John. Nicknamed 'Spiderman', he was a cultured centre-back and midfielder in the mould of Rio Ferdinand. He was also the fastest person I'd ever seen take down the football nets; I guess not so surprising when you find out he scaled a two-hundred feet tower block to kill a history lecturer and commit a robbery. He became a gym orderly; you could play an extra five minutes with Terry helping to take the nets down.

Over a period when the workshops were closed, we were asked to try to keep the prisoners busy. So, after a discussion, Kev and I decided to run a big five-a-side football tournament out on the sports field. We had two pitches marked out and around ten teams. It was the usual feisty prison football we were used to. When we started, the Governor said, "Great idea, but try not to get too many injuries out there."

Kev was refereeing a game at the same time as me when we had two players go down within minutes of each other. You could see Craig, the player on my pitch, straight away, had suffered an open fracture (compound fracture) where his bone came through the skin. Whilst trying to sort this out and get health care, there was a scream on Kev's pitch. To be honest, I thought nothing of it when I saw who it was. Like the professional players, that prisoner had a history of diving around a bit. It turned out though, he had also broken his leg. Two off to the hospital. Craig was a gym orderly then and had to have a big operation to save losing his leg. Prison football for you.

After serious debate, we were allowed to finish the tournament that had been a great success, apart from the odd broken leg.

Anyone for ice cream? Caner Karakas

I had built up a reputation for wind-ups at Lartin by now but also for legitimately helping the odd prisoner with a bad back or an injury. I was in the office when I was approached by Karakas, a prisoner I knew but not well. He'd been in the sports hall playing five-a-side. In the first few minutes, he'd pulled his back. He asked if I could help him; I told him to take a seat, which he did very gingerly. I clarified how he'd injured himself and if he'd had a history of a bad back. I put on a pair of the searching gloves and assisted him in taking off his shoes and socks, "It's your lucky day," I told him. "I've just finished my reflexology course and can get this sorted for you immediately."

Big John McKenzie, one of our gym orderlies at the time, shook his head and left the office. He positioned himself at the window to the weights room, so he could still watch. Madgey came in, so I informed him what had gone on and asked if he could bring me the toe spacers from out of the cupboard at the back. He looked a bit confused; I explained exactly where they were. He returned with my toe spacers, which were ice cream wafers we used for making up treats for the special needs group once a week.

I hid the labelling from Karakas, and after placing his foot on the desk, I put a wafer between each toe. I saw big John, the orderly, bend over. I couldn't see or hear his laugh, but I knew it well enough by now that it felt like I could.

I told Karakas I was about to gently squeeze each toe and asked him to tell me which one, if any, felt sensitive. I felt each toe, giving his third toe a bit of a pinch. After doing all his toes, he told me it was the third toe. "Ha, just as I suspected," I said. "This toe is connected to the erector spinae muscles."

I took a can of synthetic chain lubricant we used for the machines in the Gym, sprayed it along the toes, and massaged the third toe for a few minutes. Then told him to just relax for a few minutes. I got him to put on his shoes and socks; the one sock must have slid on quickly with the amount of oil I'd put on his foot. At the end of the session, I went into the sports hall to check on him, and he was running and kicking a ball around. He told me it felt so much better.

I never actually did a reflexology course, but maybe I should.

Arrivederci Ferdy

Ferdy had now left, and I could breathe a sigh of relief. Start to relax and enjoy my job – that was a joke by the way; I was loving life. Don't get me wrong, we had our moments in the Gym and answered some pretty horrific bells, but nothing had changed; I was in my dream job. And things were about to get better; we had a new PO. Tony Wright arrived in the Gym from Hewell, where Ferdy had gone, and we had a new SO, Mark Blackham. Mark was a little fiery character, but also a really funny guy. We became close, both professionally and socially. He came to Cyprus for my and Stomper's wedding.

The Department had been good to work in; it was about to become great for those who wanted to do their job. The PE courses were the first on the agenda when I spoke with Tony, and we soon implemented a PE course employing the prisoners full-time. We also implemented a course mentor job, where we selected the better candidates from the courses to stay on for the following course.

I continued my risk policy that I always had from day one, and it still paid off most of the time. Even when one of the risks didn't complete the course, you could still quite often see how it positively affected their attitude towards staff and other prisoners.

We had a varied PE programme with volleyball, basketball, circuit classes, and a well-equipped classroom with a new interactive whiteboard; it made teaching more professional. I'd say enjoyable, but it's always been enjoyable.

One-off the roll to a building site

Despite apparently being a non-contact sport, basketball in prison was every bit as fiercely contested and probably the hardest thing to referee in jail. Bear in mind, outside, you'd have two referees and foul judges; quite often, in prison, it was just you.

On this particular day, I was refereeing, and John Mackenzie, our gym orderly, came in to keep score. John was a huge black lad who was naturally big; although he did lift weights, you sensed he'd just be huge anyway. John reminded me a little bit of John, the prisoner off the film 'Green Mile' but with shoulder-length braided hair. He also possessed an infectious laugh, bringing his hand up to his mouth and doubling up, then letting out a big laugh with a little squeal.

The teams were often picked in the same way as we did at school. The teams were chosen, and bibs were given to one side. Everyone was against the wall; the staff would select the two best players, and then they picked the teams one by one. The only difference was a prison rule: if you had a second pick, you then had two picks to make up for it.

It was quite a strong turnout with two well-matched teams. However, one player, in particular, seemed to have one on him; he didn't like the staff very much, even the PEIs.

Delsol was a tall, gangly lad who tried to intimidate prisoners and staff. He was a loud character, to say the least. It wasn't long before he was cussing me for every decision.

John Mack was probably the first orderly I'd met that didn't care whether it was staff or prisoner; he'd say it as it was. If the staff member was in the right, he'd tell the prisoner he was out of order, and it didn't matter who they were. Equally, he'd do the same if the other way around. I really respected him for his moral stance.

Delsol continued to cuss. When I'm refereeing and sprinting up and down, I don't really take in what many of them say. If I do, I usually just belittle them for their behaviour. John though, had heard it and decided to tell Delsol to reign it in. It started to escalate to the point I felt like I had to act. I stopped the game and told Delsol he was returning to the wing. He began to square up and get irate. John stood with me and told Delsol to get off the court and that he deserved to go back. I signalled to Chris and Madgey that we may have a problem, and they came in. Delsol decided to take a swing, so we jumped on him and got him in locks.

Kev got on the radio to inform them that we had one off the roll. We walked him to the segregation unit, or what we thought was still the seg. As we entered, it was full of Works Officers up ladders painting. The old seg was being refurbished, and the new bigger seg unit had opened that week.

Even Delsol was laughing. He called us 'thick PEIs'. The weird thing was, from that day onwards, Delsol became really friendly with the PE staff, courteous and polite. None of us really understood why. Maybe big John had a quiet word. I'm not sure, but it wasn't the only time John backed staff up against a prisoner. If you were in the right, he had your back. It was the first time I'd seen such a thing, but not the last. I met quite a few that did the same. I'm pleased to say John has been out for several years and is doing really well; he and Mick Gillet, another orderly at the time, became great friends and remain in contact.

One of my other favourite memories of John was he used to bribe a gay lad on the wing everyone called Sacha. John would pay him to say which prisoners he'd had sex with. John always said a few names that would shock you.

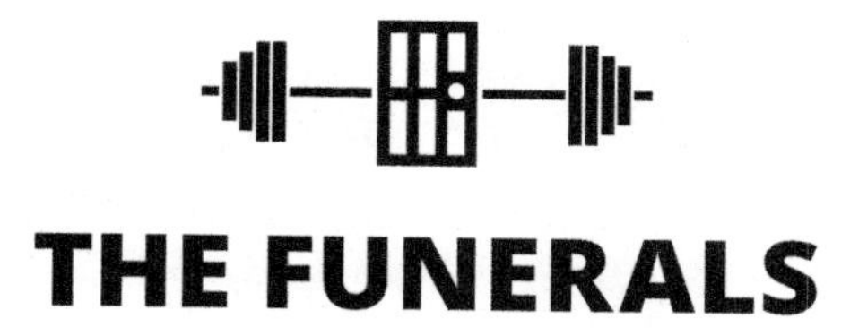

THE FUNERALS

On occasions, at the over-40s gym sessions, I would work out with and chat with two prisoners, Felix (Fraser) and Pedro. Quite often, we would also be joined by a gym orderly called Aussie. Aussie would usually just come over and have banter with Felix and me. Pedro was the more serious type but still friendly; he laughed at Felix and Aussie taking the mickey out of each other. If Felix didn't turn up for some sessions, I would train with Pedro. Over a period of time, I got to know Pedro quite well, being able to chat without all the banter flying around. All three guys were fit and strong for their ages, unlike your ordinary 40-year-old men.

One morning Felix turned up, and I asked if I could join in; as usual, he welcomed me; he was doing a chest workout. I wondered where Pedro was. Felix told me that Pedro wasn't in a good place at the minute, his son had been murdered at a nightclub recently in Birmingham, and he'd just been told he couldn't attend the funeral. Imagine being told that regardless of your offence or situation, it wouldn't put anyone in a good place. I told him to pass on my deepest sympathy and asked what reason he'd been given for not being able to attend. He just said security knocked him back.

Pedro came down with Felix the following day, and I joined them for a workout. I told Pedro I was sorry to hear the sad news about his son. We talked briefly, and although he'd seemed to accept he couldn't attend the funeral, I told him I'd have a word with security and added that I'd be happy to take him if they allow it; he shook my hand and said, "I appreciate that, Phil, but I don't see it happening".

I knew the security governor quite well and rang to see if I could go over for a chat. I went over and asked why Pedro's application had been declined. He told me that they had held a meeting, discussed it at length, and spoke to the police in Handsworth Birmingham, where the funeral was due to take place. I only know Birmingham a little, but even I knew Handsworth to be a notorious area of Birmingham. He explained that the police have even refused to man it. I smiled and said, "That's no bad thing, is it? It might just antagonise the situation."

He looked surprised at my response; I told him I would be more than happy to volunteer to take him; I explained I had a good relationship with Pedro and wouldn't be volunteering if I had any doubt. He told me he'd speak with the governor, but I'd need another officer and an SO to be willing to do it. I talked to Mackham Ralph, my colleague in the gym, knowing he also got on well with Pedro and Felix. Ralph was around five feet ten, in good shape, and I knew I could rely on him no matter how the day panned out. Outside of work, he was handy for any DIY jobs. In fact, most of his relationships were built on the back of fixing a boiler or two. Thankfully, Ralph agreed to volunteer. Next, I asked Chopper, an SO who often worked in the seg. I knew him well and thought he might have the bottle, but more importantly, the compassion to help get through what would be a difficult day for everyone.

At first, Chopper didn't seem keen, but after some arm bending, he agreed if security cleared it. I decided to go to security before they got back to me and let them know I'd got the staff. Now I just needed the green light. Time was also running out;

the funeral was in a week. Again, I went and spoke with Rob in security. He said they were still unhappy with it, especially with the information they'd received about how many would attend and the circumstances and tension the shooting had caused in the area.

Again, I told him I was confident, and they eventually agreed but finished by telling me that my job would be on the line on this call. I thanked them and left before they changed their minds. Pedro came down the next day, and I asked him if he had heard more from security. He hadn't been told, but I told him they may agree to me taking him. I also told him that my job was on the line; he gave me a big man hug and said, "Phil, I won't let you down." I just simply said, "I know."

The day of the funeral arrived. Ralph and I went to collect Pedro from his cell and met Chopper in reception. I hadn't given it much thought, but you couldn't pick three more stereotypical officers if you tried, all three of us with completely shaved heads looking like thugs.

Pedro, as you can imagine, was subdued, to say the least. Ralph and I shook his hand. I told him today would be a difficult day for all of us and told him to not be ashamed to cry. I certainly would if I ever had to bury any of my children. He touched shoulders with me and said, "thank you".

Ralph and I had spoken about the day and agreed that he would be cuffed to Pedro for a visit to the chapel of rest, and I'd be cuffed to him for the rest of the day.

We had left reception in the van and exited the gate when Pedro gave a big sigh and swore; I asked if he was ok. "Fuck!" he exclaimed. "I've left my cross that I made, in reception." Pedro had made a cross with a ribbon around it; he had shown it to me when leaving the wing and told me he would put it in with his lad at the chapel of rest. I looked at Chopper, and he just said, "We can't turn back now." I replied, "Park up on the side here, and I'll go back for it quickly." This could have a significant impact on how our day goes. I went back, and nobody questioned it despite the odd, strange look from the people at the gate.

Pedro was relaxed again once reunited with the cross he'd made. The first stop was the chapel of rest. As agreed, Ralph was cuffed to Pedro, and Chopper and I remained outside; we suddenly heard cries as Pedro broke down; it was more than understandable. I imagined how I'd feel in this situation, not having seen my child for a while, and the next time I did, they were lying in a chapel of rest. Pedro and Ralph were in there for around 20 minutes; it must have seemed longer for Ralph.

We got back in the van and headed for Handsworth. On arrival, there was a huge gathering. I thought if something was going to go wrong, it wouldn't be until after the funeral. So, I tried to relax. As per the security instructions, Pedro was double-cuffed, his wrists cuffed together and then cuffed to me. We'd agreed that I would go wherever Pedro went in the church while Ralph and Chopper would try and keep a low profile and stand at the back. As people started approaching Pedro to pay their respects and give their commiserations, he introduced me to them, saying, "This is Phil, my training partner in Prison."

Each time Pedro repeated the introduction, it had the same effect; it dissipated any tension there may have been. That's not to say it wasn't tense; the only way I can describe it was, imagine being at a football match against your fiercest rivals, and you and a couple of mates are in their end trying to keep a low profile; this was us that day. We were dressed in uniform, but I'd managed to get security to agree to us wearing a civilian jacket.

The horse-drawn carriage led by four large white horses with Pedro's boy arrived. I apologised to Pedro for having to remain cuffed. Still, I thanked him for making it easier for us with his introductions. "I wouldn't be here if it wasn't for you, Phil." Those words brought a lump to my throat. It also made me feel more confident for the rest of the day.

We entered the church, and Pedro and I sat at the front with the rest of his family; again, one or two approached to say a few words to Pedro. The service was a lovely send-off for his son, who'd been taken too soon.

After the service, we made our way out and walked over to the graveside where his lad would be laid to rest. As we walked over, a steel band started playing. I saw three large men approaching us, and I must admit, I was now feeling nervous. I knew we were reaching the make-or-break point.

The largest of the men spoke to Pedro, and again he repeated the process of introducing me. This time the tension remained. A large man turned to me and said, "We are good for going to the pub after, aren't we, Gov?" Just as I was about to explain that this wasn't possible, Pedro answered. "No, I'm not coming to the wake; I don't want to." He told the man that he was happy to have come to the funeral and that it was "because of Phil I'm here"! The men went to turn away when Pedro added, "and let everyone else know I'm cool with this and just have a drink for my lad and me".

Standing on our own at the graveside, the vicar said his final words; Pedro told me it was tradition for the dad to spade in the first load of soil on top of the coffin. I said, "Well, if you're happy for me to do it with you, I'm happy to just be a second-hand." Pedro did it. We had about 20 minutes afterwards for him to say goodbye to family and friends.

Back in the van and on our return journey, I thanked Pedro again for how he'd handled the day, and making an awkward situation easier for us all. I also told him I would write him a favourable report on how he'd dealt with the whole day, which I did.

After Pedro had been relocated to his wing, Chopper said later that he didn't think any staff other than PEIs could have carried that day off. A week later, we all received fifty pounds' worth of shopping vouchers from the governor. It was nice to receive something, but it meant little compared to the two-sided 'thank you' letter I received from Pedro a couple of months later. He was now in a category B prison after getting a progressive move.

I did the same thing with another prisoner, Michael, whom I knew from training with him in the gym. It wasn't quite as tense as Pedro's, but a sad occasion nonetheless. That time it was a long trip to Norwich. Kev and I volunteered to do the escort. His family were all from a military background. They were all very friendly and grateful to us for getting him to the funeral. Once again, he just introduced me like I was a friend. And they understood that we couldn't attend the wake. His behaviour was exemplary; I got our driver and navigator to stop to get us all a Subway on the way home. A few months after he got a progressive move, I received a nice thank you letter. There were also a few occasions when I couldn't convince security to allow an escort to go ahead. Both were also orderlies in the gym – Sean Riley and Lea Rusha. But I did try.

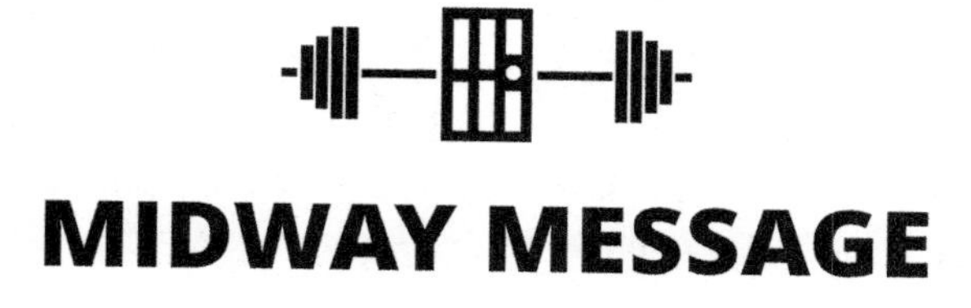

MIDWAY MESSAGE

For those of you still reading at what is hopefully just over the midpoint in this book, I'm conscious that you don't think I'm trying to portray myself as some sort of 'super screw' or hero. I'm not; if that's where you're currently at, I'm failing in my message. My story is partly written, up and down the country in every gym by all PEIs. I'm not special; I just tried to use my gift of being a PEI and put it to good use.

PE is a great vehicle to help change lives. However, it has always been undervalued by many managers of the Prison Service and even amongst some PE departments, partly due to many of the rewards needing to be measured. Prison and the press often only focus on the failures of people who return to jail. Nobody usually talks of any success stories. I won't be able to cover them all in this book, but I intend to mention enough to prove they are out there.

I genuinely believe PE is just as important as any psychology department. However, it only gets half the credence. I'll give you a classic example. One day I was training with Chris and chatting as we did about his life, what he wanted to achieve, the mistakes he'd made etc. Around ten minutes in, a lady from psychology came down to the gym asking to speak with Chris. I don't remember who came over to pass on the message. I told him to tell her Chris was busy and to ask her to come back at the end of the session; I'd get him to speak to her then.

The PEI went back and told her what I'd said. She wasn't happy, so I went to speak to her. She said, "I want to speak to Agboola about a course."

I replied, "Great. If you return in 45 minutes, I'll get Chris to speak to you."

She said sarcastically, "Well, sorry to interrupt your training." And walked off. To her and many others, she just looked and saw me and Chris having a meaningless training session. But I had what might turn out to be a lightbulb moment chat. Just because that chat is in a weights room doesn't make it any less important than if I was in an office with a file under my arm and a pen in my hand, does it?

The lady put a complaint in about me. I answered it just as I mentioned here, pointing out that I wouldn't have just turned up at her office in the middle of a meeting demanding to speak to Chris immediately. Her complaint went nowhere, and we got on really well after. She agreed with me in the end. But the gym is still undervalued in what they deliver to this day.

I've often heard the comment, 'why deliver PE courses with lifers? It's not like they are going to use the awards'. I've known a few that have, but that aside, the benefits are way beyond the certificate you give them at the end.

I've seen so many prisoners engage with the education department either to get a place on a PE course or at the end of a PE course to further their education. For some courses, a prisoner needed to achieve a basic level of maths and English; many achieved those qualifications to gain access to a PE course.

My message is to those who will read or listen, 'use PE to its full potential, and your prison will be a much better place for it'.

Danger

Danger was a huge prisoner, around six feet six and an absolute mountain of a man. He spoke just as you might expect, with a gruff gravelly voice. Generally, he was as good as gold in the gym, and most PEIs got on with him.

I'd put in for overtime to do an escort. I had yet to find out who we were taking or where we were going. Then I got told the escort was taking Danger to court over a recent serious assault he'd allegedly committed at HMP Whitemoor. I was told to report to the seg as the escort would be leaving straight from there. This was a bad sign if we were going directly from the seg. On arrival, I went to the staff office and saw Barnsey, an officer I knew well from the gym, playing football. After the pleasantries, I asked who else was on the escort, hoping it was people who could talk or fight, preferably talk. Barnsey informed me they'd spoken to Danger, and he's refusing to go. The judge denied a video link, so we had to get him there. I explained that I got on quite well with Danger and would go and speak to him.

I opened his door-flap and saw the man mountain standing in the middle of his cell. I said, "Hi." He replied, "Hi Phil, how's it going?"

I said, "I was ok, 'till I got here and found out I was taking you, and you're not willing to go." He replied, "Don't get it twisted, Phil. I know they will want their revenge back there, and I won't let that happen."

I told him if he came, I'd make sure nothing like that happened. He agreed to go.

In the court, they played a video. It was one of only a handful of occasions I've known the judge to allow a prisoner to be handcuffed in the dock; no matter what, they usually decline such a request.

I was cuffed to Danger when they started to play the video evidence. Danger whispered his own running commentary to me; whether it was true or not, only Danger and the SO concerned knew. In the video, you could see the SO gesticulating at Danger's cell door. He explained that this had been happening for days; he felt like he was being dug out over his work. After what looked like an exchange of words, Danger started to unload. The bell was pressed, and staff began to respond, but each one was knocked over as they arrived. I remember thinking I'm glad we didn't have to try and fight him on and off the van. The outcome wasn't great that day for Danger, but if it wasn't for our positive relationship, more people would have been hurt that day. That's again not to say, 'Phil saved the day'. It could have been anyone in the gym who got on with him.

It may surprise a few, even some who work in jails and fail to realise a prison runs on the goodwill of the prisoners, but that will always be the case.

I had many similar escorts; one was with a lad called Khan. I'd trained with him in the past. He was smashing up reception. Ironically, this was because he was going to Whitemoor. The orderly officer asked for a C&R team to move Khan and rang the gym; me and Brian attended.

The acting SO, who, if I'm honest, I didn't particularly like, told us to get kitted up. I explained that I got on with Khan and would chat with him; I added, "I think he'll walk". Mike, the SO, said, "Talk's over; we move him to the van in locks." Five minutes later, Mike declared, "I'm going to give him one last order." I stopped him and said, "I thought you said the talk was done? I'll speak and give him the order." Mike refused, his ego getting in the way. As I thought, I could hear Khan kicking off as the SO spoke. He then called us, the "C&R" team, in.

When we were at the door, I went number one, meaning I had the shield. Knowing I would be at the door to speak with Khan, I started talking, and he instantly started to calm down. Human nature is you don't want to fight someone you like or get on with; I'd been training with this lad only yesterday, so as I thought, he didn't want to rearrange my face, nor me his!

Yet as Khan agreed to walk, the SO cranked the door open and said take him. You usually go in and practically splatter them with the shield and pin them with it while the others take control of the arms. I put the shield down and told the other lads to hold his arms but not apply any real pressure on the locks. The SO looked disappointed as we walked him to the van, released him and got him cuffed and on the van without a fight. I left without speaking to theSO despite his efforts to talk to me.

Another example of PE helping to defuse a potentially volatile situation was with a prisoner named Shevron Smith. There had been a lot of information about a possible major incident with Shevron supposedly heavily involved. Smith said he would only speak to PE staff; I went up with Munch, and it may have been Chinny. We spoke to Smith at his cell door. To many people's amazement, I opened him up, we chatted for a bit, and he agreed to walk down to the seg. That's what PE can bring to a prison.

Have your cake and eat it!

One morning I went to the regimes' office with Richie to sort out some admin. As we entered the office there wasn't anyone around, but a huge Thornton's chocolate cake was on the table. Oriel, a lovely older lady with a Welsh accent, appeared. "Oh, what's with the cake?" I told her it was my birthday, so I'd brought it in for her office for all the work they do for us. "Oh, that's lovely," she said in her Welsh tone. I went on to say I'll have a quick piece with her if she gets a knife; off she went, returned directly, cutting us both a generous slice. "Ooh it's lovely," she said. I replied, "Well, I hope you all enjoy it." And I finished my slice.

As we made our way out of the office, Mark, the gym SO and Linda Jones, new head of regimes and governor over the PE department, appeared as we left. I heard Linda say, "Who's had the cake?"

Oriel went on to start telling her, "Phil brought it in for his birthday." Linda didn't sound impressed; I left just as I heard her saying, "Oh no he didn't! I brought it in…"

I quickly wiped the evidence from my mouth. Mark returned to the gym and asked, "What you doing?" In his Black Country accent, it became a trademark saying of his. Everyone, even a few of the orderlies, would greet him with it. Linda only worked briefly at the Prison; last I heard, she had a coffee shop in the posh part of Cheltenham. I keep meaning to call in for a cuppa and a piece of cake.

Bulldog Bash trial

Gerry Tobin was shot dead as he rode his Harley Davidson on the M40 at 90 after leaving the Bulldog Bash biker festival. I was doing overtime in black and whites, numerous times throughout the trial. It was an extremely high-profile case. We had Malcolm Bull at Long Lartin. He was giving evidence against the other six involved, having already admitted his part in the shooting. Sean Creighton, who fired the shot, had admitted murder on the eve of the trial to take the rap for the whole gang.

As you can imagine, Malcolm Bull's action hadn't gone down well with the other Outlaw members and left a price on his head. There was lots of tension throughout the trial and anger displayed by the other members of the gang who were being brought to the court by officers from Woodhill Prison. During the trial, as we arrived with Malcolm in our cat A van, we were greeted at the court by hundreds of members of the Outlaws masked, goading the armed police and throwing objects at the van.

Happy birthday, Malcolm

The prosecution told the jury how the gang had plotted the murder of Gerry Tobin, a Hells Angels member, simply because he was a patched-up member of the rival gang. Tobin was on his way home from the Bulldog Bash when Creighton shot him in the head from a car driven by Dane Garside while Simon Turner fired another shot into his rear tyre.

I was there on the final day of sentencing, coinciding with Malcolm Bull's birthday. As the judge gave them their life sentences, Creighton and some others simply turned to Malcolm and said, 'happy birthday Malcolm'!

We were all ready for it to kick off that day; apart from once again, hundreds of the Outlaws' gang waiting outside to give Malcolm a birthday send-off for his life sentence, the day passed incident free.

I have to say, talking to Malcolm throughout the trial and many times afterwards in the gym, you wouldn't think he was capable or indeed would have that side to him to plot someone's pointless assassination. Malcolm also made the best matchstick models I've ever seen, and I've looked at quite a few over the years.

Not too long after Malcolm was sentenced, I also did a bed watch out at hospital when he had an operation. I've never been on a bed watch with so many armed police around; I think the poor nursing staff thought it was someone like Robert Maudsley when in truth, they were all there for the protection of Malcolm.

The Dentist

Inductions were always a good chance for a wind-up. One of the orderlies often would say, 'Hey, Phil, my mate is on induction today. Can you get him at it?'

One day, Mick Gillet told me his mate was on induction. When he came in, I showed him around and explained the rules. Then he explained he'd only be entitled to one session a week until he got a work placement from regimes. He pulled a face. I said, "But all's not lost; you look a fit lad; we have a fitness incentive where you can earn extra sessions; all you have to do is row five hundred metres in under one minute thirty, and you get an additional two sessions." He explained that he had been getting few gym sessions at his previous Jail, so he wasn't sure.

"Where's your confidence?" I asked. "If an old man like me can do it, you can." I did the row comfortably under the time just to demonstrate. "You've got this," I declared.

Mick, the gym orderly, and Kev were both giving loads of encouragement. He set off like a train, and for the first thirty seconds, I thought he might do it; how would I give him the extra sessions if he did? Then he hit a wall; he stumbled over the finish line in one thirty-five. He was ready to admit defeat when I said, "That's brilliant, warm up done, have a blow and a stretch, you've got this."

After more encouragement from his mate Mick, he was back on and ready to go again. Off he went, starting a little slower. I said, "Time to speed up as you're halfway." He pulled hard and fast. His face changed colour like a traffic light, finishing on green. He was three hundred and fifty metres in and done! The new lad was panicking to unstrap his feet as he declared, "I'm going to throw up."

He rushed to the weights room door to reach the recess and the toilets. Panicked, he was trying to pull open the door instead of pushing. The liquid was starting to seep from his mouth. Mick was killing himself laughing. He threw up and then spent the rest of the session lying on the benches in the changing room. Mick even went in to try and talk him into one last try. Wicked!

Old faces new places

Crusher and Mary were still going strong after all the years. Mary's hair was now more grey than black, and Crusher, while still very fit, wasn't as big as he was back in Parkhurst. I spoke to Crusher regularly, but more often when I saw him on the wing or in a workshop. He was really into his cycling, so we talked about the Tour de France a lot. They were still both on normal location and in the same wing. You could always tell which landing Mary was on – it was always spotless.

It's widely believed that after a murder on their wing, Crusher and Mary struck a deal with the Home Office, stating they would give evidence about the murderer on the understanding that they had a guarantee they could remain in the same wing. Crusher and Mary have been on VP location together ever since.

Kev Brown had returned to prison after absconding from a cat D prison called Ford. He was found in a pub in Bristol several weeks after he'd absconded. Me and Kev spoke about old times and how things had changed. He never settled at Long Lartin and moved on after a short period of time. Kev had mellowed a lot from his old days, but you'd still be a fool to try and take liberties with him.

John Massey

I went to the door to get a class in the gym. We had a football competition on so it was a busy session with everyone running for the entrance. I was effectively a doorman with a guest list. If their names were not down, they weren't getting in. I had to stand in the doorway making sure I ticked the name off before they entered. I'd never seen John Massey before he arrived with the first bunch at the door. I ticked off his name and then carried on ticking the other names off.

A few minutes later, I was still getting people arriving at the door. John came by me again and started to throw a round of expletives, accusing me of extracting the urine. He got more aggressive as I ignored him to carry on ticking off the names. He then became threatening saying that I'd watched him run in with his racquet knowing it was football. I tried to explain that I hadn't noticed his racquet. He continued to be abusive, so I told him he could have a two-week ban from the gym; he went off still cussing me.

The following day I was at the door. John was coming towards me. I got prepared for another argument, or worse. To my surprise, John had come down to apologise and said having spoken to a few people he knows, I wasn't taking the 'piss' out of him. I accepted his apology and told him his ban had been lifted and he'd be allowed back down the gym. From then on, we got on well.

John and I met again, but back at Parkhurst, I had a few family problems so Mark and our Governor at the time kindly arranged for me to do two weeks detached at Parkhurst. It also provided me with an opportunity to catch up with Gary, Mick and Woody.

John told me he was going to Parkhurst on a progressive move a couple of weeks before I went back on detached duty. I asked the PE staff if he'd been down and none of them had seen him; after making some enquiries, I found out John was in the seg. I figured he must have lost his temper or something, but after checking it out, it transpired that he'd been down there since arriving.

I went down to the seg to see him. "Some progressive move this," he said. I told him I'd see what I could do. I spoke with an old SO I knew and managed to get John moved up onto the wing. I saw John interviewed recently on James English's show 'Anything Goes', and despite a couple of strokes recently, he seemed in good spirits.

Vic Dark is another old face that passed through Parkhurst before working his way down the system and out. Vic didn't really talk to the officers much, or even PE staff, but we did chat at times. Vic had been doing a lot more CV circuits etc, and I'd been doing a lot of cycling events, so we discussed the training we were doing. Great to see Vic is now enjoying his freedom.

The loan trainer (Gary Vinter)

Gary had been at Long Lartin on a couple of occasions. On the odd occasion when on normal location, he had been part of our powerlifting squad. Sometimes you see a prisoner settling much better in some prisons than others. Fortunately, Long Lartin was a prison that Gary liked being in. He loved his training and was a regular in the gymnasium. I trained with Gary on numerous occasions. Gary stood at around six feet seven and was an imposing figure, but we always got on. He was a straight-talking individual and didn't hold back in giving his opinion on anything or anyone.

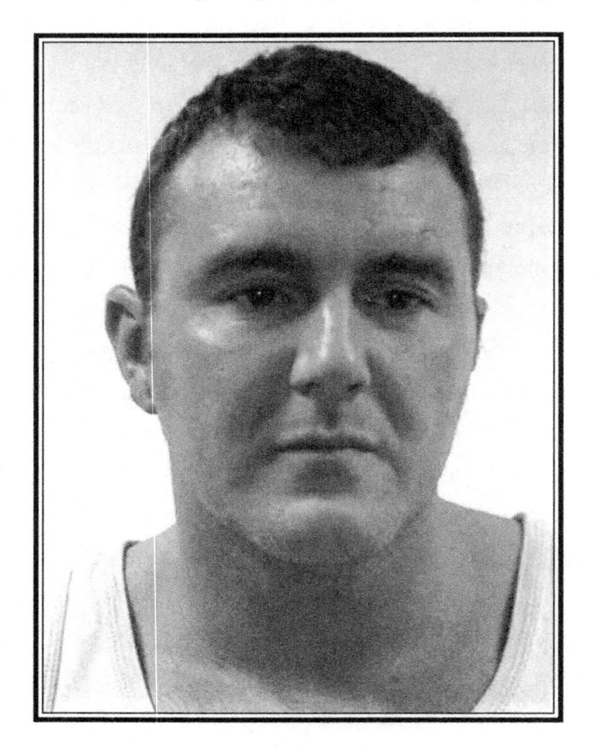

Gary Vinter.

To say Gary had a chequered past inside and outside the jail would be an understatement. Gary had previously served a life sentence for stabbing a work colleague to death in 1996 and served a minimum ten-year period. In 2008 he stabbed his ex-wife to death. In 2011 Gary stabbed Roy Whiting, the killer of schoolgirl Sarah Payne, with a sharpened toilet brush handle, at Wakefield Prison.

His time at Long Lartin seemed to be his only settled period. One thing I knew from talking to Gary and training with him was that if he warned you he would do something, you had to take it seriously. Whilst at HMP Woodhill, Gary had stated his desire to come back to Long Lartin and warned that if he wasn't moved, he would do something about it; his move had been allegedly granted but had been held up by psychology reports.

Gary decided to take matters into his own hands and attacked a prisoner called Newell. He had a chequered past of his own, having strangled child killer Subhan Anwar to death in Long Lartin Prison in 2013.

Gary had made numerous threats to staff at Woodhill regarding his delayed move to Long Lartin, including informing one staff member that if he wanted to tell him he couldn't move prisons, he'd better do it from behind a shield. True to his word, Gary carried out his threat one day with his attack on Newell; Gary punched him to the ground and then punched him repeatedly, kicking him in the head with such ferocity that it left Newell blind in one eye and with permanent brain damage. Both men were subsequently serving whole life sentences, never to be released from prison.

Gary eventually returned to Long Lartin and was located in the seg unit. He went to the gym but was escorted by a seg officer and a PEI to the Hatton Suite gymnasium, where he trained alone. The first time I saw him on one of those sessions, Gary shook my hand, and we talked about his powerlifting days in the gym. Whenever I was on that session, I would train with Gary; he openly discussed his actions at Woodhill and warned them what he would do if he didn't get his move back.

Reunited with Ferdy

I hadn't seen or heard of Ferdy Parker since he left Lartin, apart from one occasion when there was a big fire on one of the wings. The wing was evacuated to the gym, but not all the prisoners could return to the wing because of fire damage. We couldn't move them onto other wings at Long Lartin. A decision was made to transfer them to nearby Hewell, where Ferdy was the number one governor.

We arrived with our first prisoner and were locating him when there was Ferdy. "Ah, Currie, you still in a job?" I simply answered, "Yes, sir." He replied, "Well, that will change when I return to Lartin."

'Surely not; he can't be coming back, can he?' After doing some digging, it was true: Lartin's Governor was leaving, and Ferdy was coming back as our number one!

Back to looking over my shoulder, I thought. I raised my concerns with the POA union chairman and PE managers Mark and Tony Wright; I even said, "I think I'll need to look for a move."

Tony told me he got on well with Ferdy and would speak to him. I told him our history, and that was that. Ferdy arrived back, and Tony did talk to him. He relayed the conversation. Tony mentioned my concerns and reservations about him returning as number one with our history. Ferdy replied with some not-very complimentary remarks, but it was all aimed at my conduct outside of work, about how I was a ladies' man, to put it politely.

Tony told him that I was a really valued member of his staff and how good at my job I was, regardless of what he thought about my activities outside of work. It wasn't instant, but over a period of time, his attitude towards me started to change. He made remarks like, "Have you done my press-ups for me today, Currie?" And we began to chat when he came over to see Ian 'Magic Hands' Felix, our outside physio, who came into the prison to treat staff and prisoners.

I never imagined being able to work under Ferdy. Still, it was fine; our relationship improved, and I grew to like him. And fair play to him, whenever there's a staff funeral, he attends; I've spoken to him on every occasion. I never saw that coming.

The baptism

Jason was a regular gym attendee, multiple prison strongman competition winner, and a member of the powerlifting squad. He'd been studying and attending the Jehovah's Witnesses' weekly meetings and study groups for a considerable time. Jason had decided to get baptised; to do that, he would have to be completely submerged underwater.

Despite once having an orderly named Norman, who used so much bleach to clean everywhere that quite often outside visitors would ask if we had a swimming pool because of the smell. We never did, but we were about to get one!

The story unfolded like the fairytale, 'Goldilocks and the Three Bears.' Mark had arranged for the baptism in the gymnasium sports hall. Kev detailed the task of sourcing a pool and organising everything.

The first pool was knee-high at best, and Mark said, "it's not big enough," with his Black Country twang. The second pool leaked but was only noticed after Kev had filled it up. The sports hall was flooded. If the baptism had been that day, you could have almost done it on the gym floor. Kev worked his socks off, emptying the leaky pool out with buckets and was still there long after the rest of us had left.

The third pool was huge. And once again, it leaked, but only slowly. With no time left, it was patched up and ready to go.

The day before the big day, Jason came down to the Gym and told Kev he wasn't sure he could go through with it. I was crying with laughter. Kev doesn't lose his temper very often but went red in the face. Kev told Jason if he didn't, he'd be banned from the Gym for life. With Jason suitably reassured, he agreed to be down tomorrow for his baptism. Kev was still a bit put out, so he decided to top up the water with buckets of ice from our ice machine used to treat injuries. Tomorrow wasn't going to be a baptism of fire, that's for sure.

On the morning of the baptism, we all came in early to set up. Mark was a little on edge as it was a first for the Gym. He walked into the corridor where Kev and I were discussing the order of proceedings. Mark shouted his catchphrase, "what you doing?" when he saw Kev talking to me with his swimming cap and goggles on.

Jason turned up, much to everyone's relief.

The process started, and Jason and the visiting Jehovah's Witness, carrying out the baptism, climbed into the pool. You could visibly see the expression on their faces change when they entered the water. Both struggled to catch their breath. Mark gave me the nod to start the relaxation music on the jukebox. We had a double tape deck; one had Mark's relaxation music and was ready to go; the other was a circuit tape. You can guess which one I pressed. The play button on the circuit tape... 'Mr Bombastic' started to blast from the speakers. Mark went red with anger, so I quickly pressed stop and started the right tape playing.

The man in charge of proceedings was struggling to speak, me and Kev let out a little smile as Mark walked over to us; he whispered to Kev, "you're an idiot; that water is freezing". With that, Jason was dunked under the water and fully submerged; they wasted no time getting out. Mark ordered Kev to give them some towels quickly. It was a surreal moment, but one I'll never forget.

Since being released after serving a life sentence, I've seen Jason, and he's doing really well. He's still a practising Jehovah's Witness, so all that water and ice, plus the time and effort, didn't go to waste.

THE HITMAN VICTOR CASTIGADOR

Victor Castigador was born in the Philippines in 1954 and is believed to have travelled to the UK in 1985 as an illegal immigrant. Victor was dubbed 'The killer from Manila'.

Having had a row with his boss at the amusement arcade where he worked in London's Soho area, he decided to rob the arcade. With four young accomplices that he recruited, they broke into the arcade just after closing time. The manager, cashier and two security guards were still counting the money. They were forced to open the safe at gunpoint. Three of the young helpers ran off at this stage, but a young man, Paul Clinton, aged 17, stayed to help Victor.

They tied up the four hostages and locked them in the vault security cage. They then threw in white spirit and finally a burning match before leaving. The robbery haul was just nine thousand pounds.

The manager and cashier suffered bad burns but did survive. The two security guards, Ambikaipahan Apapayan, aged 21 and Kandiahkanapathy Vinayagamoorthy, aged 28, from Sri Lanka, died of burns and asphyxiation.

When staff arrived the following morning to find the horrifying scene, police were called. Victor was quickly picked up and charged with double murder. Victor was given life with a minimum recommendation of 25 years by the judge, later amended by the Home Secretary, who informed Victor he would not be released alive under the terms of a 'whole life' tariff.

I first met Victor in the gym; he never used the place, but it was when his wing was evacuated there. I spent a couple of hours chatting with him. I knew from other officers that he was always respectful to the staff. But he was, despite his small stature, a very dangerous man. He told me how back in the Philippines, he was part of a liquidation squad that would go around making evil people disappear. He had strong opinions on anyone who harmed women and children. Victor was a martial arts expert. He even displayed a few of his moves to me and my colleague Jack. Victor was lightning quick. You could see why he was something of an enforcer in jail. He was often used for this purpose to deal with debtors, working for prominent figures in prison. Victor did have another side to him; due to his exceptional culinary skills, he would be sought after by all the main food boats on the wing; in high-security prisons, the prisoners would chip in their earnings to cook and eat together. Victor was such a good cook the prisoners would allow him to eat for free if he did the cooking. This freed up all his earnings to send every penny of his prison wages back home to his family.

I remember running to an alarm bell one day. Victor had had an altercation with a prisoner called Silburn. Silburn was a known bully on the wing and picked on the wrong guy this time.

Silburn had tried putting it on Victor, but Victor prepared and produced two homemade chivs (metal spikes). In seconds he'd removed one of Silburn's eyes. Staff appeared, and Victor calmly put the spikes down and walked to the seg with the officers. Silburn might have lost his other eye or life that day if the staff hadn't appeared. Prison humour being what it was, Silburn became known as Slburn, or in other words, Silburn, without the I (eye).

In 2016, a gym orderly told me that Victor had gone on the numbers (protection). The orderly went on to say he couldn't believe it. Victor would be the last person he'd ever think of to go over to the VP wing. This tied in with my feelings; just from speaking to Victor, I knew there was no way he would run from anyone. After checking it out, though, Victor had indeed gone onto the numbers. I remember what he said about the liquidation squad in the Philippines.

Months later, Victor concealed two rocks he'd got out of the wing aquarium in socks and took them off the wing with him to his workshop first thing in the morning. On arrival at the workshop, the prisoners were placed in a holding area while changing into their boots. The following is a civilian worker's eyewitness account; she watched everything unfold from the Office.

Eyewitness statement

"The prisoners all came into the workshop as usual. I was in the Office facing the area where it happened. As usual, Teixeira stood by the door away from the other prisoners, and Castigador started attacking him. I shouted and banged on the window for him to stop, but he didn't. No other prisoner moved or said a word. In fact, a lot of them looked away. There was so much blood; it was such a brutal murder. I couldn't see Teixeira's face; I was unsure if he had one anymore. When officers came in, Castigador stood up, adjusted his shirt and did what he was told. One Officer got on his Radio to the control room to seek medical assistance and an ambulance immediately. Victor calmly said he didn't need an ambulance; he was dead. Teixeira, who was serving life for murdering his three-year-old daughter, was pronounced dead en route to the hospital after suffering multiple severe head injuries."

Victor himself died months later after suffering a stroke in prison. He suffered a heart attack in hospital and died.

THE MAGIC ROOM

I've touched on how the PE course changed many prisoners' lives, too many for me to cover in this book. It was a course that we were as a team, always trying to evolve and make better each year. It wasn't easy to choose from so many successes, some of which I know, decades later, are also making a real success of their second chance at life outside and making a positive contribution to Society.

The story of Chris Agboola typifies the magic room's powers and how the system can let people down. I'd heard of Chris, even though, at the time, he'd never set foot in the gym at Long Lartin. I'd heard about the fights in the segregation unit where his behaviour had spiralled far out of control. Like Maudsley at Parkhurst, Chris's door would only get opened with six officers in complete C&R kit undocking him. He was a six-man unlock.

Imagine my surprise one day when carrying out a gym induction and taking his name, I hear, 'Agboola'. Chris was very surly and obviously uncomfortable with me talking to him. I've seen this often where a prisoner on induction is uncomfortable talking to you and certainly isn't comfortable sitting in an office chatting. I like a challenge though. I asked his first name, and he said, "Chris". I got the paperwork and showed him around the gym, following my usual procedure for carrying out an induction.

When we finished, I sat down in the sports hall on one of the long wooden benches and started to go through my sales pitch for the PE course. Chris stopped me and said, "Gov, they ain't letting me on no PE course." He followed it up with a mixture of a laugh and a sigh. I told him we didn't have a vacancy on it at the minute as we'd just started working on the 'Fitness Industry Course' that runs for nearly two months. I added, "If you keep your head down for those two months, I'll get you on the PE course."

He asked how long it ran for and if you got paid. I told him that he did indeed get paid; I told him you get paid twice! He looked confused until I said you get wages each week off the prison and get paid by stimulating your brain. I also said, "Think about it; being down here every day has to beat the Seg."

I saw Chris from time to time in the gym after that, but only really to say 'hi'. I often talked to a few of the lads he trained with. On one of those occasions, Chris asked me when the current course finished; I told him two weeks. I asked if he fancied it and, if so, to get me an application form ASAP.

The application form arrived brought down by the gym orderly, Stevie. The process for application forms was to take them to regimes, and they would see what job the prisoner was currently doing, then juggle a replacement and forward it to security to clear.

I got the application back from security saying not recommended, in red pen. I rang to speak with Glenn, an officer in security I got on with. I said I wanted Agboola for the course. After an extensive conversation, mainly Glenn telling me Chris's history, he said, "We haven't completely blocked him, but going off his history, it wouldn't be a wise choice." I replied, "I know his history; let's see if we can stop that from being his future."

With that, Chris was put on the PE Course. The CSLA course was the first course, and at the beginning, Chris was reasonably quiet. After a few days, he started to talk with the group more. A significant portion of the course was to be able to take the class for a warm-up, stretch, and. a minor game.

By the end of the course, Chris was the standout pupil, to all the PE staff's surprise. I've seen worse warm-ups taken by PEIs to be fair.

Throughout the whole course, his progress continued. I remember taking Chris for an A&P class. It's one of the topics that usually takes a while to grasp with all the Latin names etc. That day I had been teaching the class the passage of air through the human body. At the end of the session, I asked the group to name just one section, for example, starting with nostrils or mouth. Then larynx and trachea. I asked Chris first, and he said I can go through it all. "Just one will do," I answered. The prisoner beside him, whom he had befriended, told him to do it then. I was astonished when he went through the lot.

I'd been teaching PE for years and never seen or heard anything like it. It turned out Chris had a photographic memory, which is excellent. Still, the next thing was, 'does he really understand it, or is it just purely memorised?'.

Chris proved over the length of the course, he more than understood. I know he never got below 95 per cent pass on any course. Most just scrape through with 75; the better-performing prisoners would be lucky to get in the high 80 per cent range.

Needless to say, Chris passed the course. He was also getting books out of the library and taking his education to another level. Chris became a PE course mentor and gym orderly after he proved helpful at teaching other prisoners on future courses while back on the wing and cleaning up in the gym. He also successfully completed a distance learning degree with Stonebridge University. Chris eventually moved on, and it was almost like losing a member of staff. He really was that useful to have around.

Many years later, I heard Chris was out and living in a hostel in Manchester. After a rest day, I returned to work and was called to see the corruption prevention governor, Mick. “Come in,” he said. I took a seat, not knowing what was going on. He then informed me Chris Agboola had rung me in the prison yesterday. “Did he?” I inquired. Mick questioned why he’d ring. I told him I didn’t know, as I was on a rest day. I added, “Did anyone ask him? And who spoke to him?” He told me it was Sid, a PEI in the gym. “So,” I said. “Why don’t you ask Sid then?”

It was as if I was being accused of some wrongdoing. Ultimately, I lost patience and simply said, “This is absurd; you keep questioning why he rang me at work. I don’t know. But if I was corrupt or in contact with Chris, do you really think I’d say give me a bell at work?” I added, “He would have my bloody mobile number, wouldn’t he?”

I got up to leave. Mick said, “If he rings again, I want to know.” I just walked off.

Chris did ring back the following week; he didn’t get put through to the gym; the switchboard spoke with him and correctly asked what he’d rang in connection with. As I suspected, he had called to ask if I would write him a reference, and he left his details.

As he requested, I returned to the governor. I relayed my chat with the switchboard lady that, incidentally, wasn’t Stomps anymore. His immediate response was: “You can’t write one.” I told him that was a stupid decision, I told him Chris’s history, progression etc., but he wasn’t budging. He said it was the end of the matter, and I couldn’t do it.

It was frustrating and infuriating, and one big regret. A part of me wishes I’d just written the reference, suffered the consequences, and fought my own corner on the outcome. It wouldn’t have been easy though; I didn’t have the details for Chris.

We had a real success story, after all that hard work and effort from Chris, plus everyone involved in the course, both in the gym and education. The Prison Service pulled the rug from under his feet at a vital crossroads. Chris, to my knowledge, is still out and making a new life. But had he returned to prison, what would the response be? 'Another waster, knew he'd be back, Leopards don't change their spots,' and so on. The truth would be far from that; it would have been, when it really mattered, the system failed Chris.

How many people are there like Chris? Sadly, it's not an isolated incident. Now retired, I can be in contact with ex-offenders, many of whom I consider friends. And sadly, the above is a common theme.

Fun with the yardies

Over my time in the gym, I've met many yardies. While as a nation, the Jamaicans can be stand-offish and mistrust anyone in any kind of authority, so it usually took time to build any type of relationship with them.

Once you had, though, there was a lot of fun to be had with them. Most yardies had a great sense of humour under the facade.

Some of the earlier ones we built a rapport with would speed up breaking down the barriers with others.

They'd see that Little (James) Smiley, Mema, Esko and Scaredem were fine chatting, and then they would open up.

Little, I got to know him well from me playing football for his wing in the inter-wing league games when I'd first arrived. Other wings would say, 'You can have him; we don't want a screw in our team.' Little didn't care; he just wanted the best team he could get.

Other prisoners slowly accepted it, and I ended up playing for all the wings, rotating season after season. Some of my favourite yardie stories are…

Esko Harris

Esko was a short, thick-set lad with a really gravelled yardie tone to his voice. One thing that most yardies have in common is they are incredibly homophobic. This made it very easy to wind them up. One day I spotted Esko going into the cubicle for a pee. The cubicle was only partially covered from the other one up to shoulder height. I quickly got the 'Men's Health' magazine with the topless model on the front and made my way to the cubicle beside him. Esko had a quick glance and then looked straight ahead. I made the sort of whistle-hiss noise from my mouth to get his attention, then repeated it; he looked at me, and I passed over the magazine and said, "Do you want this?" He ran out screaming, waving his hands and shouting, 'batty boy'!

Another time the gym had been closed, we were detailed to go and help with searching on the wing. I was on a cell spin with my colleagues. Esko was the next one on our list. We followed the usual procedure. Esko was taken off to the TV room while we searched his pad. On completion, one PEI went to get him, and I climbed into his bed under the sheets. Kev pulled his trousers down, pretending to have a number two on Esko's loo! Esko shouted, "Batty boy, get out." He hadn't seen Kev at this point. When he did… "Argh, both batty boys!" He was laughing though. I guess it's all about knowing your audience.

Leeshue (Java)

Leeshue was great for a wind-up; more homophobic than anyone. I used to claim he was in denial. You only needed to say morning, handsome, for him to flip. All the others would laugh; he once said, "Phil, I eva si ya in Jamaica, I burn ya 'live." Thankfully, I never bumped into him on our family holiday.

Leeshue was due to move on to another prison before being deported. On his last visit to the gym, Trevon had tipped me off, so I told him how much I'd miss him. His answer was short and sweet, although he did smile.

I told Trevon I'd got a job for him; I gave him a passport-sized photo of me that I'd written 'love you' on the back. Trevon's job was to sneak it into Leeshue's possession box that he was taking with him.

"Job done," Trevon said the next day.

A few days later, Trevon came down in hysterics with Mema, Killer, Esko, Bobba and others. He told me he'd been on the phone with Leeshue who was fuming. He said, "He told me to tell you to fuck off, batty boy." I said, "Does that mean we're finished?" I added, "I don't care; I've always preferred Esko anyway." Esko waved his hands around as the others laughed.

Esko quite often asked me for a gym orderly job. It began to be a pain. I'd have had him, but we had no vacancies then. Gym orderlies very rarely left their jobs. One afternoon Esko came in again and said, "Any jobs Phil?"

"Yes, there might be a chance," I replied. I took him into the office and told him, "We might be taking on an extra orderly; we have a Welsh orderly, an English one and a black lad, but we've been told we need to actively seek a gay orderly."

"I'm no batty boy" was his immediate response. I replied, "I know, but if you just act gay for the interview..." He cut short our little meeting and never asked me again!

One of my favourite yardie stories is one where Kev and I were rub-down searching at the gym exit. Just as we were commencing and searched the first prisoner, a yardie, Kev, got a bag of sweets out and went to pass it to me. The yardie, quick as a flash, pinched it and made off up the corridor.

The following week, Kev tipped me off; he'd got a surprise for him that day.

Sure enough, the yardie came through the door and fell for the bait. Again, he took the sweet and immediately put it in his mouth. He didn't run this time; he was waiting for his 'Bredrin'.

As the others arrived, they asked what was wrong with his mouth. All his lips and teeth were bright blue. I can still hear him now... "Bumbaclat! Me 'ave a visit this afternoon!"

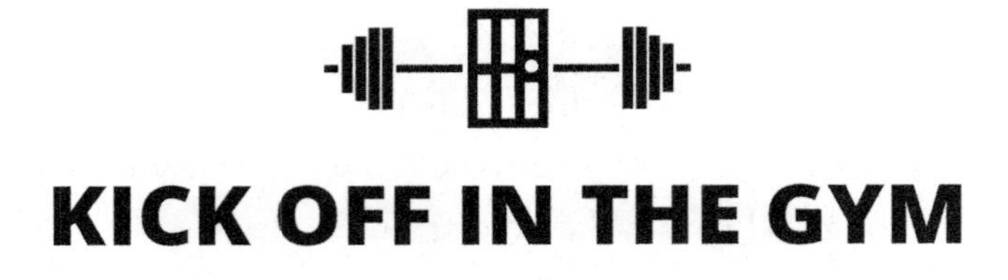

KICK OFF IN THE GYM

We used to have a specific gym session for the detainee unit that housed some of the most high-profile terrorists in the country, including the highest profile of them all, Omar Mahmoud Othman, better known as Abu Qatada al-Filistini. A Salafi cleric and Jordanian national. In prison his name was Othman, and he was a regular in the gymnasium. I even had him on a volleyball course before we had the detainee wing.

Omar Mahmoud Othman.

Once the detainee unit opened, the terrorists didn't mix with other prisoners. The unit had its own small gym with a multi-gym and an additional room containing a treadmill and a stepper-machine. They also had their own allocated sessions in the gym.

A fairly recent development was gym orderlies had been cleared to work with both VPs and the detainees.

For a few weeks, there'd been complaints from the detainees about not wanting music played while they were in the gym. They wanted Al Jazeera TV on the screens. A happy medium was supposed to have been reached that nothing would be played, TV or Music.

Aussie, one of our Gym Orderlies, and Othman had words over music. Aussie saying he'll put what he wants on. The staff weren't aware at the time, but Aussie had entered the office to put the music on. Before they knew it, matters had escalated. Othman and others were trying to get into the office with fire extinguishers being waved around.

Richie Gerrard and the other orderlies then joined in trying to stop the attack. The staff needed to use office chairs to protect themselves. The bell was pressed and eventually the incident was brought under control.

There was information flying around that a Fatwa had been put out on Aussie and Richie, the other orderly. Richie got moved a week or so later. Aussie, however, was on the wing still. One day, he'd been in the kitchen and spoken normally with a couple of Muslim lads who he knew. Aussie was then sat outside his cell eating when the same two Muslims he'd just spoken with came over and threw boiling hot ghee (Hot Fat) over him. Aussie was badly burned. Luckily, it missed his face and went all down his shoulder and back.

Fortunately, after a few weeks out at hospital and a few skin grafts later, he recovered. I've heard Aussie is out now and is a solicitor, apparently.

A much quieter day in the office

We had just got rid of a class when Mark called a meeting in the office. We were just about to start with everyone having got there when the phone rang. I picked it up and actually answered it as myself – ever the professional. Hearing it was a lady on the phone I started to flirt, we laughed and joked for ages. Mark kept pointing at his watch. I told the lady I loved her voice and could listen to her speak all day, but we had a meeting in a minute. I passed the receiver in Chris's direction and simply said, "Chris, it's ya mum!"

His face was a picture, everyone burst out laughing as Chris started to tell his mum off on the phone. Fair play to Chris's dad, he said he'd give me a tenner to take her out.

Contract put out on me again

A PO came to the gym just before lunchtime saying he needed three of us for a C&R team for one going to the Seg. As always, my first question was, "Who is it?" Aaron was the name, and I did indeed know him. I asked mainly to see if I knew him. And to see if there's a possibility of talking to him. I told the PO I was sure Aaron would walk if I spoke to him. He replied, "I doubt it."

The other two PE staff and I got kitted up as instructed. When we reached the prisoner's door, the PO instructed Aaron to stand against the back wall, a standard command. He opened the door and told him he was going to the Seg. Aaron asked if he could pack some kit and was told no, anything he was entitled to would be brought down later. Aaron just asked, "why?" and the PO gave the instructions to take him. At that moment, you're not sure if the PO's seen something you've missed – had Aaron suddenly produced a weapon – all that goes through your mind.

As we went forward, I could tell Aaron wasn't resisting. I began to talk to him, and he said he would walk. I told the other PE staff to relax their locks, which they did. The PO told us to keep control of him, which we did till we located him in the Seg. But no genuine locks were held. As far as I was aware, that was that.

A few days later, I was visited by security and told that, along with one of the other PEIs we'd had a contract put out on us by Aaron. We were told it had come from a reliable source and was being taken seriously. Having been here years ago, I would handle it differently than I did when I had little experience.

I rang Aaron's wing to speak to the SO; it was BIFFO; remember my old training SO from when I got to Lartin? "What do you want, Daft lad?" I explained what I'd been told by security and asked if he had a spare office that I could use to chat with Aaron. I went over, and BIFFO called Aaron down to the office. He asked an officer to stand outside of the room where we went to talk.

I told Aaron about what I'd been told about the contract. Aaron said that when he was being moved to the Seg on that move, one of us had put a sly punch in on him just before exiting the wing. I told him that was news to me, and if it did happen, I knew it didn't come from me or the other PEIs.

I stated, "If you remember, we didn't hold any locks on you when we moved you because I knew you weren't resisting."

He said he'd spoken to many people who said they didn't believe it would be me. He was adamant it happened but also that he hadn't put a contract out.

I explained to him that punching someone under restraint isn't what I'm about. For me, it's a cowardly act and totally unprofessional. To this day, my gut feeling is someone I don't know did it. But if you're reading this now, I hope you're ashamed of yourself.

Staff carry out challenging jobs, but that behaviour is unacceptable. And furthermore, you could get your colleagues seriously injured. Aaron ended my meeting by shaking my hand and doing the same with the other PEIs when he saw them.

Years later, during my short stint at HMP Kingston, Aaron progressed through the system and was there. We had a chat about the incident and a laugh.

He asked me who had given the information about the contract. He named who he believed it to be. He said he thought the incident was used by this prisoner who owed Aaron a debt, so he concocted the story in the hope Aaron got moved off the wing.

There may have never been a contract. But I'm glad Aaron didn't go through the rest of his sentence believing I did that cowardly act. So, I'm happy I handled it the way I did and got to clear it up.

THE EVIL IN THEIR EYES 2

A few prisoners had that cold look in their eyes, a cold vacant look, which I recognised from seeing Robert Maudsley all those years before.

John Straffen viciously strangled two of his victims days apart and killed a third time when he escaped from prison for four hours.

Straffen, who died in 2007, spent 55 years behind bars. I don't think Maudsley or moors murderer Ian Brady has served a lengthier prison sentence; it depends where you look; records are a little unclear.

Surprisingly, he spent most of his time at Long Lartin on normal location. Straffen was sentenced to be hanged, but a little over a month later, he was reprieved by the Home Secretary on the grounds of insanity.

Instead of hanging, Straffen was jailed with no hope of being released. Whenever anyone was in his company, he gave them a chill, even more so if female officers were around.

Mark Dixie

Dixie used to attend the gym regularly, usually playing football in goal. He was on rule forty-three (protection). Over the years, Dixie was known to have used the names Mark Down, Mark James McDonald, Steven McDonald and Shane Turner. I went to court with Dixie a few times about his case. He never showed remorse whenever I took him to court, and when you looked into his eyes, there was that same look I'd described. He also had a short fuse to go with it.

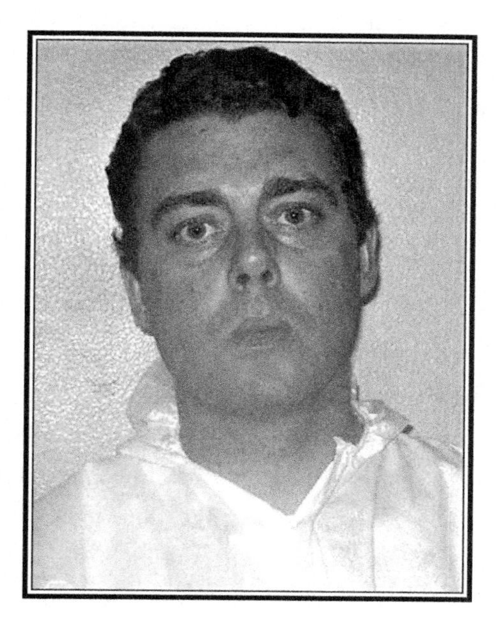

Mark Dixie.

Dixie brutally murdered and raped 18-year-old Sally Anne Bowman in 2005. Sally had been on a night out in Croydon with her older sister, Nicole, and a group of pals when she was murdered.

The 18-year-old had persuaded her boyfriend to come from Kingston and drive her home at around four in the morning.

But the couple had an argument. Sally stormed out of the car, and her boyfriend drove away. Dixie spotted her and attacked just yards away from her home. Then he dragged her body under a car. Dixie's only feeble defence in court was to claim she was alive when he raped her. I've sat through some horrendous court cases, but this was one of the most harrowing.

It is now widely believed Dixie tried to murder another lady just yards away from where Sally was attacked, but she managed to escape. So, he then stumbled on his next victim. Sally's mother tried to secure a job at Long Lartin in the visits as a volunteer, trying to get to her daughter's killer. Having heard the case unfold and what that poor woman had to endure; nobody could blame her.

Colin Ireland

Ireland, known as the 'Gay Slayer'; prisoners at Long Lartin called him the 'Fairy Liquidator'. Jobless at 37 and contemplating his next career move, Colin Ireland made a New Year's resolution to become a serial killer and went on to murder five victims in a crime spree that lasted from March to June 1993.

Ireland met all his victims at the Coleherne Pub, a popular gay venue in London's Earl's Court, where he convinced them to invite him back to their flats under the promise of sadomasochistic sex. Once inside, he bound and tortured them to death.

Ireland had studied previous serial killers like Peter Sutcliffe (The Yorkshire Ripper) and had started killing because he 'wanted to be somebody'. So much so that he called the press anonymously after taking the life of his first victim to brag about what he had done.

Ironically, Ireland pleaded guilty to his murders, so he didn't have a full trial, therefore, didn't get the same infamy, notoriety, or the exposure he desired. I'll never forget the day I carried out his gym induction when our orderly approached him and simply said, "Hey, are you that poof killer?" Ireland just nodded his head. He was a regular gym user during his time at Long Lartin. Ireland died in Wakefield Prison in 2012.

The Suffolk Strangler

Suffolk Strangler Steven Wright was arrested by police in December 2006 for the murders of five women. Few people could have predicted how events would unfold over the next month. Just before Christmas, two ladies had been reported missing from the town's red-light district in just 14 days. The bodies of Miss Nicol and Mrs Adams would be found along with those of three other women. The hunt for a serial killer began.

The grisly discoveries raised concerns, both in the media and among the people in the town, that a serial killer was targeting Ipswich's sex workers.

Those fears were confirmed when the body of Anneli Alderton, 24, was found in woodland in Nacton ten weeks after she went missing. Another shock was just around the corner two days later when two more bodies were found. Wright's DNA was found on three victims, and fibres from his car, home and clothing were found on all five.

Wright's DNA had been added to the National crime database in 2002 after he was convicted of stealing £80 from a pub till.

The former pub landlord was arrested on suspicion of murdering all five women.

The jurors took just eight hours to reach their decision. Wright showed no emotion throughout the trial and just answered when questioned, if you say so, yes, or it would appear so. He claimed the evidence against him was circumstantial. His main defence was that he had a professional relationship with all of them. The judge sentenced him to a whole life term the following day. It has been widely reported that Wright may have killed before this spree. He was questioned at Long Lartin Prison regarding further murders.

Wright's demeanour in prison was the complete opposite of Dixie's; Wright attended the Gym regularly on the VP sessions but would always train on his own. One thing that both men had in common was that cold look in their eyes.

David Bieber

A former US marine and bodybuilder, Bieber used a potentially deadly homemade, pronged iron bar to repeatedly stab Officer Alison Smith in 2017 while serving life for the murder of PC Ian Broadhurst and the attempted murder of two of his colleagues. Alison was a good friend and colleague of mine. She was lucky to be alive after a totally unprovoked frenzied attack.

Officer Ian Harper RIP, who sadly passed away just months later, was one of the first on the scene and undoubtedly saved

Ali's life that day. Attacks like this on female officers never happened years ago; they went against the moral code of old-school criminals. The moral code appears to have disappeared as the old-school criminals have gone.

Nathan Matthews

Nathan Mathews, the stepbrother of Becky Watts, was sentenced to a minimum of 33 years; despite Matthews' attempt at an appeal against the length of the sentence, the sentence was upheld. Matthews, 28, had a fixation on young girls and tried to kidnap his stepsister for sexual purposes. Matthews murdered Becky, suffocating her, dismembering her body and hiding her remains in a shed. Matthews' girlfriend, Shauna Hoare, 21, was sentenced to 17 years for manslaughter.

The Court discussed whether Matthews should be sentenced to a whole life tariff reserved for Britain's most notorious killers. Matthews' lawyer argued that his crime didn't meet the level required for that sentence.

In Court, Matthews was accused of being obsessed with violent teenage pornography. He is believed to have watched a film titled "Virgin teen gets raped in her own house", before he throttled Becky and dismembered her body.

During his first few months at Long Lartin, Matthews made several complaints that the staff didn't talk to him.

In 2017 Matthews was attacked at Long Lartin by another prisoner named Jackson; Jackson used the familiar method of using a jug of boiling hot butter known as "ghee"; the ghee was thrown partially over his face and neck. Matthews was quickly doused with water by the same staff Matthews had complained about previously. Matthews, although trying to come across as vulnerable and requiring staff protection, wore that same cold look of a cold-hearted killer. Personally, I think he fits the criteria befitting a whole life sentence.

His girlfriend Hoare was acquitted of murder, but convicted of manslaughter, conspiracy to kidnap, perverting the course of justice and preventing a lawful burial. She always denied any involvement and said messages sent to Matthews discussing a kidnap were just sent to placate him after he was violent towards her.

In one message, Hoare wrote: "Just went into Costcutter and saw a pretty petite girl. Almost knocked her out to bring home lol xoxo".

A message from Matthews 20 seconds later said: "Don't you 'almost' me ... Now DO IT b*****!!!xxxxx".

Steven Griffiths The Crossbow Killer

Stephen Griffiths, the Crossbow Cannibal, cooked and ate parts of his victims. One Monday morning in May 2010, the caretaker at Stephen Griffiths' block of flats checked CCTV footage from the weekend. To his horror, he saw Suzanne Blamires running terrified from Griffiths' flat before he appeared and knocked her unconscious. Griffiths disappeared from view, returning moments later with a crossbow. The PhD student lined up his weapon and fired a bolt through the unconscious woman's head before dragging her lifeless body down a corridor. Then, holding the bow above his head in triumph, he raised a bottle of drink to the camera.

The caretaker phoned 999, and Griffiths was arrested within hours after he had dumped Suzanne's body in the nearby river Aire.

The monster admitted killing Suzanne, 36; Shelley Armitage, 31; and Susan Rushworth, 43, after luring them to his flat on the edge of the red-light district in Bradford, West Yorkshire.

In his flat were hundreds of horror films, books about serial killers and blood-stained crossbows, samurai swords and 30 knives. When Griffiths' mobile was handed to police, they found a video showing one victim naked in a bath, then tied up on a bed with the words 'my sex slave' spray-painted on her back.

A rucksack holding Suzanne's remains was found on the bank of the River Aire. A crossbow bolt and a knife fragment were embedded in her skull. She'd been hacked into 81 pieces.

Griffiths told police he dismembered the women using power tools, a hammer, an assortment of knives, and a samurai sword. Police divers also found parts of Shelley Armitage and a black flight bag holding knives and hacksaws. He bragged to detectives that he cooked parts of the first two victims, but when his oven broke, he ate raw pieces of the third victim.

When he appeared in court in May 2010, Griffiths gave his name as the Crossbow Cannibal.

When you looked into Griffiths' eyes, you saw that now too-familiar look; I often thought you didn't need to be a qualified psychologist to see the pure evil in these men. It smacked you in the face as soon as you looked at them. These are just a tiny sample of prisoners I met over the years who all shared that same dark cold look.

The governors

You would be amazed at the difference a change of Governor has on the overall smooth running of the jail. As I said previously, all prisons run on the goodwill of the prisoners. But the goodwill of the prisoners is usually won and lost by the number one governor and how they run their jail.

During my time in the Service, I have seen the prison I work in improve almost overnight. I've also seen governors have a negative effect with sometimes devastating consequences for staff and prisoners.

The best analogy is that the effect may be similar to a poorly performing football team. A new manager comes in, and the performances can improve instantly; just by having someone who can man-manage players. It's the same players on the pitch (or staff in prison), but the performance improves. And it can go the other way just as quickly. A great manager leaves, and a new one comes in, which can have a harmful effect.

Over all my years in prison, in the main, I've been lucky to work under some fantastic governors, some not-so-good, and a few terrible ones.

My first two governors were totally different in style and personality but were fantastic man-managers in their own way. John Marriott was very liberal in his approach and not afraid to take a risk. Tell me of another governor who would give Charlie Bronson a pick axe?

Jim Mullen, my first governor at Long Lartin, had a firm but fair approach. He kept you on your toes. If you went to see him and he took his glasses off, you knew it wouldn't go well for you. You knew you had to take cover if you crossed him.

Dai Williams wasn't a number one governor but has to get a 'shout out'. He was a regular gym user and a real staff man, one of those governors you'd run through a brick wall for. I had only briefly been at Long Lartin when I discovered you could leave an answering machine message on the gym phone. I left a message leaving gaps for the caller to speak, pretending that the phone was faulty, asking them to speak up. Then, 'can you bang your phone, I can't hear you'.

Dai had been trying to contact the gym; he shouted down the phone and banged it on the table. Eventually, he rang A-wing and spoke to fellow Welshman John Davis on the desk, explaining what was happening. He asked him to go down and tell us the phone was faulty. He said, "I can hear Phil, but he can't hear me."

I was in John's sight getting a class in, so he said, "Phil is at the door here." Dai immediately put the phone down and rang the gym again. The game was up. He had a good laugh about it. Today I'd probably be dismissed.

Dai's son works at the prison and is working through the ranks. The apple doesn't fall far from the tree; he's also a great staff man and has organised numerous charity events for staff and families.

Nick Dann, this may surprise a few people, but as I've said many times, I take people as I find them. Nick was acting Governor when I got diagnosed with cancer. He gave me unwavering support till the day he left and beyond. I also have to applaud him for 'sussing out' a few people close to him that others never did or have since.

Nick Leader and Tom Wheatley; I'll describe those men together; they have similar work methods and ethos; that's not to say they didn't have different personalities. When both arrived over separate periods, Long Lartin was going through a difficult time. Both turned sinking ships into flagship prisons almost overnight. Both men could galvanise the staff below them and allow their managers to make decisions. Both encouraged healthy prisoner and staff relationships and set up consultation groups that had a purpose. If prisoners came up with reasonable requests, both men would consider their merits carefully and then calculate well-balanced decisions.

There were no knee-jerk reactions with those two governors. It also helped that both valued the positive impact a PE department can have on the smooth running of a jail. I always believed, 'if you get three things right in prison, you're halfway to a smooth-running place. Food, gym, and visits'.

They also implemented family visits held in the sports hall, a big perk for prisoners and a massive incentive for them to conform. Those visits were a huge success. We would organise little mini sports days for the children. Still, more importantly, it provided a natural setting for kids to spend quality time with their dads.

I know Tom is currently the Number one governor at Wakefield Prison, but I'm unsure where Nick Leader is or whether he's retired. Still, both will be a success wherever they are. I would work for both again in a heartbeat.

Chameleons, a lot of governors that work under a number one are like chameleons. They instantly blend into the governing Governor's style, whether they see it as a way of jumping the ladder or fear being their own person. I've watched many a governor who I previously thought was good change their whole demeanour and values under a new governing governor. Conversely, I've seen some poor Governors become almost average under a decent number one.

THE ORDERLIES

I could write a book on orderlies and success stories. Still, the media or newspapers want to refrain from publishing news about them. For this chapter, I can't think of a better place to start than four gym orderlies that I remain in touch with, and it gives me great pleasure to see how they are turning their lives around. I asked if they could write a few lines about their experience in the gym. Kindly they've all agreed to do so.

Stevie Fountain

Stevie was our gym orderly for a considerable length of time; he came to the prison as a young lad straight from young offenders with a history of a chequered past. Despite his slight frame, Steve was an outstanding amateur boxer growing up. I recognised Steve as almost still a young boy at heart who lacked guidance and a role model. Over time I built a positive relationship with him, competing in every sport you can think of.

One day I was getting a volleyball off the racking in the Sports Hall to go through some drills with Steve. I lost my footing and slipped and broke my arm; I also cut my head open just above my eye after hitting it on a weight training stand on the way down.

Steve heard the clatter and sought assistance from the SO, Mark Blackham, after putting me in the recovery position. I was told later that Stevie had kept asking staff on the wing and in the gym if I was ok. Bear in mind that it could have been a considerable security risk, me with keys and unconscious.

Years later, I was contacted by a solicitor who asked me to write a letter of support explaining the above events. Remembering my regret with Chris Agboola, I just wrote an accurate account of it. And I'd heard Steve got his move sometime later. Since retiring, I hear from Steve regularly and still try to offer my advice as he continues to settle into building a new life outside.

One funny memory of Stevie was, one day, I was refereeing five-a-side football. Steve came in to keep the score using the whiteboard on the wall. One of the most notorious prisoners in the Prison System, Gary Nelson, was playing. Gary, similarly to Dennis Arif, wasn't the best of footballers but always got plenty of time and space because nobody dared get too close to him or put in a decent tackle on him. I always got on with Gary; he always gave me his gold studded Rolex watch to look after when he played, and at the end of the Game, I always gave him my cheap sports watch in return.

Stevie owed me a Mars Bar from a bet on one of our many basketball challenges. As the game drew to a close, I told Steve, I'll quash the bet if at the end of the game, you say to Gary, "it's time you packed in playing, Gary, you're shit". Steve agreed to the deal, entered the pitch at the end, and shouted those words to Gary. To my disappointment and Stevie's relief, Gary didn't react at all. Steve was walking back, looking all smug, when I shouted to Gary, "Are you going to let him get away with that, Gary?" Gary suddenly ran after Stevie, pinned him down, held open his eyes and licked his eyeballs. Stevie returned, not looking so smug this time; I said, "now that was worth the Mars Bar"!

STEVIE'S PERSONAL LETTER

I arrived at Long Lartin as a 21-year-old fresh out of YOI under a big cloud, I was facing a second life sentence and, I'd been accused of taking a prison officer hostage, and trying to escape from Swinfen Hall young offenders.

I was taken to Long Lartin as category A prisoner and put straight into the SCCU, I was put in a high control cell where I stayed for 3 months only coming out of my cell for exercise and shower under SO and 4 unlock. These were some really dark times and at this time I didn't know how it could ever improve, Eventually I was allowed onto the wing on normal location, so I started to use the gym on a regular basis and successfully completed various PE qualifications.

I had the category A status removed and the escape risk so I made the most of my time, I eventually managed to get a role as a gym orderly where I performed daily tasks such as cleaning and tidying up the weights after sessions, this is where I met Phil, he was a gym officer and we formed what I can only say was a friendship, he took the time to train with me and play sports, we used to compete over everything.

One day whilst playing basketball and taking turns at attempting 3 pointers, we had a friendly bet on the outcome.

I won and as the forfeit, Phil had to wear my Derby County shirt for a full day. Phil hated this not just because he was a big Leeds fan but because I was half his size ha-ha, but he did wear it. This just showed the kind of man he is; he wasn't just a prison officer he was my mentor and a silver cloud in a dark and extremely dangerous environment. I worked in the gym for some years up until I got a progressive move and transferred to a category B prison. During my time working in the gym, Phil helped me to stay focused and positive even when a lot of the time, I felt there wasn't a lot to look forward to.

In my time at Long Lartin I developed bulimia, Phil helped me to try and get this under control and eventually talked me into seeking help from a nurse he knew and trusted. This really helped me to address this. Phil worked with me and the nurse to help me get my health back and for that I could never thank him enough. Who knows, if he hadn't, I may not be here now, my relationship with prison staff wasn't always the best but Phil was one guy that I always had as a friend and mentor. I can honestly say I never met anyone like Phil in my 17 years in Prison, he made an otherwise terrible place more tolerable.

Steve Fountain.

James Gilligan (Gilly)

Gilly was a gym orderly for many years at Long Lartin. Gilly was a tall, good-looking lad with a great sense of humour and quick wit. One fond memory of Gilly involved Steve, who I mentioned earlier.

Steve was doing some Jehovah's Witness study with Jason, the lad who got baptised. So, Gilly said, "Have a practice at doing your spiel, you knock on my cell door, and I'll answer, then you give me your sales pitch." Steve agreed and knocked on Gilly's door. Gilly answered, and just as Steve started his opening line, Gilly slammed the door in his face shouting, "get used to it, ya crank".

Like me, he shared a love for football. I recognised a bit of myself in Gilly in that he changed once he got onto the pitch. He was a fierce competitor, a commanding centre-half with a knack for scoring important goals. Gilly completed various courses and was an intelligent lad.

Gilly got a progressive move to Oakwood Prison from Long Lartin, where he put all his experience and mentoring skills to good practice. He set up a mentoring project called The Big Project, Basic Intervention Group. This group started with five mentors who would take prisoners off the Basic wing, where prisoners were previously banged up for 23 hours a day. They would take prisoners off to the Gym, Gardening, Painting, and a Joinery workshop. The Project went from strength to strength, with Gilly proudly having over 600 successful mediations to his name, with 40 mentors working under him.

The Project won the National Mentoring Awards event at Manchester Cathedral, which Gilly and his family attended. Governors from prisons from all around the country visited Oakwood with a view of introducing the Project in their prisons. Also introduced by Gilly was a pupil referral scheme (PRS) that saw selected pupils referred to have days visiting Oakwood, where Gilly and other mentors would talk about drugs and their own experiences of being in prison and the consequences of making the wrong choices.

I monitored his progress with keen interest as he progressed through the system until his recent release from prison.

I had no doubt that Gilly would use his qualifications and personal qualities to the full after leaving Long Lartin. And he did all that and more. I gained a lot of great friends in my career, and a few didn't wear a uniform. Gilly was undoubtedly one of them.

GILLY'S PERSONAL LETTER

Anyone who's ever met Phil will tell you the same thing. You will never meet a better bloke; I've never met a single con that has a bad word to say about him. An absolute legend and the fittest man I have ever come across. This man helped me personally get through some dark times at the beginning of my sentence, as I know he did many other men.

None of us ever saw him as a screw, we just saw him for what he is, a genuine, honest, and fair man. And to be honest that's all we ever asked for. I consider him to be my friend, as an ex-con, I realise that's some statement to make. But anyone who's met Phil would say the same. I spent 6 years with Phil, working as a gym orderly at Long Lartin, he truly is an inspirational man. My time was filled with tears of joy and happiness and a few of sadness.

I remember after leaving there and some of the lads wrote to me telling me of Phil's plight and his battle against cancer. They told me how they had all decided to do a Triathlon Charity event for Phil. They also told me how many prisoners were getting involved, to be honest it came as no surprise it was just a measure of how much everyone respected him. They raised thousands of pounds and told me how they weren't ashamed in admitting they shed a tear when to their surprise Phil came in on the day of the event to support the lads. And again, later when they presented Phil with a cheque.

The one sadness I have is on hearing how Phil stood strong against some of the poison behind him, and against the poison in front of him, and most of it was making a stand for us, the cons! Only to be let down by so many. That said how many of us can honestly say they'd have done what Phil did? This is why every Prisoner, or person that met Phil would say, "Phil is proper stuff". As we would say, "A fucking minority".

Never change Phil,

Respect always James (Gilly) and the rest of us.

Reuben

My first memory of Reuben was of him regularly attending the gym and training with a prisoner off his wing that I knew as Papps. They trained together over quite a long period. Papps was a friendly guy, passionate about keeping fit and staying healthy. Incidentally, he's another ex-prisoner now released and making a new positive life. He's integrated back into society, building his own business.

I'd noticed Reuben had been training alone and asked about Papps; it turned out he'd got a progressive move. I started to train regularly with Reuben. Naturally, we would talk about training, his background, and, eventually, his case. Over weeks and months, it became pretty clear after numerous discussions that Reuben had deep regret about his actions, which resulted in him serving a very long life sentence.

We became training partners daily after Reuben completed the PE course and became a Gym Orderly. His thirst for knowledge was quite clear; he was also keen on yoga and meditation, something, despite all my years of training, I'd probably underestimated. He would practically live in the gym, even coming down to work on his rest days.

Everyone who commits serious offences must be seen to serve their punishment. But, with Reuben, I felt, unlike many other prisoners I'd spoken with, they took years to get to a similar mindset of where he was already at.

Clearly, the Reuben being locked up today isn't the Reuben who committed the crime. Undoubtedly, he will spend the years he has left continuing to grow and educate himself. Still, I would have no doubts about releasing him back into society. It almost felt like his time being served was a waste of another life.

Since retiring I went to visit Reuben at Dovegate Prison, he's currently awaiting repatriation to Iraq – Kurdistan. It was a strange feeling going through the gates as a visitor; the time passed by in the blink of an eye, just chatting about training, what he was doing in the gym etc.

A few prisoners recognised me and broke from their visit to come and shake my hand. Staff may read this and question why and find it suspicious that I would go out of my way to visit a prisoner, but I have nothing to hide and had no ulterior motive. I was simply continuing what we'd started and wanted to check that he was still on track.

REUBEN'S PERSONAL LETTER

I was a young man who had arrived in England, I had always been restless and eager to make a difference in the world. I took a wrong turn and made a really bad decision, and made a huge mistake, I took a person's life and as a result was awarded a life sentence and found myself in a High Security Prison in the UK.

For a considerable period of time, I was filled with despair and hopelessness. I then attended a gym Induction; where I first met an Officer PEI named Phil Currie. Phil took an interest in me as he showed me around the Prison Gym, he invited me into the Office to chat after the induction and informed me about a PE Course that he was currently running. Something made me feel that he saw potential in me, the way he spoke to me filled me with enthusiasm to apply for the Course. I completed an application form and asked a gym orderly off my wing to take it down to the Gym for me.

I later started on the PE Course, and found a real thirst for knowledge, I enjoyed learning more about the human body and how it works. I found myself going to the library and studying in my spare time in my cell. I started to work out with Phil when I came down on a weekend or if we were given a free session. As we trained, we got chatting about life in general and our backgrounds, and even about our futures. I hadn't even thought about having a future to be honest, whilst I had so many years to serve. Phil broke my sentence down into smaller chunks discussing possible targets, one of which was to complete the course to the best of my ability and aim to become a Gym Orderly, or even a course mentor. Here I was suddenly starting to look forward and not back.

I took Phil's advice on board and gave the PE Course my best, also continuing with my private studies. I was amazed at how much I'd learned in a short period of time. Phil also educated me about offence related courses and encouraged me to take part. My life seemed to be turning around for the better and seemed to improve daily. I was learning so much from Phil and not just in the classroom he had become a role model, a mentor and I'd even now describe him as a friend.

My confidence grew throughout the PE Course, and I started with Phil's help to plan and take part in Charity events, raising money for those in need. I found a purpose in life and was finally able to make a positive difference in the world. I am extremely grateful to Phil for showing me the way, I now truly believe that I can achieve anything with dedication, determination and hard work. Despite the mistakes I had made, I was now determined to live a meaningful life and make the most of my time in Prison. With Phil's guidance and support I became a better person and started to learn to forgive myself for my mistakes. I knew there was a long road ahead, but I was now determined to keep moving forwards.

Years have passed since I first met Phil, but I have never forgotten the kindness and compassion that he showed me. I continue to grow and build a successful life, on the sound foundations Phil helped to put into place, I'll never take for granted the positive impact he had on my life. I now pay it forwards and volunteer and help others in the way Phil had helped me. My life changed forever when I met Phil the extraordinary mentor who helped rehabilitate me and change my life around.

Reuben Kareem.

Bobby

Bobby became our orderly/painter and was in the gym for several years before getting a progressive move. After going to his cell one day, I came away believing, "you could eat your dinner off his floor". It was immaculate; never had I seen a cell so clean, not even Mary's, and up to this point, she was the best cleaner I'd ever seen.

I got to know Bobby well over a period of time, training and chatting. It became apparent a lot of Bobby's problems stemmed from him punishing himself for his crime, believing that he didn't deserve to have a future. Getting Bobby to come to terms with that position took a long time. Bobby had suffered a harsh childhood. I'd defy any child having suffered his experiences to go through them and come out unscathed. If Bobby had been given an ordinary childhood, he would never have come to jail. If any government is serious about levelling up, money needs to be pumped into the deprived areas. It's no coincidence most crime is caused by people in the suburbs like the ones I grew up in. It's nothing new; you can go back to Robin Hood's days for a classic example; deprived people will use other means to go out and get them.

Bobby was a real grafter with a tremendous work ethic and a lovely lad who had been given a really poor deal, right from being a baby. If we see a baby or child in this situation as a society, we have sympathy for that child. Why does that sympathy and desire to help get reduced as they age?

I recently managed to contact Bobby, and seeing and hearing how well he's doing brought me great pleasure. Another thing that has yet to change is Bobby's cleanliness. I saw a video of his home, and it was spotless. Bobby has continued to be a conscientious worker, gaining three promotions in his place of work.

BOBBY'S PERSONAL LETTER

My name is Bobby. I'm an ex-prisoner or should I say ex offender, I prefer the latter. I have spent all my teenage years and adult life behind the door not to mention growing up in the care system so you could say I've been under the care of authorities since I was born. Firstly, I'd like to say I wasn't born a bad person, my environment and learnt behaviour shaped my life.

I used drugs and alcohol from a young age and hurt many people along the way both outside and inside those walls, including myself. I felt lost for so many years and pushed away a lot of support because, I didn't feel worthy enough. My time in prison was spent fighting staff and inmates and hurting myself; you could say I was stuck on repeat.

I was now serving a life sentence for murder and was shipped from jail to jail, finally ending up in a high security Prison due to a staff assault and continued drug abuse, I was tired of running from my demons.

I then became ashamed of myself and the things I'd done. I had a feeling of dread and shame so decided I needed a change and that's where I met the real me, and a man called Phil Currie. Phil installed in me trust, respect, responsibility and self-belief, he gave his all to each and every person he came into contact with, I had never felt anything like the care that he showed me.

I became super fit and more confident and got the job as a gym Orderly/Painter spending most of my day in the gym. I stayed in Long Lartin for 4 years and eventually got a progressive move to a category C jail then a cat D. There was light at the end of the tunnel for me, I managed to secure a job and I've been promoted on 3 occasions.

I was released and met my Mrs. Without doubt a great deal of credit goes to Phil and all the gym staff, I'm forever in all your debts. I often actually miss the place because I wasn't in prison when I was in the gym. I'll love you all forever.

Thanks, BOSS x

Bobby O'Dell

Happier times, meeting up with Bobby and his girlfriend Kelly. Bobby was well on his way to becoming everything I knew he could be. He keeps doing me, and himself proud

That's just a handful of orderlies that used their time and experience in prison and made the most of it. They educated themselves and are now out building a new life for themselves. There're too many orderlies of this nature to mention here.

One of my favourite stories of the orderlies was two characters we had, Martin and Rickard. As always, the staff had been down during lunchtime playing badminton or doing personal training. Straight after, we would get the first class of the afternoon in. The orderlies would be down to do their cleaning and tidying around.

Unbeknown to us, Martin and Rickard found a pair of white polka-dot knickers in the female changing rooms. They decided to keep them for later on the wing; they took turns having them in their cell. Martin had them for the first night and decided to wear them and kept them on overnight. He was still wearing them in the morning when the staff opened the door to take him to a hospital appointment. Even Martin admitted dying of embarrassment.

A similar story happened when two orderlies washed some staff kit out the back. For some reason, they thought it was the kit of our female PEI. Just as one of the orderlies was joking about sniffing the shorts, Sid, one of our PEIs, walked in and said, "Oh, thanks for washing my kit; let me know when it's done." The orderly was nearly sick.

Occasionally, I would bring in a malt loaf to split between the orderlies on their break if I had them cleaning the classroom and doing other duties. At the time, we had an orderly called Dave Kerwin. Dave was a slightly built lad, extremely fit, who loved doing a circuit. I would often join in with him. Dave was a proud cockney and spoke with an extreme cockney accent. I brought a few malt loaves to work one morning to keep in my drawer. I often had one as a snack before training. I put it in the office to save for later for eating between sessions and before my workout. My colleague Kev Phillips was in the office at the time. I was in the weights room when Dave came over to chat; I asked if he was training on the next session, and he said he was, but he was returning to the wing first to get some food because he was starving. I told him I had a malt loaf in the office if he wanted one, but said keep it to yourself though I haven't got enough to give all the orderlies one. Dave said "sweet". I went into the office to get my malt loaf and told Kev to give it two minutes before coming out to ask us if we'd seen his malt loaf from in the office. I returned to Dave, slipping him the malt loaf and told him to keep it hidden. Just as he put the package down his tracksuit bottoms, Kev appeared and asked the question, had we seen his malt loaf out of the Office. Dave went white and whiter when Kev added: "if I find out who's got it, they will be banned from the Gym"! Kev returned to the office. Dave, who by his own admission, is a bit "para" (paranoid), went into full cockney mode. "You cunt, you'll get me the sack." Kev started to come around again, and Dave promptly disappeared. When Dave returned, Kev was back in the office; I told Dave: "he's fuming, mate; give it to me, and I'll sneak it back into the office". He replied, "You're too facking late, mate; I've eaten the evidence," and said, "trust me, the packet is never being found."

Several weeks later, I offered him another malt loaf, insisting that it was genuinely mine this time. He said, "Fack it; I'll have it because I'm starving, but don't fack about, Phil; you nearly got me the sack last time." I told him again that it was mine. He was still unsure and wasted no time getting it down his throat. He returned and said, "It's gone; you may as well tell me now. Was it yours?" I told him it was. I found it in the recess under the benches; after doing a search, security rang and said they had information about drugs in the recess; I did a search but only found this malt loaf. He instantly flipped into full Cockney mode again, dashing off to the recess. I went to the doorway and saw him enter the cubicle. As he came back into view, I asked what he was doing. In his strong Cockney twang, Dave said, "If in doubt, get the fucker out, mate." He added, "You said it was facking yours." I replied, "It was, Dave, I found it, and as you know, possession is nine-tenths of the law."

Another high-profile prisoner and Gym orderly who recently got released has gotten married and is building a new life. That orderly, on several occasions, came to the rescue of a female officer and very good friend of mine on the wing. He often stopped things from happening. He told me it sometimes caused him a problem, but he knew she was my friend, so he wouldn't let anything happen to her. He was one of a dying breed in prison that still possessed that moral code where you don't hurt a female. As stated earlier, with the attack by Bieber on Ali Smith, the moral code is sadly becoming a thing of the past.

Getting along with an Orderly would also assist you in getting along with their friends. One that really springs to mind is a friend of our Gym orderly, PJ McGuire. PJ was a Gloucester lad who I really got on with. He was a straight talker with both staff and prisoners. He was well respected by prisoners. PJ lifted for the Long Lartin powerlifting squad and was one of the strongest lads I'd met in prison. PJ would often train with a couple of other prisoners, Sean Jackman and a Manchester lad called John Gray.

John was a no-nonsense guy with a fearsome track record; and head of a strong Manchester firm at Long Lartin at the time. Through my relationship with PJ, I started talking to John occasionally. He never said too much, but it was still more than he spoke to other staff. I remember answering a bell on the wing one day when I discovered the side of John that I'd often heard about. I answered an alarm bell on the wing, after a prisoner had allegedly had his lip bitten off. The staff were trying to take John off the wing in connection with the alleged attack. I entered the wing, to hear John threatening to break the governor's jaw. I knew from talking to other prisoners that you didn't want to get on the wrong side of him. Over the coming months and years though, after John had returned from a stint in the segregation unit, we again engaged in brief conversations.

John eventually moved on after starting to really keep his head down. Since retiring, I've learned John is not only out of prison but has set up a few successful businesses and is not only settled into the community but is making a real positive impact in society. I spoke to John recently, and he's talked about going to schools and advising on how to stay clear of the path he took for a large part of his life.

It was a real pleasure to meet up with both John and PJ recently and hear their success stories. John and PJ recently set up their own protein drink company, Combo Shot, endorsed by numerous famous athletes and footballers like Kieran Trippier. They kindly donate 20% of all proceeds to charity. They are both living proof that there is always time to make positive changes in your life.

Left to right John Gray, Myself and PJ McGuire

Convicted without a Jury

Barry Hibberd was jailed for 17 years and six months for his role in a £1.75 million raid on a Heathrow warehouse in a trial that made legal history: it was the first time in 400 years that a major criminal case was heard by a judge alone with no jury.

Barry and three accomplices, John Twomey and Glen Cameron, both from New Milton, Hampshire, and Peter Blake from Notting Hill, who was also in Long Lartin with Barry and a real character, were all found guilty of robbery and firearms charges at the Old Bailey.

Hibberd, Twomey, Blake and Cameron were part of a six-strong gang that gained access to Menzies World Cargo after being taken airside in a van by an employee on February 6, 2004.

Armed with handguns, the men entered the warehouse and stole several bags containing cash after gaining access to the vault. They left the warehouse, stealing a white van and a gold Ford Focus at gunpoint. During the raid, 16 employees were tied up with plastic handcuffs; allegedly, two were pistol-whipped, and one was kicked in the chest.

The thieves had taken seven bags of banknotes from the vault containing thousands of pounds worth of Danish Kroner, Swedish Kroner, Norwegian Kroner and Australian Dollars. The amount stolen was worth a total of £1,772,852.53 sterling.

Parts of the foreign currencies are believed to have been exchanged for sterling at a foreign exchange bureau in central London; 260,000 Australian dollars recovered by officers was traced back to a Bureau-de-Change in Notting Hill.

Detective Superintendent Stuart Cundy, head of MPS Flying Squad, which had the men under surveillance, said: "These are dangerous individuals who organised a complex armed robbery to steal a substantial amount of money and expected to get away with it. They were prepared to carry guns and use them to ensure their plan succeeded.

"I pay tribute to the victims of this violent robbery who provided evidence in this case. I have no doubt that these men would have continued to pose a risk to the public if they had not been caught."

Four trials had previously failed for the Heathrow robbery; previous trials had to be abandoned due to sickness and the Jury's inability to reach a decision. The third trial was abandoned nearly halfway through after the judge said information had been received that pointed to "a serious attempt at jury tampering". The prosecution then applied for a trial without a jury. The key element to the successful prosecution was evidence given by a supergrass. Menzies supervisor Darren Brockwell had been dreaming up the raid for months after discovering bags of currency were held in a vault inside the warehouse in 2003.

After being put in touch with Twomey's gang, Brockwell studied flight patterns for weeks to determine when the vault would be full. But on the night of the robbery, he misread flight documentation and believed £10m would be in the vault rather than just £1.75m.

Shortly after the raid, he was arrested at his mother's house in Woking, Surrey. In his Vauxhall Vectra were two drawn maps of the warehouse.

At first, he denied involvement, but following discussions between his solicitors and the police, Brockwell agreed to turn supergrass and reveal all about the robbery. He ended up giving evidence in all four trials.

In March 2007, he was given a reduced sentence of six years, having admitted conspiracy to rob, in recognition of the help given to the prosecution. He was released later the same year. But Brockwell will spend the rest of his life living under an assumed identity, and his former wife and two young children have been moved to a secret location and given new names.

When this fourth and final trial began in January, all the defendants were initially on bail, but Blake walked out of the court and disappeared for three days. He returned to apologise to the judge and was remanded in custody along with his co-defendants to await a verdict.

The "hallowed principle" of trial by Jury was set aside by the court in the first case using powers under the Criminal Justice Act 2003. Still, campaigners called the decision a dangerous precedent.

Evidence seen by appeal judges of alleged jury tampering was kept from the public and defence lawyers because of what senior prosecutors described as the "sensitivity" of the information.

The total cost to the taxpayer of the aborted trials is estimated to be at least £25m – more than 14 times the amount stolen.

Barry completed the full-time PE Course at Long Lartin and became a Mentor and Gym Orderly. He was one of the funniest prisoners I'd ever met. We often spoke about football. Barry was a massive QPR fan and told me of the time he went to my club Leeds away. He was arrested after a fight between rival supporters. On his return to Leeds to appear in court, he expected the Leeds fans to have a reception committee waiting for him. To his surprise, the opposite happened. The Leeds fans were there waiting, but they took him on a night out, paying for his drinks. He said he always had a soft spot for Leeds afterwards. Barry also spoke openly about the repeated collapse of his trial. He told me how he told the Jury that he was an entertainer, not an armed robber. He even broke out into song for them on several occasions.

He said the Jury was in stitches laughing; a week later, the judge declared yet another change of Jury. Both Barry and Peter Blake were model prisoners in their time at Long Lartin. Barry always lightened the mood at the right time during his time mentoring in the classroom.

The Dream team.

Over the years we often got a group of Gym Orderlies that formed a tight bond, none more so than this group of Gym Orderlies, Lea Rusha, his Co-defendant Jet Bucpapa, Carl Burgess, Sean Riley and John Beere. A great group of completely different characters but all good lads. Jet and I became as close as good friends you can possibly be whilst being on different sides of the fence. I would often train with him, Lea, and Carl. I was pleased to hear recently that Jet was now back home a free man in Albania and had recently got married. Carl has also been out for some time now and doing well, he was a huge man with a great sense of humour and was a very gifted sportsman, professional rugby player and one person even I struggled to live with on a rowing machine, once he mastered the technique. Their routine was brutal; one exercise in this routine was to stack 20kilo rubber discs up to waist height and perform reps of sergeant jumps up onto the top of the stack. And then other times, after a warm-up, the pile just got higher each round until failure. I witnessed Lea jump almost his height onto the weights from a standing jump. Trust me, it's no mean feat to achieve. Once the stack got above waist height, it would play tricks with your mind, knowing that a failure could end with some seriously grazed and bruised shins.

Sean was ex forces; this could sometimes cause problems for people especially in the ever-increasing political world behind bars with many Muslim prisoners forming a large new formidable gang. It's no real secret that many people either chose or were forced to join the Muslim faith for protection; I heard many tactics of how prisoners were forced to become Muslims. One tactic was when a new and vulnerable lad would appear on the wing, the Muslims would pay one of the non-Muslim prisoners to go into his cell, rob him and smash his TV. Then one of the Muslims would befriend him the next day, asking how he'd settled in, and ask where his TV was. They then offered him protection if he was to become a Muslim. The robber would then be told to be nice to him and he then saw the Muslims had sorted his problem for him; before you knew it, he would be attending Muslim prayers. I must add at this point there are many Muslim prisoners that I met who are nice people and not interested in the culture just to be part of the fastest growing gang culture in the Prison Service.

Having prisoners like Lea, Jet and Carl around, helped to address this balance.

I remember talking to Jet about a charity bike ride (Ben's First Steps) I'd recently been involved in for a local lad to purchase a new chair for him. Jet straight away decided to help by doing a brutal rowing challenge of his own. Sean, Lea, and John all got involved, raising over 2,000 pounds towards the charity. Ben's Mum came into the prison to be presented the cheque. It was a proud moment and one me and Jet spoke about for years to come; he often asked me how Ben was progressing.

Above. Governor *Tom Wheatley, Emma (Ben's Mummy) and myself*

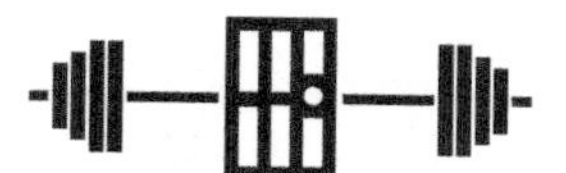

STANDING UP TO CANCER

It was September 2012, and I was training harder than ever, still doing my weights and circuits, but I'd also gotten heavily into road biking and had completed quite a few hundred-mile sports events with colleagues from work. I wish I'd gotten into it earlier in life; as a kid, my record times around the block should have been a sign; we'd also invested in some spin bikes in the gym and set up spin classes for staff and prisoners.

I often volunteered to take classes at lunchtime and a couple of sessions with prisoners. These were really great classes. They were ultra-competitive, and the classroom at the end of the sessions almost looked like the sports hall after a baptism! Occasionally, I would even cycle down to my daughter's house in Portsmouth, and back to my home in the Midlands the following day. I loved it; the route and roads I rode along, you'd never go in your car. For miles and miles, I'd cycle, often seeing more horses in the streets than cars.

I had recently noticed I'd developed a strange-looking lump on the left side of my neck. I asked Ian the physio's opinion; he seemed confident it was a cyst. I left it for a couple of weeks, but it didn't disappear and had started to weep a little. My wife convinced me to go to the doctor and get checked.

The doctor reassured me that she was sure it was a cyst but also told me to go back and see her if it didn't clear up in a week.

A week later, it showed no sign of clearing up, so I made another appointment.

The doctor told me to err on the side of caution; she would refer me to have a needle aspiration on it.

I got a date through, and a week later, I attended the hospital to have the procedure carried out. They would scrape some cells away and test to see if anything more sinister was going on.

We received an appointment to return for the results. Stomps and I drove over to Warwick to see the specialist again, Dr Cable, who had initially seen me many weeks before. The drive over was hard. I had a bad feeling about it all, and told Stomps and my eldest daughter Emma that I feared the worst and thought it was throat cancer, which had killed my dad 12 years before.

We sat in the waiting room and agreed that I would go in alone. I walked towards the lady. My name was called.

"Bring your wife with you," she said. That confirmed my fears for me.

We took our seats, and the doctor said as he first thought, I had a tumour on my tonsil. Sarah had to say the word: "You mean cancer?"

The doctor looked at her and very calmly said, "yes".

I felt a tear roll down my cheek and just nodded as he explained that this had spread to five nodes in my neck. I knew this news was coming, so why did I feel I had been hit by a truck?

The doctor explained his disappointment that it had not been sorted before. He had marked it as urgent when sending me for a scan and the FNA needle aspiration. Sarah and I were then invited into a room with a Macmillan nurse who gave us some information.

The drive home that teatime was a blur, but I insisted on driving to stop myself from falling apart. Both Sarah and I were in tears. We went to Sarah's mum and dad's home and broke the news. Dawn gave me such a big hug it calmed me for a moment, and then I just blurted out, "I'm so scared!"

Sarah's dad, bless him, just didn't know what to say, and I felt sorry for him. It must have been hard for him with his own previous cancer experience, when diagnosed with testicular cancer that was thankfully caught early and was subsequently cured, as well as seeing his little girl hurting.

That night Stomps and I cried buckets... and more buckets. I had to give my older children the news. Emma was the first one I contacted and I asked her to explain to Sheri and Jack – I couldn't bear going over it several times. I then broke the news to my brother Mark, sister Julie and spoke of how best to tell Mum.

Julie arranged to go to Mum's the next day when I rang to tell her the news. My mum is a very strong lady but I could tell the news had hit her very hard.

I was given an appointment at Birmingham QE soon after. Every advert on TV suddenly seemed to be about cancer, and the Channel 4 campaign, 'Stand UP To Cancer', had just been launched; there appeared to be no escape. I was told I would have to return to Warwick for a scan – in two weeks to see if cancer had spread anywhere else in my body; it felt like a lifetime away. 'What if it spread in that time?' I thought.

I was given an appointment to see Dr Pracey at Birmingham QE. He was very blunt, but I instantly liked him (thankfully). He reiterated that I had a tumour on the tonsil and nodes in the neck. I told him I had been given a scan date for Warwick. Fair play to Dr Pracey; he told me he would organise one for me that day. I asked Dr Pracey what my chances were. He replied, "Around thirty per cent, maybe a little less, as it's in your nodes." I was both relieved and scared at the same time.

I was given a date for a pre-op to have my left tonsil taken out. I'd never had an operation before, and the thought of it filled me with dread! The operation date came around quickly; still, I was worried about the scan, and I didn't know if it had worsened.

I had my operation and suffered for a few days after. My mum came down and helped look after me and the house, bless her. No amount of pain stopped me from worrying about the scan results though.

I rang and asked. I was told I wouldn't find out till the next consultation with Mr Pracey. It seemed forever, but the appointment date came around, as all things do. I felt physically sick with worry on the way there. I started to think of how I had promised Henry to train together in the gym when he was fourteen; was I still going to be around? 'Worse still,' I thought, 'Dolly wouldn't even remember her daddy if it happened soon.' My grandson Morgan would have little or no memory of me.

I don't really fear death. I just don't want to go yet. I have had the best two years of my life getting married. I love married life and being with my beautiful wife. I had never felt so happy and content.

Dr Pracey said they had removed both tonsils (BOGOF)! But couldn't really say how big the cancer was. He didn't think it was as large as he first thought. It had spread to five nodes on my neck, the largest being two and a half centimetres, so he gauged it at a 3B. I gave out half a smile. Strange, really, the news had floored me two weeks before. After that chat though, I felt like doing cartwheels!

"Better than we anticipated," said Stomps.

"Me too," Pracey said.

Once I recovered from surgery to the back of my throat, he wanted to give me chemotherapy and radiotherapy treatment. Now for what was the next ordeal. Mr Pracey continued, "We are running a clinical trial; the trial nurse will discuss it with you."

We moved to another room where two nurses explained about the trial. They gave me some info to read through and to decide. If I agreed, I would be the first in the UK to enter it.

It was the worst few days. Apart from not knowing the scan results and feeling nervous at every twinge, I discussed it with Sarah. Her gut feeling was not to do the trial; I must admit it was mine too. I googled and googled. We saw many conflicting reports, and I didn't sleep for three nights, continually running it over in my head. 'What if this new trial ended up being the bees' knees, and I miss out? Then again, it could be a disaster, and I'm the guinea pig!'

We had an appointment again in the oncology department at the QE. I told them I was not doing the trial, and a massive weight was lifted from me. Sarah and I both felt that Dr Hartley was almost relieved too; his hands were not tied by the constraints of the trial now. He could just do as he saw fit.

I felt so much better. I felt like I'd got too much to live for. Sarah has been a rock through it all, and my family and friends would get me through it if anything would. So, I would start the standard treatment plan of 35 sessions of radiotherapy, Monday to Friday, and five sessions of chemotherapy (Cisplatin, one every week).

Staff funeral Pauline Wright (RIP)

After the removal of my tonsils, I received news that Pauline had lost her long battle against cancer. I was really saddened by the news. I liked Pauline a lot and, on many occasions, would walk into work with her, and she would always ask me how Snowy, our pet rabbit, was. Snowy was a present off Father Christmas for our boy Henry, three years ago. I would often walk into regimes to hear Pauline's infectious laugh from her office; she was a very bubbly lady, but straight talking too, which I liked. If her office was free, I would always pop in and usually chat about a holiday she'd been on, or the one she and Tony were planning.

Tony, Pauline's husband, had been my boss for a few years and someone I also liked. He was an old-school PEI, proud of the badge and PE staff's work. It was nice to have a boss who understood PE, and Tony brought about some good changes for the gymnasium. He also managed to smooth things over with Ferdy for me. Tony too had been through a challenging period, having had a knee operation and almost losing his leg after complications. He was back on the rowing machine in no time at all.

I had to decide whether to attend Pauline's funeral. Could I hold it together? I wasn't sure, but I knew I wanted to pay my respects. I held it together despite the pain etched on Tony's face. It was a sad occasion on the day; Munch picked me up and took me, but it was good to see many old faces. Family members said a few words that confirmed what I already knew of Pauline.

On leaving the crematorium, I approached Tony, shook hands, and then embraced. I felt tears running down my cheek. I just wanted to hug him. Tony looked at me and said, "Fight this fucking thing, Phil, just like Pauline did."

I didn't know Tony knew about me; honestly, my legs buckled a little under me as he spoke. Not just because of what he said, but the fact that at a time with the grief he must have been filled with, he was still thinking about me; those words ran around in my head and still do.

On the way home, Munch must have read my mind during the service. He said Phil, don't think this could be you anytime soon; honestly, it was in my head as he spoke.

The spa

Jules came around with something me and Sarah thought was another get-well card. I cried just reading the words in the card, yet within was another card, a gift voucher for Malvern Spa; somewhere Sarah and I last visited on Valentine's Day. What a lovely thought, what great friends we have.

People at work chipped in to give us a fantastic couple of days, and for the first time since being diagnosed, I managed to forget things for a while at the spa. I can't thank people enough for that mental break, and it wouldn't be till later that I realised just how valuable the spa time had been.

I received a dental appointment at Birmingham Dental Hospital before my treatment started to assess my jaw and teeth. A side effect of the treatment can be rotting all the teeth, so they evaluate you beforehand to see if they need to carry out work before treatment commences. Thankfully, I was all good, so there were no delays.

Friends from work were nothing short of amazing in their show of support. I always received messages giving me a lift when I needed one the most. I was humbled by how people supported me, volunteering on rest days to take me to the hospital.

I had numerous lovely messages of support from prisoners as well. Cards from them lifted my spirits. They say in hard times, you find out who your friends are; I have many, and their support through my health problems proved invaluable. Too many names to mention, but all the gym staff and many, many more.

The mask

I found another use for my mask after treatment.

I had googled radiotherapy for head and neck cancer and discovered, much to my despair, that I would have to have a mask fitted. I would have to wear it for every radiotherapy session. That was a genuine concern for me as I am claustrophobic. It's something that seemed to get worse as I got older. I'd noticed it more at work lately whenever we did smoke hood training. Having to wear the hoods made me panic a little. And sometimes, even on escort in the back of a Cat A van, I would have to control my breathing to lower my stress levels. I kept all of this to myself though. I asked Mr Pracey about the mask and whether it meant me having to have one, and he confirmed my worst nightmare.

While I awaited an appointment for the mask to be fitted, I devised a training exercise to desensitise me from the fear. I wrapped a Leeds United shirt as tight as I could around my head and face as close-fitting as I could get it while playing music.

I was told I could bring my own music with me. I didn't get off to a great start while practising. Within seconds I found myself ripping the shirt off in a panic. My son Henry even joined in trying to help. The day of having my mask fitted arrived, I wasn't sure what to expect or how long it would take. From the information I'd googled, it said the mask fitting was around 30 minutes! I'd built up to being able to complete one or two songs on a good day with the shirt around my face.

I went to the hospital, and they tried putting me at ease after I warned them of my fear. They said it was common for people to dislike it and that Mr Pracey had made them wear one to understand how it felt.

They laid me down and said my upper torso would be bolted to the bed. I wasn't prepared for that at all. I sat up immediately and said, "I'm not sure I can do this."

One of the doctors advised me, "You must try because the alternative isn't good."

I knew what he meant. The alternative would be less than the 33 per cent chance I'd been given. I eventually let them bolt me down; then they placed a warm, wet plastic mould over my face. I had my eyes closed, so I didn't know what it looked like. The doctor then pushed it firmly onto my eyes, around my neck, and to my surprise, over my upper chest and shoulders. My legs kept coming up. To be honest, I wanted to kick out. I managed to get through it, but it was horrendous, one of the worst things I've ever endured; I'd almost rather be potted.

The nurse said after unbolting me that I should think about getting some medication from the doctors to help me get through the radiotherapy sessions. I told her I was hoping I would be ok, having gotten through this and now having an idea of what to expect. I then discovered my ordeal for today wasn't over. I would need a scan in the mask to enable them to mark the mask-up to show where the radiotherapy blasts would be given.

Again, I was bolted down to the bed in the mask. The scan lasted around 20 minutes. It felt like an hour at least. They played music, but I couldn't hear it because of the machine's noise. The nurse again mentioned getting medication for my sessions to keep me calm. She also informed me that my daily sessions would last around 40 minutes! 'Forty minutes! Oh my God!' I thought. 'How the hell am I going to do that?'

Honestly, I returned to my car and just broke down in tears. I wasn't sure if I could do it. I arrived home a wreck. Stomps asked how it had gone and I explained, finishing with, "I'm not sure I can do this".

Stomps doesn't lose her temper very often, but she did on that occasion. She reminded me in no uncertain terms why I had to have the treatment. I needed it, and she reminded me why I must get through it.

Start of treatment

My eldest daughter Emma had bought me a gift an iPad that I would be able to use if, as expected, it became difficult/impossible to speak further down the road. This became a real godsend as I used it to make notes daily throughout my journey.

At the end of week one, I still felt surprisingly good. Even managing to train through my first two weeks of treatment. The mask was still a massive obstacle for me, but I managed to get through with the help of four Diazepam and my CD playing at full blast.

I adopted the 'I may have cancer, but cancer hasn't got me' attitude. Going to the gym and training made me feel like I was throwing a few punches back at cancer. One of the problems with the mask was it fitted so tightly, especially on my eyes. It quite often left me with a severe headache. In the second week, they decided to cut holes out where my eyes were, which thankfully resolved the issue.

Gym Julie took me three times in the first week and was tremendously supportive. Years earlier, I had been part of the decision about Julie taking up a position in the gym as a potential PEI. Tony, our PO, and Mark, our SO, asked me to run a mini-selection course for two future PEIs. I felt honoured to be asked to be a big part of the process.

A few days before the selection, Tony told me we were only looking for one because Julie would be given one place. After all, we still needed a female working in the gym. I told Tony if that was the case, I would not be running the selection; he looked a bit stunned at my response. I doubled down on it though, when questioned. I told him if I did it, I'd take the best candidate regardless of gender or race. "If that's Julie, then so be it, but it will be because she earned the position, not because of her gender."

He reluctantly agreed. The selection also included the madman, Brian; everyone had written him off, saying he was wasting his time. I ran the selection, and two candidates stood out at the end of delivering their ten-minute lectures. One was way out in front, Julie, followed by Brian and then a gap to the others. Both were sound choices, and both went on to add real value to the department in their own ways. Both are still doing so at the time of writing this.

During one of my first visits to the QE, I picked up a charity brochure and read about their campaign to raise money for a new state-of-the-art cancer treatment called cyberknife. After reading it, I contacted Munch and asked him to get the staff and prisoners to do something to raise money. I knew from experience just how well these events go with prisoners. We'd held loads over the years. I rang Munch to ask him to organise an event for such a worthy cause. I dropped a booklet through his door, and he wasted no time in getting to work on it.

I saw a dietician at the end of week two. I couldn't help but think she should take some of her own advice; she was a lovely lady though. It's a little bit like the builder who is too busy improving other people's houses to do the repairs on his own home. I left with a bucket load of build-up shakes for future use.

Chemotherapy (Cisplatin)

Each dose of chemotherapy lasted five hours; afterwards, surprisingly, I felt ok, although I did feel a little strange. It felt like a warming sensation through my veins. Stomps came with me, and although she couldn't do much, it was a massive help to me without her realising it. Work had been marvellous, drawing up a rota to take me to and from the hospital. Taking some pressure off Sarah, who was still trying to carry on with her job.

In the evenings, after treatment, it hit me. I started to feel extremely tired. I remember looking at all the tablets I had to take just to prevent myself from being sick and feeling overawed; I don't like to even take a headache tablet to be honest!

The best news was I felt like I might be on the road to conquering my fear of the mask. I remained calm throughout two sessions and only needed one Diazepam, which got me through with relative calm. As silly as it may have seemed, my practice sessions of tying my Leeds shirt around my face seemed to pay off; it helped to desensitise me to a degree.

The morning after my first chemo, I woke up feeling really heavy. Like I'd been filled with lead, not chemo. One thing to come out of the nightmare was I never needed to doubt how many great friends I had. They were all unbelievable. Munch organised a spreadsheet for everyone who had volunteered to take me to the hospital daily. Also, organising not one but three charity events for the Birmingham QE cyberknife fundraising appeal. I was incredibly humbled by it all. When I glanced in the mirror after chemotherapy, my face looked yellow, like I had jaundice. The sickness wasn't too bad after my first session, but I had no energy to train for a day or so.

Sunday 23rd December Stomper's message

I came downstairs to find my darling husband laying on the sofa with the most pissed off face I have ever seen. No sleep for him again last night and as he rightly said yesterday if that was me, I would be going mad by now. This has got to be the worst thing people have to go through as there is nothing worse than seeing the man you love with all your heart go through so much pain and there is nothing I can do to help. I can't fix him and that breaks my heart! All I know is that we must do this, we have to get to the end of the seven weeks of treatment as we have two beautiful children who need their Daddy and love their Daddy very much xxxx

Sunday pm reading Stomper's message

I Just had a cry after seeing the message on my iPad off Sarah. That morning was the worst place I have ever been in my life. The most pain, the most scared. I thought, 'I just can't do this.'

I had just gone nine days with pretty much no sleep and constant pain. It drove me into a dark corner. But that morning Sarah got me back on track, not just from her note... she rang the hospital, then we ended up going to the hospital. They gave me something stronger for the pain and that night, for three hours after taking it, I was in a much better place. Not pain free, but compared to where I had been, it felt like it. If it continued, I hoped to force a smile Christmas morning.

I was conscious I might ruin Christmas for Henry, and Dolly's first Christmas. It should be a special time for all of us.

More importantly, I thought I could face chemo the following day. I felt like I could get through it knowing only one more time to face afterwards. Then a little bonus of a couple of days off from radiotherapy after the chemo. Although I did have radiotherapy twice on the Friday – I couldn't win 'em all!

So, I replied to Stomper's message…

It must be horrible for you Sarah. I can hardly face seeing you go through anything like this. I know it must be so hard and you must just feel helpless. Well, you can stop feeling helpless now, cos today you got me back on the path.

I LOVE YOU SARAH-JAYNE xxxx

Treatment through Christmas

I had an extra roasting on Saturday during Christmas week to make up for missing Christmas Day. That meant radiotherapy in the morning, followed by another one six hours later; it was incredibly hard. I was certainly fully cooked for Christmas! By then, I was on my new appointment card, and I would be done when that one was full. That spurred me on a little; I had never felt so tired and drained.

Henry came with us and went into the room and saw the machine and my mate the mask. I was forcing the shakes down, but they became more difficult to swallow almost daily. I was even more motivated to gulp them after being told that if I lost too much weight, they would have to refit the mask.

Christmas Day wasn't great, but I managed a little chicken soup and stayed awake for the opening of presents.

By the afternoon, I was tired, so I went upstairs for a rest; when I came down, Dave (Sarah's Dad) was asleep in the chair with a set of reindeer antlers on his head. Henry was playing Hoopla onto the antlers, and Dawn was doing photography. Brilliant!

By then, my taste had gone entirely, and I was really struggling to swallow. I had Boxing Day off, and then it was back on with the treatment plan.

Week six of treatment

I was really struggling. The pain was so intense. Swallowing had become a real problem; just getting half a glass of Solpodol painkillers down took me nearly an hour instead of the ten minutes it had before.

Eventually, I asked Sarah to ring for help. Julianne, our good friend, was around in a flash, and it wasn't long before I was packed off into an ambulance. Henry, bless him, was so upset seeing me in pain. He was such a brave little boy, the last thing I recall seeing out of the back of the ambulance was Henry's little worried face, and then he crossed his fingers at me, and I just about managed to do the same back to him.

The ambulance planned to take me to Redditch Hospital, but my temperature was over 39 degrees, so they headed to Birmingham QE. To be honest, I preferred that; they knew my treatment plan, and I was due for radiotherapy again on Monday.

The ward was a sombre place to be. I saw one bloke ringing someone up earlier to tell them his mum had been given only a short time to live. Then there were two alarms in the night. It was a little like being back at work. At the end of the day, it's true; the only guarantee in life is death.

I prayed to Jesus and asked him for some more time on Earth. I had so much to see and do. My grandson Morgan would have very little memory of me if any at all and Dolly, bless her, would not remember me. Henry would be scarred and miss me so much. We had made plans for the next few years – to train together and a million other things. I couldn't wait to take him to the gym and knew he couldn't wait either. My married life had only just started; I was the happiest I had ever been. I felt content and loved married life. My wedding day had been as it should be, the happiest day of my life. I needed to build more special memories with my lovely wife and family.

Eating had become almost impossible. The nursing staff arrived for the second day running, to attempt to fit my feeding tube; after checking my observations, my temperature had gone back up and was above 38 again. They said it was a concern, but my blood count was still quite good; I took that as a positive. The decision was made to try and fit the tube up my right nostril because of my complex wonky shaped nose. Experience told me that this was the best option. It had been the one decided by Mr Cable and Mr Pracey, who had both put the camera wire up there in the past. Mr Cable struggled a little, but it was pretty pain-free, just not very comfortable. The worst part was the top of my nose and then down through my throat. I was worried at the start with Mr Pracey as he didn't use any local anaesthetic, but he did it with relative ease, which surprised me.

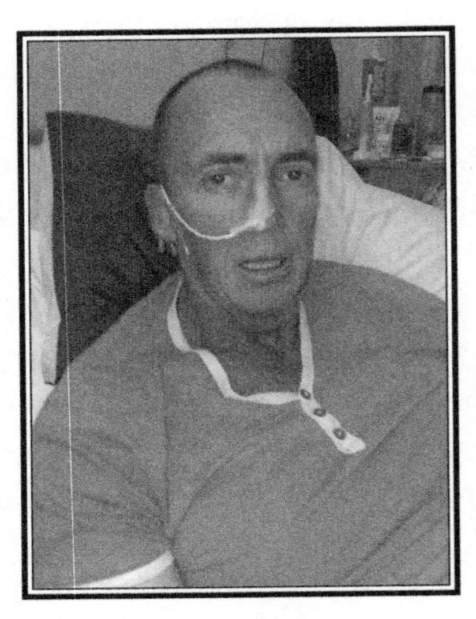

With the right nostril finally tubed; to be honest, I've had better days.

The nurse was lovely, but there was no way the tube fit would happen on either side. The result was me on the bed, tears streaming down my face; it compounded what had already been a bad day.

"Never mind," she said, "we will try again later." Yet they didn't try any more that day. And I was relieved.

After the nurses' failed attempts, I was informed that the ENT team would attempt to fit my feeding tube.

I felt weak through the lack of food, although I'd started being able to swallow tiny amounts of water again.

After a week in the hospital, Stomps had a crash course in setting up my feeding machine and testing my PH levels – to check the food was in my stomach and not my lungs. That needed to be done before each eight to 12-hour feed and a flush of water before and after the bag of food. She did amazingly well.

It wasn't long before I discovered it didn't look or taste great when I brought it back up. This was to be a common theme over the next few weeks, which I needed to get used to. One of the problems with being sick with a feeding tube was that it increased the chances of it coming out and entering my lungs. The last thing I ever wanted was to have a refit of that tube.

Sleep was virtually impossible and non-existent, with the feeding machine going all night. I was propped up on the sofa, trying to stop myself from being sick. Some nights it would be coming out as quickly as it was going in. I'd now lost so much weight my wedding ring constantly just fell off my finger.

Saturday, end of treatment

My last journey to the hospital was eventful; there had been heavy snow, but it wasn't too bad in Evesham. We set off with what we thought was plenty of time because of the weather; the snow just got worse and worse as we got nearer Birmingham, and we were stuck in bad traffic. There was also an accident on the way so we didn't move for about half an hour. As we crawled up the hill, the snow was coming down heavily. I could sense Sarah was getting stressed.

Sarah said we would have to turn back; by now, the roads were covered, and snow coming down so hard you couldn't see where you were going. I told her I'll drive if I had to or even walk but going back wasn't an option. There was no way I wasn't going to make my last appointment. I felt terrible because Sarah got really stressed and had a little cry at the wheel. Fair play to her, though; she stuck at it and got us there safely and almost on time. As I checked in, the receptionist lady said they had had many people ring up and cancel their appointments.

The last one you would think would be a doddle, but it wasn't the case. I'd had a tough one all week, and that last day was no different. Just for good measure, the scanner went down twice during treatment, extending the time in the mask. I took the group who treated me a box of chocolates. Emma (Scouse), who had helped me so much initially, had recently worked in another room. She came back to see me, and that was nice. I left my CDs for one of the ladies who had commented many times on how much she really liked all the songs on it. On Fridays, I always made sure I played 'It's Friday I'm in Love' by The Cure.

Dolly's First Birthday

Little Dolly's first Birthday. I'd had another bad day, so Dolly's birthday passed me by. I was gutted to have missed her first birthday and not to be able to kiss and cuddle her because she had a habit of grabbing my feeding tube. My consultant told me that the last two weeks after completing treatment would be the worst due to the radiotherapy still building up in my body. I had become really sick, and the lack of sleep was taking its toll on me.

I tried forcing some Müller Rice down, but it felt like swallowing razor blades. I had been told recovery would be a slow process. They weren't lying.

Four weeks post-treatment, the first signs of recovery

Henry, bless him, came up with the idea of doing a charity event of his own, doing laps of the local running track for Red Nose Day. He aimed to complete ten laps over three miles, a good achievement. He roped in some school friends and local children. It made me so proud.

It had been 11 weeks on the treatment journey, but it felt much longer. It had been a gruelling time, to say the least. I was starting to turn a bit of a corner, though, showing more signs of recovery, a little less phlegm coming up and less blue roll required. Being able to lie down flat in bed and get a little sleep was a massive help. I needed to catch up on some sleep, having not had a decent night for weeks and weeks.

I went for my appointment with the dietician. I was apprehensive about the trip; I'd been sick all the way there and back last time. This time? No sickness. Then surprised as the dietician said, "How do you feel about having your tube taken out?" I was gobsmacked; I think Stomps was too.

So, my tube had gone. I'd still not felt that hungry feeling, but the medical staff said it should return soon. We could start trying to get our life back, going to bed at night instead of during the day. I managed to eat a whole tin of chicken soup that evening, and it wasn't too bad.

The first thing I thought about the tube coming out was: it would allow me to cuddle Dolly properly again without constantly being on my guard; fantastic! I knew having the tube removed didn't mean I had it cracked. I still had many bad days ahead, but they could be no worse than those I'd endured.

Prisoners' charity event

I went into the prison for a charity event organised by the prisoners. All the prisoners were genuinely pleased to see me, and it was great seeing the PE staff that had given me so much support throughout; I entered the sports hall. The prisoners cheered, and I had to fight back the tears. It was such an emotional day and one I never will forget.

I spoke to some old faces I hadn't seen since my treatment commenced. Seeing the orderlies was incredibly emotional.

Dave Smith, our gym orderly, informed me that there were high-profile Muslims at the event that missed Muslim prayers to be at the occasion because of the respect they had for me... humbling, to say the least. I went around and thanked everyone for taking part. I was absolutely amazed by the effort the prisoners had put into raising a considerable amount for our charity appeal.

The day after, I became poorly again and was in bed for a week, being sick and feeling terrible. Once again, my wedding ring fell straight off my finger because I had become so thin. It really knocked me back, both mentally and physically.

After a week, I gradually improved again and even came off all my pain relief. I managed to swallow rice pudding and the like.

The first all-clear

My big day came around. I remember Mr Pracey telling me at the first consultation that he would see me sometime after treatment, probably around April; that conversation felt like a lifetime ago. So much had happened, so many low points in the hardest thing I have ever experienced, harder than I ever imagined.

We arrived at the QE; I was nervous but kept telling myself, 'apart from him putting the camera up my nose, I didn't believe I would be given any news that day...'

Mr Pracey greeted us; he was a likeable bloke but very deadpan. He asked how I was and where I was at, then explained the meeting was classed as my week nine post-treatment. He said the radiotherapy was still working in my body until week six, so recovery took place after that. He expected gradual improvement from then on. He ran a few checks looking into my ears, then looked in my mouth with the light and pushed my tongue down. Then came the moment I wasn't looking forward to at all. He said, "Can I look down with the camera?"

Not the nicest experience with my road crash of a nose, but he got the camera up a nostril and then down to my throat. Pracey confirmed the hard part was done; he'd got to my throat. I could feel it pushing.

Pracey said he couldn't get a good view as too much mucus was at the back of my throat. He then felt my neck, almost like playing the piano with his fingers and pulling at the skin. Then he sat down and looked at me.

"It's all clear," He declared.

I looked at Sarah and she at me.

"When do you scan?" I began.

"I don't need to scan. I can tell better by feeling because the radiotherapy leaves too much scarring, so it doesn't give a clear reading on a scan."

Sarah asked if there was any cancer at all? Pracey just gave his smirk and said no, it's clear.

We left the room, and I don't think it sank in with Sarah or me for a good while. His words kept repeating in my head the same way the words did all that time ago when diagnosed and told I had cancer. I kept asking myself whether I had heard him correctly. Had I got it right? Had he really said I was clear of cancer? We got to the car park. Sarah and I had a big hug.

I texted all the fantastic people who had given me so much support throughout and rang my sister and Mum.

Henry and Dolly were at Sarah's mum's; I rang to say we were returning and gave them the good news. Henry straight away wanted to know off Nanny how Daddy got on. She told him I'd been given the all-clear; his face was priceless when we got there; he gave me so many big hugs. I will never ever forget that moment.

Sarah went out that night for a 'hen do' but was driving, so she didn't celebrate. I got the kids into bed, got in the bath and had a bit of a cry. Don't ask me why; it just happened, relief.

FIRST ARM MEETING WITH GOVERNOR CARTWRIGHT (MR ANGRY)

I received a letter through the post from the then Governor Simon Cartwright. It filled me with dread simply because I knew of his record of dismissing officers for medical inefficiency, regardless of their records in the past. I knew from others that his favourite phrase was 'can you provide me with regular and effective service going forwards?'.

I started feeling better and could walk a little without feeling I needed my bed. But, if I was honest, I couldn't return to work there and then, I simply wasn't strong enough. Even eating was still a struggle. I hadn't come all that way, strived for normality, planning everything around a return to the job I love, just to have the rug pulled from underneath me.

The Prison Service and my beloved team, Leeds United, had one thing in common: they made some bizarre managerial appointments. You could have a really calm, well-performing prison under the style of a governor like Nick Leader, who was very much a staff man who allowed the managers underneath him to manage.

Nick Leader, one of the better governors.

He concentrated on everything that made for a smooth-running prison, creating a safe environment for staff and prisoners. When people like Nick moved on, usually after three to five years, the powers would decide to drop a hand grenade into a prison. On that occasion, the grenade was named Cartwright. One thing I would give him credit for was that his strange behaviours only affected staff and their morale. So, the actual safety of staff and prisoners wasn't unduly affected. I think he probably influenced a lot of staff in other ways. Cartwright was just a permanent Mr Angry. To be honest, that management style becomes like white noise and totally ineffective after a while. In my experience, the best Governors have that anger switch, but they know when and when not to use it.

My first real encounter with Cartwright had come in the run-up to my wedding in 2010. We were planning my stag do, and one of the PEIs had compiled a list of staff intending to attend my do on a whiteboard in our office at the rear of the gym. Someone had written Cartwright's name on the board. I can't even remember being aware of it at the time. A governor who I had a lot of respect for came down to the gym one day and was chatting in the office with a few of us. He looked at the board but said nothing. The same governor came down with Cartwright the following day, and they both made straight for the whiteboard.

In what I later became accustomed to as classic fashion, Cartwright hit the roof. He told Richie he wanted him to report to his office on the way out, and he wanted the name of who had written his name on the board. He then did his trademark action of going to check the noticeboards to see if they were up to date and check to see if he could spot any dust anywhere. He was more concerned about noticeboards being up to date and the walls being painted magnolia than any good work staff may have done. I can honestly say if staff had dealt with an assault or incident, he would first check that the floor had been cleaned suitably afterwards.

I told Richie not to do his job for him and not to bother trying to find out who did it. I didn't know who was responsible; I'd presumed it was one of the PE staff. I would have told Cartwright he better get the handwriting police in because I didn't know who it was. Richie did find out a name, and I was surprised to find out it wasn't one of the PE staff, but it was a very good friend of mine from another department. Richie had rung around and spoken to their department, and my friend being the kind of guy he was, just owned up and said he'd go and tell Cartwright it was him. I would have rung and told him not to do it if I'd known. My friend went and owned up, and Cartwright went completely overboard, holding an investigation into the matter. The whole episode showed up a couple of things. Cartwright's lack of man management skills and a junior governor who I respected showing classic chameleon traits; he could have just said, 'look, lads, I know it's a bit of fun, but take his name off the board'. Instead, he chose to run back to the number one governor with his information, seeing it as a way of getting a feather in his cap.

There was also an incident where Cartwright set off the geophone alarms in the control room. Him not being so happy with the dog section because of the untidy appearance around their section. That resulted in him kicking the fence repeatedly in anger.

My fondest memory of that governor was when I was on a court case, and the judge requested Cartwright attend the court.

Cartwright was doing his level best not to attend and, in the end, sent the security governor Rob Luxford to do the dirty work. The barrister's response to this was hilarious. He said, "I am disappointed Mr Cartwright can't make it. I have seen him many times before but never in person." He added, "You couldn't fail to know who he was because as one walks through the prison, his photo is on every wall."

He was right, paint the wall magnolia and sticking his photo on it was to be a common theme. A trait also shared by the last governor I worked under; if the ever-expanding psychology department were asked to conduct an assessment about this, I'd be interested in the results.

You can see why I was slightly worried about this attendance review meeting. The day arrived, I hadn't slept much, but that was nothing new. It was simply due to my dry mouth keeping me awake all night. I arranged for a POA rep to come with me. Cartwright invited me in, and he was accompanied by Chris Jones. A useless waste of space, in my opinion, but I'll leave that one there.

I took a seat, and he asked how I was doing. I decided to take the wind out of his sails and hit him with his own punchline.

"I'm getting there slowly. I'm still weak due to lack of sleep because of the side effects from my treatment, but each week has shown improvement in me getting a little stronger. I'll be able to offer regular and effective service moving forward soon."

Cartwright looked confused, me having used his opening line on him. He didn't seem sure how to react. He fell silent for what seemed like an age, then simply said, "I need you to return to work, or we will have to look into medical inefficiency." In other words, dismissal on medical grounds.

I told him we were singing from the same hymn sheet, and my main focus through treatment, apart from getting well again, was to return to the job that I loved. I reiterated that I hadn't said I can't come back; I simply said I was not physically ready. I added that it's physically impossible for me to return right now. So, he hit me with the 'if you're saying you can't come back, then we have to proceed with medical inefficiency'.

Cartwright said, "Well, I want you back on Monday even if you just do an hour a day." This was the point I realised all he wanted was me off his sick list, so when he sends his monthly figures off to headquarters, it shows a reduction, and they see it as him managing well.

With that in mind, I said, "I've been off all this time, so I have lots of annual leave that I haven't taken...."

The POA rep interrupted and advised, "That's your leave, and you're entitled to it."

I replied, "I know, ok, so how about I take that leave? I'm no longer on your sick record, and hopefully, it gets me to where I need to be to fully return to work."

Both Cartwright and Chris Jones looked shocked. Cartwright said, "If you're prepared to do that, then yes, I agree; but you must sign to say you agreed." He got his secretary to print off a letter, and I signed it. The POA rep tried to interject, saying this wasn't right, but I cut him short by just saying I'd been off for ages; when I got back in the gym, I wanted to be back properly, and the last thing I wanted to do was repay all the support I'd had from my colleagues by saying 'I'm back, but I've got all this leave to take', I didn't want to do that.

Well, I'd managed to kick that can down the road; now it was time to concentrate on being ready to return after my leave. It gave me almost six weeks. I left feeling lifted at having that chance to get back, regardless of how it was achieved.

May 2013

So much had happened since my last appointment, and eating was slowly improving, but there was still one thing that really got me down: the boredom with the same foods, the lack of choice. But it still beats being fed through a tube.

The charity ride went ahead and was a fantastic weekend, fair play to all the riders who stuck to the task despite it being a gruelling route. All being well, one day, I would ride that route. My wife and I followed the bikes the whole distance, supporting the riders.

The photo shows the riders at the finish by Birmingham QE hospital.

Munch and I and the Cyberknife Radiotherapy machine

We were invited by the charity to attend an open evening at the hospital for the Cyberknife, showing it working. Knowing we had helped the hospital acquire this state-of-the-art treatment that would change people's lives was a great feeling.

Munch had put so much effort into organising the charity bike ride, a 12-hour circuit by the prisoners and an auction of promises night. It paid off by becoming an event that people would talk about for years to come.

By the time we attended the opening evening, we had hit over twenty thousand pounds, an unbelievable achievement.

My consultant and a couple of radiographers were there; it was quite an emotional experience seeing them, and comforting that they thought I was doing so well.

It was a fantastic, rewarding night, making us proud of what we had helped achieve. We couldn't thank Munch enough and everybody involved for making it all possible. I did note that Dr Hartley, who I'd now nicknamed Shipman, my oncology consultant, had lost none of his bedside manners when I approached the buffet supplied, and he said, "probably nothing you can get down"!

I also went back to work on a phased return a couple of mornings a week and just for an hour or so a day. It confirmed my thoughts from my meeting that it was just a case of me not appearing on the governor's sick figures. I was placed over in security doing some filing, which was mind-blowingly dull, so at my own request, after the second week, I went to work in the offices at the rear of the gym, working on updating PE courses etc. I was at home again from my point of view, and because of that, in no time, I was increasing my hours.

I was extremely touched by the welcome I received from all the staff I bumped into, but what really overwhelmed me was the greetings from prisoners, hugging and telling me how I had been missed; one telling me how he had had letters from numerous other inmates who had left the prison and some that had been released years ago, all asking how I was. That I did find overwhelming.

Prisoners also said that when they did the charity event, everybody got behind it; not once had they had a negative response. They might have expected it off a few, saying, 'it's for a screw,' but on the contrary, they said nobody had a bad word to say. Nice to hear, especially considering the role we have to play. When I told the gym orderly, he said, "It's the respect that people have for you." How do you answer that?

~

Sarah's birthday, and the day I was going back for another check-up; I was just praying for good news. It's horrible building up to the day; try as I may, all I could do was worry. 'Get this out of the way,' I thought, and then our holiday to Ibiza, on the 11th, with my mum and Pete. A holiday we had all been waiting for since treatment started. It seemed a lifetime ago when it had all started, to be honest. Henry deserves the holiday more than anyone; he's handled all this so well.

Sarah's birthday, and neither of us slept too well worrying about my check-up. We travelled to the QE, and it was, as always, a quiet journey filled with our thoughts and fears. When I was called in, it was not Mr Pracey, my usual consultant, but one I'd not seen before. I instantly thought of the camera and wondered how skilled he would be at directing it up my road crash of a nose!

Well, I was pleasantly surprised. It was good news. He could see this time, and it was all clear and normal. I also had to have a hearing test as the hearing in my left ear was not too good. We sat waiting to be summoned, and then a man came and called my name; typically, I didn't hear him. As we entered his office, I said, "I guess I've just failed the hearing test."

He smiled, unlike my kids, who never find my jokes funny.

My hearing was affected on my left side, but there was no real nerve damage, so again, it was good news. The hearing should get better in time.

On the way home, Sarah drove, and I made the phone calls and texted family and friends who had given us so much support.

We could look forward to our holiday in only 12 days.

Ibiza, here we come

We'd promised ourselves that a holiday would happen once I felt up to it. My mum and Pete, her husband, flew out with us. It's the first all-inclusive holiday where I came home lighter than I went. However, I didn't drink shakes, although I did manage to eat pretty well. The place was fantastic, just the type of location me and Sarah both love.

I treasured every minute of it. Two weeks of bliss! Spending time with Henry and Dolly. I had missed so much quality time with Dolly when I was poorly; precious time that cancer robbed me of. The time I can never get back. My little girl is only just beginning to see her real daddy. And our bond grew along with my strength. I could get through most days without a nap; there was a time when I thought Dolly would be doing that before me.

It was almost the countdown to my next test, six months post-treatment. I could tell I was getting better as time started going quickly again. I often thought of some of the lovely people I had met in treatment and wondered how they were getting on.

One year on

It was just a year since my treatment had started, and to be honest, it really felt like at least two. My eating stayed the same for ages, not getting any worse or any better. My mouth remained so unbelievably dry that my tongue got really sore and still does to this day. I was waking up most hours through the night with my mouth so dry. I drank and sprayed, but in no time, it would dry again. I often needed to peel my tongue off the roof of my mouth.

I was managing at work despite my lack of sleep. Fortunately, I was always someone who could get by on four hours. It was the broken sleep all night that got to me. Despite that, I managed to get back on the spin bikes, taking classes and courses. My voice was a little weaker, but I managed.

The gift that keeps on giving

I'd just been to the dental hospital in Birmingham and been told I would need to go to Plymouth for hyperbaric oxygen therapy for eight weeks. Six weeks before my operation and two weeks after, which involved being treated every day for two weeks, twice a day, two hours at a time. The treatment was to try and improve blood flow to my jaw and hopefully avoid my jaw crumbling when they removed my teeth. I was dreading it, to be honest, being away from my wife and family and going back to soups and shakes; just the thought was depressing me.

I kept trying to tell myself, 'Think bigger picture; if someone offered me this last year to be rid of cancer, of course, I would have taken it!'

But then I got back to just thinking about the here and now. The reality of no teeth, not being able to eat properly again. On top of that was the worry of going to half pay. We wouldn't have been able to cope with half the salary. Or worse still, if Cartwright went down the medical inefficiency route.

I picked Henry up from school; it was the first thing he asked when he came out of school. "How did it go, Dad?"

He looked as gutted as me when I told him. It had been a tough year for all of us, but we had come through it, and if anything, we were stronger for it.

Work and my mates in the gym had been fantastic; once again, they made plans to give me a lift down and come to visit me.

Henry had gotten upset at school and again that night. We both had a good cry and had a big hug; nobody gave hugs quite like Henry does.

ARM MEETING NUMBER TWO

I was called into another absence review meeting (ARM) at work the day after I saw Mr Pracey. No doubt someone would ask me again, 'Can you provide regular and effective service going forward?'

I found the meeting a little strange. Both Chris Jones and the then Governor Nick Dann knew full well that I would be off again for hyperbaric oxygen therapy, and the best-case scenario left me needing to be away for another eight weeks minimum.

One of the questions I asked was, 'I had an interview with Stella, the Attos lady, employed by the Prison Service, and at the end of the meeting, I received a report that stated she was closing the case and recognising that my latest absence was connected to the cancer treatment and was ongoing treatment.'

I thought that was that. Then the following week, I got an e-mail regarding the ARM meeting. I questioned the point of paying Stella's wages if her report and medical opinion were just discarded for them to implement their local rules.

My concerns were raised somewhat after a meeting with Steve Hamilton, the POA rep, somebody I trusted and respected, who looked at all my paperwork. He hit me with a bit of a bombshell, telling me I would be dismissed, in his opinion! He was well versed in this area as his partner Jane had just been through the same, eventually winning her case and getting medical retirement.

It wasn't what I wanted, I still loved my job, and I enjoyed working with prisoners and the staff I worked with. But if they went down that road, I wanted the best package I could get… medical retirement.

To be forewarned was to be forearmed. So, I put what I needed in place just in case. I told my consultant about my pending ARM meeting and the question: 'can you guarantee to provide regular and effective service going forward?'. His response was very typical of him but also absolutely correct.

"Who can guarantee regular and effective service going forward? Your sick record was exemplary pre-cancer. Who can predict what your future holds, health-wise? It's nonsensical."

Other major fears for me were returning to liquid food and being unable to train again. Sarah rolled her eyes at that; however, I did feel a little vindicated during my last check-up when I saw someone who was treated at the same time as me. I couldn't help but notice how thin and ill he'd still looked. Wanting to train again had given me a goal, and training again had made me stronger and happy in myself. I wasn't ready to give up or slow down just yet! I've trained all my life.

I would not have teeth for at least three months, which meant returning to the soft diet. If there is one change in my life brought about by cancer, not being able to eat everyday foods and what I want must be the worst.

I hide my frustration and disappointment and think I do well hiding it most of the time. The other side effect I hated was not being able to enjoy food like I did. Food didn't taste like it used to at all. I would sweat profusely as I ate, either finding the food too hot or spicy for my throat or through the effort it takes just getting it down. I was quite often willing myself to just eat a few more spoonfuls.

Sarah, once again, was a tower of strength. She's always supportive and says the right things. She was even responsible for giving me a kick up the backside when needed. She said to me, "What about doing this?"

She showed me details of the Tour de Yorkshire, a bike ride covering 122 miles, the first stage of the Tour de France. I wasn't sure, as I sometimes struggle with my dry mouth just cycling to work.

"Text Munch and ask him too," Sarah said.

Knowing it was for cancer research, with all entry fees going to the cause, made me think I could do it.

I texted Munch, and as always, he was on it! He gave me motivation and encouragement. I would get round it by hook or by crook. It would be the most challenging, longest ride of my life, but nowhere near as hard as my journey over the last year or so. Sarah was there with me (not riding) but helping me get through it, just as she had with cancer – Munch the same.

The effect of entering the Tour gave me a focus again that I hadn't had post-cancer. I got back on the spin bike at work, going through the pain barrier, forcing myself to cycle through the dry mouth on limited drink, as when I would do the ride. I couldn't have 20 water bottles strapped to my bike!

I took my first spin class with prisoners_and felt the old buzz again. I loved it, hurting myself but hurting them more. Wanting to still be able to lead through example.

It worked; most of the eight prisoners who started the class were not too keen, and at the end of the class, they all wanted to be put down for a regular spin session. I was gutted; I would only get a few sessions and then be off work again. I felt like I'd just grabbed a piece of my life back that cancer had taken away. I was determined that cancer would not leave me toothless in every sense of the word. I'd got my mojo back and was ready to push myself to the limit again. The more I did, the more comfortable the ride would be on the day.

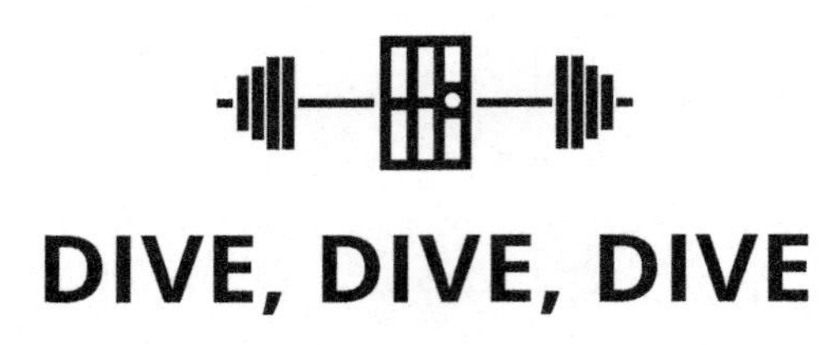

DIVE, DIVE, DIVE

I left home in the morning to go on my first dive. I would travel to Plymouth for Hyperbaric Oxygen therapy where I would go into a diving chamber every day. The chamber was used for divers who had been suffering from the bends, I would be given the treatment to strengthen my jaw in preparation for all my teeth being removed and implants fitted. As I departed all of us were in tears, apart from Dolly; bless her. I hated being away from home, although the six weeks seemed so long, it was better than the eight weeks that they had first stated. It was changed to four weeks before treatment, then two weeks after removing my teeth.

I was caught in two minds, just wanting it all to be over and be back home with my family, dreading the four-week point when I would have no bloody teeth. The eating, or rather a lack of it, I felt sure was going to kill me.

The dive went ok, although the goldfish bowl was worse than I had imagined, with it fitting tightly to my neck. All the people were very friendly. And I managed to find out there was a gym nearby; things were looking up. I settled down after about 20 minutes and got through it by reading a cycling magazine.

It was the end of the first week, and it hadn't gone as quickly as I had hoped. I had a wobble mid-week; it started when I got an abscess on Tuesday, Followed by a bad dive on Wednesday. I ended up in quite a bit of pain and got a little freaked out again by the goldfish bowl on my head. I am convinced it wasn't helped by being told to cut back on my training by half.

There was one man I'd spoken to who insisted on a morning dive each day so he could venture into Plymouth in the afternoon for a few beers. You weren't supposed to drink during this treatment, so I thought if he could bend the rule and drink, I could train. So, I did!

Maybe it was the same for him with the drink. Sarah and Pracey both said I'm like an addict. I guess it's true, but there are worse things to be addicted to. It's hard to explain, but it puts me physically and mentally in a better place when I work out; training is what I've always done.

By midweek I could have quite easily gone home, I felt down, so I went to the local Gym and did a weights session in the morning and spin and a kettlebell session in the evening. That got me back on track. I even managed to get another quick blast in the Gym before heading home on Friday.

One of the biggest mind games was wanting time to fly by and get home, but, on the other hand, I was dreading week five, where I would lose all my teeth. One thing it made me realise when talking to others who have been through similar treatment was that I'd done well in my recovery. No one else had been able to return to work, and they all felt exhausted all the time. I felt for them, but it did make me realise I was doing well. I knew I may never get back to where I was pre-cancer, but I would have a bloody good go. They said the hyperbaric treatment makes you very tired, and one or two said they'd been in bed by six-thirty most nights after week one. I hoped that was not the case with me in the coming weeks. One chap said it kicked in after four sessions; I'd had four now and still felt great and had plenty of energy for going to the Gym.

Teeth out

The day came around. All my teeth would be removed because of radiotherapy damage after an eight-hour operation and a few complications of trying to get the eight metal implants into my jaw so they could later give me some teeth. Wearing dentures wasn't an option because my dry mouth would be too sore, so it was either implants or having to do the Steptoe look forever. Being unable to eat again and thinking of those shakes five times daily turned my stomach.

Arriving home with no teeth is an experience I'll never forget; Henry came to the door to greet me, and his smile soon changed into inconsolable tears. I've never been the best-looking bloke in the world, but the difference in my appearance was staggering. It didn't help that I also had blood all around my mouth. It broke my heart to see him hurting all over again.

Day after op

I was sore and swollen, and although I was tired, I couldn't sleep all night. God knows why; it wasn't the pain. Not being able to pee kept me awake for ages. On what was my fifth attempt, Stomps called out, "You're going back to the hospital in the morning if you haven't been." That must have spurred me on. I did manage to pee at last. It seems to affect me whenever I have an op. The nurse on duty was a bit slack, letting me go, not having 'been'. I was confident I would 'go' by morning, so I hadn't told her anyway; I guess they're not mind readers, are they?

It was Henry's birthday. What a birthday surprise seeing me that morning and realising he hadn't dreamt that his dad looked like he did.

During the night, I got my hopes up in bed. No, not in that way; Sarah's eyesight isn't that bad. I usually drink and spray almost every hour because of my dry mouth when lying in bed. But it was two in the morning that night, and I still hadn't used my spray. My mouth was moist, and I had dribbled for the first time since radiotherapy had fried my saliva glands. I thought that having my teeth out had stimulated them back into full flow until I got up for the toilet and realised all this time it had been blood in my mouth, not saliva. Back to the spray when I stopped bleeding.

Recovery dives

Back down in Plymouth for a further two weeks of recovery dives. I knew the routine. My dental consultant told me not to train for the first week. I managed to talk him into reducing that to a couple of days on the understanding if my mouth started to bleed, I would ease off.

I didn't recognise myself when I looked in the mirror anymore; to say the change in my appearance was immense would be an understatement. I remember seeing my Grandma without her teeth in for the first time when I was a child and being surprised at the difference it made to her appearance. The change in me was a stark comparison. I looked a good 20 years older overnight. Stomps used to watch that programme on TV called ten years younger, where they would take a person, replace their teeth with new ones, and give them a makeover. The results were often astonishing. Well, I'd literally just done the same, in reverse.

Toothless returns

It's strange how returning to work didn't hold any fears for me. I was just looking forward to getting back – straight back into the gym. I turned down a phased return; I wanted to be back doing what I loved. I hadn't even thought about the reaction of the prisoners. I guess I thought I'll continue being myself without my teeth while speaking a little funny. A few colleagues had already seen me, so it wouldn't be a shock for everyone.

As I walked into the prison and was in a queue at the gate, a female colleague approached me and said, "Phil, you can't possibly come to work looking like that!" She was lovely, and I knew it was said with the best intentions. I just said, "It's fine; the alternative is to lose my job, and that's not what I want."

She asked where I would work, and I replied, "In the gym, of course." She looked horrified. I wasn't sure whether it was from my reply or because I attempted a smile.

I got to the gym, hugged all the staff and started the day as usual. A few of the orderlies came down and shook my hand. They enquired how I was getting on and how long I had to wait before getting my Simon Cowells. One of them said, "Bloody hell, Phil, your modelling career is over." No argument from me.

Carl Dobson (Crazy Titch) and half-brother Nathaniel

Carl Dobson, better known by his stage name Crazy Titch, known to me simply as Titch, or when I was ticking off his name on a class list, Dobson. He was serving a life sentence for murder, allegedly over song lyrics by another rapper named Shaba Shak.

Shaba had released a song with lyrics that had disrespected Titch's half-brother. As a result of Shaba's music producer being shot dead, Titch was serving a life sentence with a tariff of 30 years.

Carl Dobson – Titch

I'd got on with Titch well. We always chatted about football, and while he could sometimes be a challenge to referee, we always shook hands at the end of a game, and he'd thank me for refereeing. I know some PE staff had a different experience with him than I did though.

I'd known Titch for quite a few years. I had spoken to Nathaniel about a family fallout they had had and a relation who had cancer. I'd managed to talk Nathaniel into getting in touch with the relation; I'd encouraged him to try and build back a relationship or, at least, let bygones be bygones before it was too late. Nathaniel followed my advice and thanked me. I did try to help him convince Titch to do the same, but Titch was a little less willing.

Following my return to work, as the prisoners came to the gym, I spoke with quite a few about my treatment. One of our orderlies was asking when I'd get my new teeth. Nathaniel came over, and we started talking; he was asking me about one of his gym sessions and seeing if he could get it swapped for another time. As we got further into the conversation, he said, "Shit! It's you, Phil, isn't it?" He gave me a hug and said, "Phil, I'm so sorry, man, I hadn't recognised you."

We spoke about cancer, and he told me more about his relative. I asked if Titch had made up yet, and he said no, he won't do it. A few weeks afterwards, Nathaniel was down again, and he was getting other prisoners to sign his brother's birthday card. Titch had been transferred to another prison; he approached me and asked if I would mind signing it. His mate exclaimed, "You're getting an officer to sign your brother's card?"

Fair play to Nathaniel, he replied, "Titch likes Phil and will be pleased that he signed it." I did the deed and said, "Tell him not to use it to enhance his music career when he gets out." He laughed.

I sometimes question whether I believe in fate. However, driving up to the Leeds game that weekend, my son was playing a song by Stormzy, a friend of Titch who used to visit him regularly. It had an interlude with Titch and Stormzy chatting. It was strange hearing him talking in my car. The last time I heard him would have been his questioning my eyesight on the five-a-side football pitch.

Tour of Yorkshire

The Tour of Yorkshire was over one hundred miles of hilly terrain; despite my lack of sleep and permanent dry mouth, I was determined to complete it. I also had the added complication of having no teeth, so I would be really handicapped when it came to eating. I trained how I meant to survive: wine gums, gels, and energy drinks. A few others were riding the race, Munch, Steve McGrath and Tom Hill.

I battered the training at home on my turbo. I thought, 'If I can't sleep, I'll just train.'

Near the start line with Henry.

Sarah and Henry came up to see me off on the start line. During the ride, I found myself feeling stronger and stronger. In fact, I was being told to ease up a bit. I felt like all my months of frustration were being taken out on my pedals.

I hammered every climb, thinking of where I'd been during my battle with cancer. Each climb was a walk in the park in comparison.

Despite only having my jelly babies, I got stronger as the ride went on. It felt amazing. I felt alive and completely forgot all the recent ordeals while on the bike... I must have looked like a crazy Freddy Krueger with my toothless look. Pedalling like crazy!

Now you see them, now you don't

After weeks and months of going to Birmingham Dental Hospital to have multiple moulds of my mouth taken, I finally saw myself with teeth again. They weren't the finished article but a test to see how they fit and gauge my bite.

When they showed me in the mirror, the difference was amazing. I would never have swapped them for my own, but it significantly improved my Steptoe look. I looked more like Freddie Mercury!

My dry mouth still drove me mad, especially at night. I saw every hour, usually waking up needing to drink or use a synthetic saliva spray. It gave a bit of relief for ten minutes or so, and then I'd be dry again. If I did manage to sleep beyond an hour, I ended up peeling my tongue off the roof of my mouth.

Sometimes I'd wake up absolutely exhausted, having blurred vision from sleep deprivation, and at work, I could fall asleep on the spot; well, I felt like I could. I've never needed a lot of sleep, but I really did feel like an insomniac.

I didn't look like the old me, but honestly, I was long past caring about how I looked. I was more bothered about being able to chew again once I got used to the pearlies. It felt like I was breaking them in for Red Rum for a while. It filled my face out, though and made me look a lot better than I did without teeth, that's for sure.

When I returned to work, the reception I got from staff and prisoners was amazing. Our gym orderly Tufty said about getting some himself. He said, "I've got one more job in me to pay for them."

Even refereeing was more straightforward; I could hold the whistle in my mouth correctly again.

MONT VENTOUX AND THE RETURN

I had a fantastic week cycling in France with some good friends, including the inspirational Ray Harris. I hope I'm as fit as him if I ever live to be his age.

Cycling up Mont Ventoux was two years in the planning. I'd just completed the three-routes-in-a-day challenge, Club des Cinglés. It was a fantastic experience.

Thanks to Munch for organising that memorable trip with a great group of friends. I will never forget seeing the top on that first ascent and putting the hammer down. Every turn of the pedal felt like a stab in the heart of the disease that had taken control for a period of my life – even though I always tried to think, 'I may have cancer, but cancer hasn't got me'!

Left to right: Steve, Bertie, me, Ray Harris and Munch.

At the top of the mountain: Steve McGrath, Munch, and me.

When we returned, I could feel soreness in my neck where I'd had radiotherapy. It wasn't like a standard sore throat or a stiff neck that you get occasionally. It felt tender to touch. I was worried. I went to the doctors who, after an examination, couldn't see any infection, which I thought probably wasn't good news. It's almost like cancer must keep reminding you that the fight is ongoing and will never be over. I guess one-day cancer will get its victory, but I really hoped it wasn't upping the ante just yet!

I went to see Mr Pracey for a check-up. Before seeing him again in September, I hadn't had time to put as much weight on as I'd hoped. I knew I'd get that look from him on one side and Sarah on the other.

Fortunately, Dolly doesn't remember much about my battle with cancer, only the fact that I had no teeth for a while. I didn't want her to endure what Henry did...

We arrived back from the hospital, and it felt like we had been catapulted back three years; I never thought it possible to again feel like it had back then, but it felt the same, if not worse. We sat in the car, reliving that day again, awaiting the needle aspiration test and a head and neck scan. It brought me back to that day in October 2012.

The only real positive I could draw on was when Pracey put the camera down; he said my throat looked clear. Then he said I had a nodule, a lump on the left side, the same as before. He also said that it could be a reactive lump from treatment. The best I could hope for was an operation to have it removed. That would interfere with my eating and swallowing again.

So many thoughts were flying around in my head; the idea of it all was draining. Sarah, bless her, seemed to pick the baton up again and start running.

Fortunately, after an agonising wait and a minor operation, the results came back all clear. We all breathed a huge sigh of relief.

CALM WATERS

The chaotic period with Governor Cartwright was soon forgotten. The arrival of a new governor Tom Wheatley, son of the well-respected former Head of the Prison Service, Phil Wheatley, was a breath of fresh air.

Tom Wheatley was just what we needed on the run-up to implementing the ban on smoking in prisons. It would be one of the most significant changes to impact prisoners for a long time. One that needed a governor like Tom to steer the prison through what would be a real challenge. Tom was a governor who, from day one, valued the PE department and was going to utilise our strengths in the build-up to the ban being implemented.

We set up smoking cessation meeting groups in the gym classroom twice a week, working closely with health care. It was surprising how many prisoners were looking forward to the ban, knowing it would be the only thing that could get them to stop smoking. The date for implementing the ban kept getting pushed back by headquarters. At times I questioned whether it was going to happen.

Tom let his managers manage and questioned them if they weren't, but gone was the micromanaging, dictatorship-style of management we had endured previously. We also all knew who the Governor was, not from seeing his A3-size photo on every wall. Tom also knew all the staff by name and everything workwise he needed to know about you.

As I said, get three things right in prisons, and you'll see a smooth-running jail. Visits, food and gym. The waters were suddenly calm for staff and prisoners, with that 'authority line' just where it needed to be.

Family visits started up again, utilising the PE staff to organise games and entertainment for the kids on their visits. Prisoner consultation meetings were held. Tom would attend and listen and not just dictate what would happen. If he was changing something, he would explain why it was happening.

What most people reading this would think is basic communication skills. Trust me, they were sadly lacking in many managers over the years.

Those calm waters allowed 'the line' to be thrown out, and many prisoners grabbed it. I continued my two-risk method and am pleased to say most paid off. We had a fantastic period of running PE courses with the usual success stories.

One of my risks on a course was a lad called Hirsi from Somalia. He hadn't long been sentenced to life and was somewhat surly. To be honest, I was guilty of throwing him 'the line' a little early. However, even though he got sacked from the course before completing it, we had many conversations afterwards. He still learned a lot from the experience. He went from being surly and not wanting to engage with staff to coming to the office and spending most of his gym session chatting. It shows that even out of a failure, there is success to some degree.

La Marmotte, France, me and my older brother Les

La Marmotte is one of the toughest sportives in Europe, with a total distance of 174 kilometres then nearly 6000 metres of climbing in a day. After completing the three ascents of Mont

Ventoux, it would be the new year's challenge. I'd got myself back to a really high standard of fitness on the bike. Hammering spin classes, often three a day, a weights session, then a session in the evening at home, all on a pocket full of jelly babies. My older brother Les was joining us for the ride, and there was no way he was getting to the top of any climb ahead of me.

My Brother Les and I on La Marmotte route.

The day's first climb came after 11 kilometres with a short ascent via two hairpin bends to the Lac du Verney. There are then roughly two kilometres of flat before the climb of the Col du Glandon starts.

The Glandon is a 24-kilometre climb at an average of five per cent, which is a slightly distorting statistic. It's mainly because in the middle of the climb, after just over 11 kilometres, there is a steep descent followed by about three kilometres of quite a gentle climb. The good thing about the ascent of Glandon is that we did it relatively early in the day. So, not too hot and had plenty of trees to provide shade.

We have some protection from the elements. The bad thing is that it's just a long, challenging climb. We scaled this one together, I think, just checking each other out.

The only other ride we had done together was in the freezing cold on a testing sportive near where Les lived. That day I had to keep waiting for him all the way around. After the last feed station with two more big climbs to go, I was waiting at the top of the climb, only for Les not to arrive!

I rode back down, looking for him, but still no sign. I eventually rode round to his house to find him back home, refusing to come out and finish the ride. I went off to do the climb again and finish; by now, though, I was at the back of the ride. The broom wagon stopped me and told me I had to get in. I told him no way. In the end, I agreed to get in if I hadn't caught anyone by the last climb. I was not getting in that van; I caught several before the previous ascent, called the Cat and Fiddle, and then passed hundreds on the way up. The van pulled over at my side near the top with the passenger saying, "you fucker, you just cost me twenty pounds". He'd bet his mate that I wouldn't catch anyone.

Les was at the finishing line waiting for me. So, France was his chance to even the score; he had been training hard, but I knew he hadn't trained as hard as me. And even on Jelly Babies all day, I wasn't going to be behind him up any climb!

By the time we were heading towards the next ascent, the temperature had hit the mid-thirties as we rode along the valley to Saint-Michel-de-Maurienne, where the Col du Télégraphe ascent begins. At Saint-Michel-de-Maurienne, we passed a sign that says the Col du Galibier is 32 kilometres away with over 2000 metres of climbing. This was a clear indication of the road ahead.

Unlike the Glandon, the climb of the Col du Télégraphe is a steady climb with few surprises. Unfortunately, you can only use the right side of the road and miss out on a lot of shade. It was a warm climb. I noticed Les starting to feel it, so I tested his legs by putting the hammer down for a few minutes. Before I knew it, he was dropped. Now it was just me against myself to the top. To be honest, I thought it was a relatively easy climb.

I had learnt from the previous descent that Les came down the climb quicker than me, so I wasn't going to give him that satisfaction again. I decided to wait at the bottom rather than the top.

Next up, and the best climb I've ever done, it had everything, straight hard inclines and hairpin bends. From there, I decided the pain would really start for Les. The climb to the top of Galibier is totally exposed to the elements, and at high altitude (the Galibier is the highest paved road in the Alps at the peak of nearly 3000 metres) takes the breath away.

When we hit the final four kilometres of hairpin bends to the summit, which runs at around nine per cent, I decided to put the hammer down. It wasn't long before I could look down on the hairpin bend and see Les, a dot down below.

That was where I saw people pushing their bikes for the first time. The final kilometre is very tough, especially if you're hammering the pedals as I was. But I could at least see where I was aiming for and just kept pedalling. At the top, I stopped for some photos of me in the snow and of the magnificent views before heading off for a nice slow descent. I lay on a wall having a sunbathe and had almost fallen asleep by the time Les arrived.

The final ascent of the route was Alpe d'Huez, 21 hairpin bends and 14 kilometres of climbing at an average of nine per cent. It's a brutal way to end the Marmotte route but a great climb. The first four bends of the Alpe d'Huez are the hardest, but once that's out of the way, you know you can finish.

I got to bend five and developed a problem on my bike. I had to roll back down the hill to the local bike shop as Munch, Paul, Ray, and Les carried on up the climb.

With my bike repaired, I restarted back up the mountain. The first three kilometres are at over ten per cent. It takes over a kilometre to hit the first bend (which is bend 21; they count down in reverse), and mentally it makes you feel like it's never going to end. After bend four, there are sections of the climb which are less sharp a gradient, and you could ease off if you chose. I had nobody to race but myself, so I just got in a good rhythm and enjoyed the climb to the top.

I eventually reached the edge of Alpe d'Huez, not to be confused (like I did) with the village of Huez, which is about four kilometres from the end. Then you have the final glorious kilometre-long ride to the finish. The gradient eases off a bit, and you can sprint to the line. What a fantastic day.

One of the best of my life.

At the end of the final climb Alpe d'Huez

Cartwright in a skirt

All good things must come to an end. When a governing governor announces they are leaving, especially a good one like Tom Wheatley, it leaves a degree of uncertainty. Whenever a new governor comes, their reputation usually precedes them; lots of rumours flying around, it must be said they are usually pretty close to the mark. Rumours typically travel from the staff at previous establishments. This occasion wasn't any different. Rumours were rife; many described Governor Pearson as Cartwright in a skirt. Others stated you'll be begging for Cartwright back in six months. We were told about her time at Woodhill Prison as a deputy governor under a governor of a similar ilk called Smith.

All those rumours had gone around before Cartwright took up the post, and unfortunately, they were all true. All we could hope for as a staffing group was this time, they'd be unfounded. Or the new governor would learn from past mistakes.

The rumours continued circulating – how our new governor referred to Officers as landing rats. And how she had a record of dismissing people at the drop of a hat, only for many of them to win their jobs back on appeal.

I had just completed a PE course on one of her first days of being the number one governor. I saw it as an opportunity to invite her down to give out the certificates, an invitation she accepted.

I introduced the governor and continued describing the courses the prisoners had succeeded in. I went on to talk about a few of the previous success stories who had gone on to further their education, completing degrees. I spoke of a few doing well upon release. The governor gave the certificates out as I read out the names, and I invited her to say a few words. It wasn't lost on the prisoners or me that she declined to speak. I hoped that it was more down to nerves and not a lack of interest.

Full staff briefing

It was always customary for a new governor to hold a full staff briefing upon their arrival. One was announced, and all staff congregated in the visits' hall. Governor Pearson told us how proud she was to be the first female number-one governor in the high-security estate. And went on to notify us of her vision for the prison; from nowhere though came the words that received almost an audible gasp from all the staff: "If you don't like working here, go and find somewhere else to work."

I remembered thinking of Brian Clough coming to Leeds and saying on his first meeting with the players, "you can throw all your medals in the bin; you've cheated to win them". It wasn't received too well. The governor's words had landed a similar message with an identical impact. Her standout message was clear from all the good she may have said in that briefing. Notably, there was no opportunity for staff questions at this or any future briefings.

It didn't take too long for her A3 photo to start appearing all over the prison, a familiar trait now. Within a few weeks, stories of the morning meetings of the SMT (senior management team) began to leak out. The governor would dictate the morning meeting, and she would publicly ridicule any manager who spoke or made suggestions. Prisoners also mirrored the same message when talking to them. Consultation group meetings either didn't occur anymore, or the governor dictated what would happen. Prisoners no longer had any input; many of them came off the groups.

It soon became apparent that Pearson would micromanage everything. Nothing would go ahead without her knowledge. She had to be the one making the decisions. You can imagine how the SMT were all weighing up their options. The governor had a clear approach: "you either ride with me or collide with me".

Again, this made me wonder what goes through head offices' minds when they make such appointments. Who decided that going from Tom Wheatley to someone like Governor Pearson would be a good idea? Good for the staff or prisoners?

Suspensions galore

Within months almost every day brought the news of yet another member of staff being suspended. I'd never seen or heard anything quite like it, often over the pettiest things. Slowly, after months off suspended, many simply returned to work. Despite winning their case and their jobs back, some were ordered by the governor to go work elsewhere because she didn't want them in her prison. Staff morale was starting to plummet. I had never known the mood of a jail to change so dramatically in such a short space of time.

Two in the pocket

The suspensions kept coming at an alarming rate. The then POA chairman, Aaron Stowe, was suspended for allegedly failing to carry out any of his nightly observations on a prisoner in the segregation unit who was supposedly on a 15-minute watch. He was also viewed on CCTV footage walking around in pyjamas and slippers. Staff were amazed when he managed to keep his job and return to work. However, it turned out to be a masterstroke by Pearson. His position as POA chairman was now severely compromised. You could visibly see how his support for colleagues going through disciplinary hearings had changed.

Several staff had been misrepresented and wrongly advised not to pursue a tribunal case. Overnight the poacher had become a game-keeper. The deputy chair of the POA would also go down a similar path, but for different reasons. It was no secret that Dave Monger had been trying to gain promotion for several years. The governor secured his loyal services by giving him the promotion he so craved. The consequences were that no staff had any proper POA representation, or indeed none they could rely on or trust.

The general mood of the whole prison started to change. It wasn't helped when many staff who had been on 'work-life balance' hours found them removed at short notice. Many appealed, but to no avail.

I was told by Gary Nelson, a high-profile prisoner and a regular user of the gymnasium, how the governor had turned his wife away from a visit. His wife had turned up in a skirt above the knee and high-heeled shoes. Governor Pearson had implemented strict rules on visitors and their clothing. Attending the visitors' entrance, Governor Pearson told Gary's wife she wasn't coming in dressed the way she was and would have to go to Tesco to get a change of clothes if she wanted her visit. Gary's wife correctly pointed out to the governor that her skirt was shorter than hers and her shoes had bigger heels.

Gov Pearson responded: "I'm the number one governor, and I do what I want."

I checked with a few visits staff to see if that story was true. To my surprise, not only was it true, but there had also been several occasions where children of visitors had been told to go to Tesco to change their footwear, having been informed by the governor that anyone wearing sandals or open-toed shoes was not allowed entry.

Full staff briefings and 'graffitigate'

Full staff briefings were called on a regular basis. The Governor was customarily joined by her shadow, another female governor who had 'absolutely' chosen to ride with her rather than collide.

It had become common practice amongst the PE staff to have friendly bets on how often Gov Pearson would say 'absolutely' in her briefing. One regular message was still, 'if you don't like working here, go and work somewhere else'. Sadly, quite a lot of experienced staff started to take her advice. Quite a few left for the Border Force and to work on the trains. Some, after suspension, were told to start work at HMP Hewell. Others simply lost their jobs, many over something petty.

Another fun pastime for staff would be counting the 'umms' between the 'absolutelys'. They came at an alarming rate, but it was an excellent way to concentrate the mind.

Much to our surprise, we were in for a particularly interesting briefing one morning. The Governor had discovered someone had defaced one of the many photos of her in the administration block. Someone had written 'cunt' across her face on the photo. It was 'Absolutely' clear the Governor was 'absolutely' not happy.

Quite bizarrely, the Governor spent almost half an hour trying to convince us that she knew who it was but would allow them the opportunity to report to her office. She finished by informing us that it had only happened because she was a female and the first female to be the governing Governor of a high-security prison. I'm unsure why, but she loved reminding us of that fact. I've never met a single officer who cares whether their boss is male or female; no one cares about that if they're good at their job.

Gov Pearson had made one of her SMT the prime suspect; he'd been told so. He turned up at her office for what she thought was a confession. To her disappointment, he told her to take him off her list because it wasn't him. Just for the record, it wasn't me, either. I recently discovered that a female had defaced her photo; I wouldn't mind betting the Governor didn't have any females on her shortlist. Her amusing attempt at bluffing her staff had failed, and nobody came forward. I also heard afterwards she allegedly had a falling-out with the police liaison officer because she didn't think he was doing enough to find the culprit.

Red shoes

I was on duty in the sports hall with two of our gym orderlies; a Geordie lad, everyone called Sausage, and another prisoner, Reuben, who I previously wrote about in the book. I was chatting with them as they cleaned the gym floor.

Sausage was a quick-witted lad with a great sense of humour. As we chatted, the governor came in. We all said good morning. She awkwardly, just out of the blue, asked the orderlies what they knew. If anything was happening in the prison, she needed to be aware of, being the Governing Governor. Sausage, being Sausage, just jumped back, making a remark about her bright red stilettoed shoes with white polka dots. The governor wasn't too impressed; she turned and walked away. Reuben made a joke about how Sausage would be in Parkhurst tomorrow.

By the end of that week, both had been shipped out to HMP Belmarsh in London with no explanation. I asked security what the reasons were, but nobody seemed to have a reason. It was clear why they had been moved; Reuben was one of the best orderlies we ever had. He hadn't even made the remark but was clearly being punished for just being there. I heard that they won a case against Pearson a few weeks later and were both moved to HMP Dovegate with a small payout from head office.

I remember being surprised that Terry Adams had yet to be moved. Adams had previously won a case against Pearson and liked to remind her of it. Whenever he was in the gym and she visited, it would always result in Terry having a few digs at her. He quite often took the 'mickey' out of the governor.

I PREDICT A RIOT

Over the coming months, the mood of the prison continued to slip to an all-time low. The segregation unit was constantly full. I'd been down in the seg a number of times helping out after a few incidents in the prison. Speaking to staff and prisoners, I was told how the governor and her shadow would do their rounds, which would always end in mayhem, regularly with a prisoner ending up in a special cell. On many occasions, the Governor would insist that one of her SMT sign it off, not doing it herself. Eventually, a few of them got wise to this and refused to sign off the paperwork. The use of special cell figures went through the roof. I was informed that the seg staff and the Governor had differences of opinion numerous times when she ordered them to 'box' a prisoner.

I came on duty one morning, and the PE staff on duty were told to report to C-wing. It transpired there had been a major incident during the night. Two prisoners, while out on night sanitation (a system where prisoners are placed in a queue and could come out twice through the night for a quick shower or slop out. That was due to the old-style wings still not having in cell sanitation), had come out on their respective landings, the twos and the threes. They smashed up the wing, causing significant damage; smashed glass was everywhere, so it was unsafe to unlock until it was cleared up and made safe by the works department, which took a couple of hours.

Cell bells were going off everywhere. Prisoners who had visits wanted to know if they could come out to have a shower. Almost every prisoner I spoke with at their door said they were pissed off with the two idiots who had gone on the rampage. One prisoner even told me, "Phil, if' you'd let me out last night, I'd have got them behind their door, trust me."

The inmates' mood was very much against the two insignificant prisoners that had caused the damage.

I answered another cell bell, and when I opened the flap on the door, it was obvious he was rattling. He said, "Gov, I need to get my methadone."

I informed the PO on the wing and asked if I could take the prisoner to health care. In prison, inmates on methadone must go to healthcare to get their prescriptions. It can't travel to the prisoner. At the same time, I asked if we could do a controlled unlock, unlocking those who had a visit in the afternoon. This would keep the mood of the wing favourable. The PO agreed to ask the governor in the morning meeting.

On his return, I again asked if we could get the inmate to health care to get his methadone. He was really struggling now. He'd been ringing his cell bell a few times.

The PO told me Gov Pearson had said no and told him she didn't want people on methadone in her prison anyway. She also refused to allow us to carry out a controlled unlock for the inmates' expecting visits. As we went to inform them, the mood of the prison started to shift. The banging of the doors began, and before long, the whole wing had turned toxic.

Eventually, when the prisoners were unlocked, there were several alarm bells. There wasn't any room in the seg, so there was nowhere for troublemakers to be taken. They were kept on the wing but under a segregation routine. That could have been avoided with a simple decision to unlock those with visits, even if it was just one or two at a time. Under previous Governors, I know that the

PO would have made those decisions himself. But it seemed every decision had to be run through the governor, or everyone felt like it did, because of the repercussions if she disagreed with the other managers' decision. The wing was unstable for weeks afterwards.

China in your hands

The tension within the prison continued to mount. We found ourselves running to more and more alarm bells on all the wings. In all honesty, the gymnasium is quite often the last place for these tensions to show due to two main reasons: prisoners want to be in the Gym, and they don't want to risk a ban from the gymnasium by expressing their frustrations while in there.

However, you could see the tension in a football game that might spill over from problems on the wing. The game I was refereeing on one particular day had started to show the tension that seemed over and beyond any of my refereeing decisions or any tackle on another prisoner that could sometimes ramp up the tension in a game. The needle was there from the first whistle, mainly amongst prisoners off the same wing. At one point, it threatened to spill over into a full-blown fight. I managed to get between several prisoners as they squared up to each other in the sports hall. I told them it was their last opportunity to either get on with the game or the game would stop, and they'd be returned to the wing.

I've refereed too many five-a-side games over the years not to realise that the tension was different than a few bets riding on a game. I spoke to several prisoners individually and a few as a group to ascertain the problem. Every conversation I had led to one inmate upsetting the whole wing. A prisoner named China Walters. He attended the Gym regularly whenever he was on normal location.

I got on ok with him, but he could be a nightmare.

Walters was a very loud individual, one of those you hear before seeing him. The best way I could describe him was a young prisoner (YP) trapped in a man's body. A few convicts on D-wing were from his area; they felt like they had to stand with Walters whenever he inevitably upset other prisoners on the wing.

China had been moved off D-wing to the seg on several occasions. Each time he was moved, the wing started to settle back down. China openly discussed how the number one governor would always have him back. Even claiming that Pearson had promised a return to Long Lartin after him being shipped out to another prison. On his arrival at the other jail, China even told the staff that he wouldn't be there long because Lartin's governor had said he was going back. Upon his inevitable return, he even told staff, including me, that he wrote to the Governor, and she had been influential in his move back to Long Lartin.

The words of China Walters could be taken with a pinch of salt. But, I do know that it was baffling to staff and prisoners on D-wing why he kept being moved to the seg and back to the wing when it was so apparent that he destabilised the whole place.

The day after the football game, I had a conversation in the Gym with a prisoner with whom I had a good relationship; he was playing in that game of football that had almost gotten out of control and was a regular player. During our conversation, he told me of the problems on the wing and how they all stemmed from China Walters being brought back up from the seg. I had jokingly promised him that if he ever managed to score a hat-trick in a game, I'd get him moved onto another session where all the better footballers were playing. I was still waiting for his hat-trick to arrive years later, although admittedly, I was worried once or twice when he scored two and reminded me of my promise.

The prisoner pleaded with me to do something. He said, "I've spoken to everyone; what am I supposed to do?" He told me that he and another prisoner, who I knew, had to try and protect Walters every time he came back up on the wing. He finished with, "Do they want someone to get killed? Because that's what's going to happen."

I did everything possible, ringing security and even putting it on paper. Unbeknown to me, the next day, the governor and her shadow were up on D-wing assessing China's cell, which he'd smashed up before being moved to the seg. Obviously, the prisoners observed this and later asked what was going on. The governor had made the decision that the cell wasn't too bad. China would be allowed back up onto the wing the following day.

Alarm bell D-wing. All available staff to D-wing

That evening, the alarm sounded on my radio in the Gym. Running to answer the bell, a considerable distance away, and a few gates to get through, I heard those dreaded words, 'all available staff to D-wing'. I knew that wasn't good. My thoughts immediately went back to my conversations with the prisoners from that wing.

Arriving at the wing, I could hear the commotion of raised voices upstairs coming from a landing. I ran up to find all the staff were locked behind the doors to the landing. There was a standoff between two groups of prisoners. I knew if that got into a full-scale fight, we would never get back on the wing and would then be waiting for the national C&R squads to arrive. It would escalate to a full-blown riot. The deaths that had been spoken of could possibly happen.

I quickly spoke to the PO orderly officer, Mike Winkley, who was effectively in charge. I said we needed to get on the wing. He agreed, and we entered. I spotted the prisoner I'd had the conversation with and made a beeline for him. He and his mates were considerably outnumbered by the other prisoner, so I figured if I could convince them to go behind their doors, the others would have nobody to fight unless they turned on staff, which wasn't out of the question given the mood of the wing.

They agreed. As I locked him away, the prisoner reminded me how he'd told me what would happen. He told me about the Governor coming on the wing and deciding to bring China Walters back once again. He said, "It's like they wanted this to happen."

To be honest, I couldn't find any words to say to him. I just gave him a look, and a sigh that I hoped said it all. The following day I heard that the prisoner I had spoken with was on the wing but under segregation conditions after the incident. So, not only had he tried to warn numerous staff of the consequences of bringing Walters back, but he had been placed on report and locked up for 23 hours a day on the wing.

I went on D-wing to speak with him at the flap through his door. I asked how he was doing, and immediately, I thought, what a stupid question. He would have been well within his rights to tell me to 'get fucked', but to my surprise, he started talking. I felt bad having the conversation through his door. Suppose it had not been on the old-style wings where you had to request an unlock from the control room. In that case, I'd have opened his door to have the conversation and offered him a handshake and my apology for failing him like many others had. Again, to my surprise, he spoke calmly, and despite his obvious disappointment, he was polite and courteous. I found it quite humbling. I'm not sure I could have reacted as he did.

He told me he knew I had done what I could; he said it was on the governor to keep insisting on bringing Walters back to the wing. The lad was shipped out sometime later.

Incident at height

A few weeks after the above incident and countless alarm bells later, I had been informed by numerous prisoners on different wings that the weekend could be a busy one. Many told me that the Governor had caused much unrest within the prison and that the consultation meetings were now a complete waste of time. The segregation unit was still constantly full, and the special cells were in frequent use, especially after a visit by Pearson and her shadow.

I was on duty in the Gymnasium and was getting a class in (a procedure that meant going up a long corridor and standing at an electronic door with a list). It used to be that a member of corridor staff joined me to assist; however, corridor staff no longer existed after someone in their ultimate wisdom deemed we didn't require them because there was CCTV coverage in the corridors.

Even with the best alarm bell response, though, a member of staff could be killed before the 'cavalry' arrived. An incident with Ali Smith and Bieber and his attempt to murder her in the corridor didn't even change things. I guess it was a sign of the times and only going to get worse and not better due to staff shortages.

So, I was up at the door, getting the class in and ticking off the names one by one. I'd got the bulk of the class in when a member of staff came to talk to me about football. As I was ticking the last couple of names off, a prisoner I knew well from completing the full-time PE course recently came back past me, returning to the wing. As I scrubbed his name off my list, I asked why he hadn't stayed for the gym session. He told me there weren't enough people to play football. I asked what had been going on with him; I was told he had recently smashed his cell up.

Jewell, Jewelly as I called him, had been one of my risks on a course that had paid off. He passed every part during the year and had performed excellently throughout. I'd even mentioned him as a future mentor on a PE course and informed him. He thanked me at the time and then said, "Thanks for all you've done for me, but this prison is fucked!" Before walking away, he shook my hand and said, "Get yourself straight off tonight, Phil; otherwise, you may be late home."

PE Staff got off earlier than the uniform officers due to shift pattern times. On Jewell's wing, they were aware of that fact; they would regularly have a bit of banter from the end of the wing as we walked out on our way home.

As I said, many had already told me it could be a busy weekend, and then Jewelly told me that. When I returned to the gym, I asked the other staff if he'd said anything to them. He hadn't, so I told them and said I would ring security, which I did.

I spoke to the PO in security and relayed what I had been told. He informed me that he got along with Jewell and would go to the wing to speak with him. I asked if he wanted me to inform the duty governor, a chameleon called Jo May; she'd gone from being everyone's friend to jumping on board with the Governor (ride or collide). The PO said it was okay; he would handle it from there.

Alarm bell F-wing

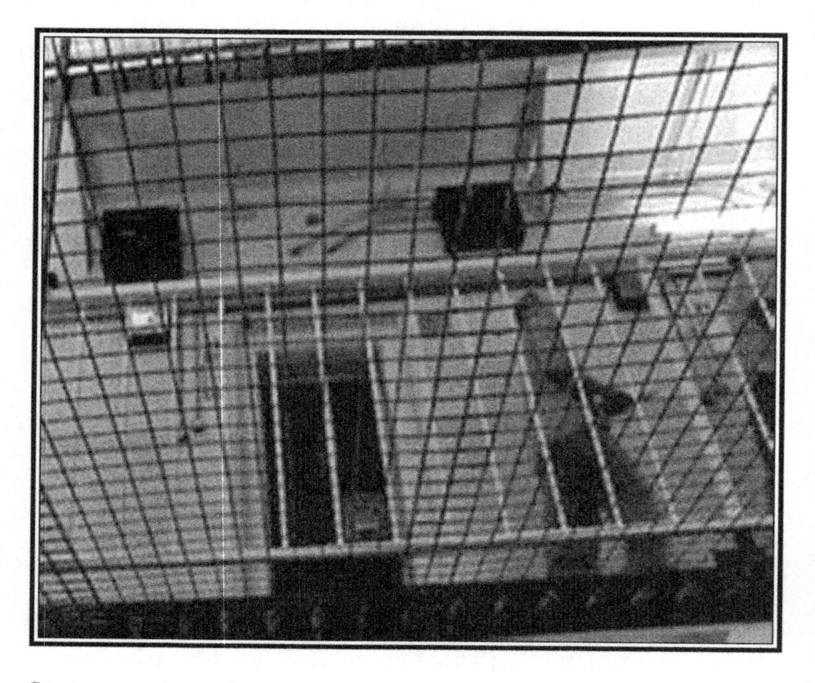

Sitting in the office, I had just completed my report when my radio went off, 'alarm bell Foxtrot'. We didn't have enough staff on duty to respond; naturally, I wondered if this had resulted from the PO going over to see Jewelly. It transpired that Jewelly and two other prisoners had gone onto the netting, which covered the landing, to prevent prisoners from jumping to the ground floor in a possible suicide attempt.

The alarm bell concluded after around 20 minutes, with all three returning to their cells. Just after that, I received a phone call in the gym; it was Jo May, duty governor, questioning whether I could have handled the situation better. I asked her in what way she was suggesting.

"Why didn't you take him to the seg?" she asked.

I replied, "For giving me information that I might be late home?" I added, "Are you telling me I should take anyone who tells me anything straight to the seg?" I also told her as far as I was aware, the seg was full.

After a silence, she repeated that maybe I could have handled it differently and asked me to see her on the way out of work. What made the conversation even more bizarre is I was fully aware that an officer I knew well was working in a workshop when a prisoner there threatened to kick off. He took the prisoner to the seg and was lambasted by the governor for doing so.

I went to Joe May's office on my way out as arranged, and we had the same conversation. I reminded her of the situation in the workshop and how it had been viewed by the governor. The conversation ended, and I left, believing we'd agreed to disagree. Two days later, I received a disciplinary letter stating I was being placed under investigation for causing an incident at height. Even after the conversation I had had with Governor May, I was amazed. I bumped into Governor May in the corridor that day, and she said, "Hi, Phil, how are you?"

I hadn't slept due to my dry mouth and had had a dreadful night. So, I let her have it; numerous staff passed us in the corridor as I unloaded on her. She tried to say it wasn't her decision to take it to an official investigation. I knew she and the PO from security were particularly close. Rumour had it, more than just friends. So, I asked the question if he was also under an official investigation? After all, he was the last person to speak to Jewell before entering the netting. Of course, the PO wasn't.

The gossip went around that I was under investigation and how it had come about. Many staff told me they wouldn't be reporting anything in the future. The lad standing at the door with me said he couldn't believe it; he'd heard the conversation

I had had with Jewell and said he hadn't thought anything of it because he was thanking me and shaking my hand.

John Barry had been given the incident to investigate, and he arranged an appointment for me to see him.

A few days passed, and I was still being stopped by staff regularly asking if the rumours were true. I always said, 'yes, they are', but when they added, 'I won't be reporting anything in future', I always tried to correct that train of thought. I was being investigated, but I would do the same if I faced that situation again. It was worrying staff took that mindset when the prison, in my opinion, was on a knife edge.

My meeting with the governor

A few days later, I was just behind the governor, coming through staff search at the gate. I said good morning and asked if I could have a few minutes of her time at some point. She agreed and asked me to make an appointment for that morning with her secretary. Arriving at the gym, I phoned and made an appointment for 11. I informed the other gym staff, and we arranged for my duties to be covered. We were fully staffed because we had one additional PEI on duty, meaning nothing had to be curtailed.

I went over and arrived five minutes early. I sat in the secretary's office; the governor was in her office but was conversing with the deputy governor, Mark Allan. To be honest, I'd almost forgotten he was the deputy. If ever there was a classic chameleon, Mark was it. I've since heard he's now the number one governor in another prison. I wouldn't have a clue if he made a good one or not; his identity changed completely to fit whoever the Governor was. The conversation was discussing the new work phones they had recently received. At 11.40, I was called into the governor's office.

She requested that I take a seat across the desk from her. She asked what I had come to see her about. I relayed the above story, or attempted to. She stopped me once I'd mentioned what it was about and said, "It's absolutely right and proper that you're investigated, so why are you here?"

I put across the same argument I had with Joe May but also added my concerns about the message it was giving to other staff. She then went completely off on a tangent. Her demeanour changed, and she was getting visibly angry. She asked why I'd left my colleagues in the gym to come and see her? I reminded her she had asked me to make the appointment for that morning. The Governor then added angrily, "You self-roster in the gym, don't you?" Meaning we didn't follow a shift pattern, we didn't but only because it hadn't worked when they previously tried with the number of PE staff we had. I asked what this had to do with the investigation. "Oh, you've brought a lot to my table today," she replied; by now, she was red in the face, almost as red as the stilettoes she had on her feet. She then went on to talk about our downtime between sessions, making veiled threats to change things; at this point, I stood up and said, "I think we've exhausted this conversation." As I left, I looked at her irate face, smiled and walked away.

On my way out that evening, I was called to see the gym manager, Dave Grant. Dave was also someone I would have classed as a friend; we knew each other socially. He told me the Governor had spoken to him and said she felt like I'd tried to intimidate her in our meeting. I thought he was trying to wind me up at first. He went on to say she thought I had sat too close to her; I just said, "Well, I'm not sure how that works when she told me to sit where I sat. And it was across the desk from her." I told him to tell her to show CCTV footage of our meeting that displays I acted wrongly in any way. He told me she wasn't happy, so I said, "tough, neither am I".

I also told him how she had finished the meeting, threatening to remove self-rostering.

Investigation

Governor John Barry rang me and asked me to discuss the investigation he had been told to carry out. John was an ex PEI and a good friend of mine. You might remember me mentioning him earlier in the book; I referred to him as half-glass empty John.

John would be the first to admit it himself, he's almost the opposite of me that way, but we were good friends. I was confident there was nothing to answer on the investigation. Even if I got some stupid award off the Governor, I felt sure I would win any subsequent appeal.

John went through it all with me; he was as baffled as I was about why it was being investigated. I covered the whole episode from beginning to end, and John made notes. I knew he was going to recommend no further action; despite that, I never received an outcome from the Governor. She would have been quick to let me know if the recommendation had been different.

Alarm bell Perrie-wing

The disturbances continued at a rate I'd never known in all my time at Long Lartin. The mood of the prison had plummeted to an all-time low from both a staff and prisoner perspective. Many seg staff that had worked there for years were requesting to come out; they'd simply had enough. The governor refused to let two well-liked and respected staff have their requested moves. It was a horrible time, watching staff with years of experience walking around broken; those were men that had been to war for their country and not been broken. So, to see them like that was a sad situation.

I was in the gym when the alarm bell went off on Perrie-wing; I responded to the bell. When I arrived, the governor's shadow was sitting at the end of the corridor, smiling and telling staff as they arrived to get the prisoners behind the door using any means necessary.

As I approached the far end of the wing, six prisoners were holding a peaceful demonstration. I recognised a couple of them, so I asked what was happening. I spoke to a prisoner called Paul Mapps, Mappsy as I called him. He told me they'd had enough of the way the governor and, pointing down the landing at Shadow, "her down there speak to and treat prisoners". He continued, "We haven't got a problem with staff; it's them causing all the problems." He finished with, "Ask her to come down and speak to us."

I asked Shadow if she was happy to come down with me to hear their concerns. "No, get them behind their doors" was the reply.

I returned to Mappsy and said to go behind your door, put in a request complaint, and get the other lads to do the same, raising your concerns. He wasn't happy, but he spoke to the others, and they went away. A lad called Deano, a good officer with a good rapport with prisoners, talked to some of the other prisoners.

Mappsy said as they went away, "If that's the way they want it, then we will ramp it up next time."

I know Officer Deano and numerous other staff requested those prisoners to be moved to help settle the wing back down. But that request was refused.

As promised, the prisoners ramped it up on the wing with a small riot where pool balls were thrown at staff. It was just a sign of things to come.

If someone had told me within eighteen months after Tom Wheatley left we would be in the position we were, I'd never have believed them. It was obvious where we were heading. The only thing uncertain was which wing would riot first.

Rattle those pots and pans

That was the second mini-riot in the space of weeks that Shadow and the governor had been instrumental in causing. We suffered numerous staff assaults and another major disturbance after Shadow walked onto the wing one morning and, after noticing cookware had been left out in the prisoners' kitchen overnight, ordered DST (dedicated search team) to come and take it all to reception before unlocking the wing.

As soon as the prisoners were unlocked and noticed all their cookware had gone, it kicked off.

Riot F-wing

After the peaceful demonstration, the calls from staff to disperse the prisoners around the system were ignored. Mappsy's promise to ramp it up was followed through. If I'm honest, I believe that dispersing the prisoners may have delayed the riot for another day.

But, the way the prison was being run, it was a case of when, not if, a major riot would occur.

Throwing that Governor into a high-security jail with a smoking ban looming was like throwing in a hand grenade. As I've said many times, it's not always the message you deliver to prisoners but how you deliver it that causes the problems.

I am sure if Tom Wheatley had been left to steer the ship through those waters, we wouldn't have faced all those problems, left with an uninhabitable wing and fifty-thousand pounds' worth of damage.

I was on duty in the gym on the night of the riot. We hadn't long got the class in when the alarm bell went off. I'd been training with a couple of prisoners in the evening. At around six, the bell went. Then, the all too familiar call of "all available staff..."

We had minimum staff on duty that evening, so none of the PEIs could respond to the bell. It's always difficult when that is the case knowing that your colleagues were probably in danger and just listening to the radio to hear it all unfold.

The long delay without any updates told us something serious was happening. Around 20 minutes later, I took a phone call from one of the managers on the centre, asking how many prisoners we had in the gym off E and F-wings. I was also told the wings had gone up, and staff had to withdraw. The prisoners were on the wings, rioting.

Our prisoners were all preparing to return to the wings after their workouts. We counted them off the affected wings. Obviously, these prisoners wouldn't be returning to their normal locations, So I told them, if they wanted to shower, 'have one now'. Many usually waited to have one back on the wing. Terry Adams was one of those who went to shower with a few others.

A few prisoners asked what was going on. I saw no reason to hide it from them as it would soon be apparent. I told them we had a major incident on the wings. Terry Adams, one of the high-profile prisoners I mentioned earlier in my book, and a few others talked about their food being on the stoves back on the wing. They asked if we could get someone to turn it off for them.

The wings had gone up, and staff had been chased off with pool cues and snooker balls thrown at them. So much for the food!

After the prisoners had showered, we counted them all into the PE classroom and sat them down. The mood in the gym was relatively calm. A CM (custodial manager) had been sent down to the gym with a handful of staff. We had a few prisoners off E and F enquire about needing their medication in their cells after being told by the CM that they wouldn't be returning to their cells that night. There were further discussions about being placed in the detainee unit where they would have no bedding. Once this was sorted, the CM told them he would ensure they got any medication they needed and that bedding would be provided. One or two also asked why they couldn't return to their wing if only one wing had problems.

They didn't realise at that point that we had lost one wing completely. We escorted the other prisoners back to their wings. And the E and F-wing inmates were taken to the detainee unit for the night.

The Tornado teams arrived at around 2.30 in the morning. The flashbangs could be seen and heard as they went in to take back control of F-wing.

At around four that morning, we congregated in the chapel for a hot debrief from the Governor after the wing had been taken back. The wing was still being decanted to other jails by numerous prison vans that had arrived.

The Governor started the debrief by thanking staff. She got some feedback from some of the wing officers. Much to my surprise, she then asked about our second incident in the gymnasium. I volunteered to speak; I stood up and said, "What second incident are you referring to, Governor? Because I wasn't aware, we had one."

I saw her expression change instantly to the face I recognised when she didn't like what she was hearing.

"Well, that's not what we saw from the gold commander suite and what we had been informed," she replied.

"There were a few reasonable requests regarding medication; once that was clarified for the prisoners, there were no problems. They all went back to the wings without any trouble," I finished.

I couldn't understand why, when the Governor had just lost a wing for the second time in months, she wanted to create another incident where there really hadn't been one. Towards the end of the debrief, she intimated that two high-profile prisoners were behind the riot, Gary Nelson and Terry Adams. I then understood her narrative. Both prisoners she had problems with.

The following day I was contacted by a CM that had also come down to the gym that evening to assist in getting the prisoners back to the wings. She informed me that the Governor told her she had to place all the prisoners that were off E- and F-wing that night on report. She refused to do it, having the same view as mine on how things unfolded in the gym. I pointed out to her that if they checked the CCTV footage of the classroom for that evening, they would see that at one point, I'd got the skeleton out in front of them and was making a few jokes about it. I wouldn't have done that if we had an ongoing incident in the gym.

The writing is on the wall

F-wing was out of use for 12 weeks. The following day at work, all the gym staff received an email from Aaron Stowe, including an attached email from the governor to him, giving notice for our self-rostering to be removed. That was no real surprise after the Governor threatened me at the end of my meeting with her. The real surprise was the timing of her email. It was at five on the morning of the riot, while the wing was still being decanted and the smoke from the flash bangs had hardly cleared.

I found it strange that this could be at the forefront of a governing Governor's mind at that time. Later the following day, I went over to look at the damage to the wing. It was like a warzone. I couldn't help but notice the graffiti everywhere on the wing, clearly indicating why the prisoners had rioted. The writing was on the wall for anyone who wanted to listen or see.

Date with destiny

Over the next week in the gymnasium, things returned to as normal as things could, given the recent events. The staff did go back on a shift pattern, but it only lasted for two weeks before the Governor conceded it didn't work and put us back on to self-rostering. It clearly indicated that it was a decision based on anything but the business needs of the prison, as the Governor had tried to claim in her email.

We were told that Ed Cornmell, the deputy director of the Prison Service, would be attending the prison in two weeks for a meeting with staff. There would be a meeting in the morning and one in the afternoon. Both were designed to ascertain the problems in the prison. The centre was compiling a list of staff who wished to attend. I called into the centre to put my name down when Richard Vince, the director general, was talking to the deputy governor, Mark Allan.

I had met Richard Vince several times; the last time I had met him, I treated him for a back injury. Watching Allan try to manoeuvre him out of my way was quite amusing before I spoke. I simply said 'Hi' and requested to be put on the list for the meeting. He agreed, and that was that.

I made it clear to everyone that I was going to attend the meeting and that I was going to tell the truth, whether they wanted to hear it or not.

My symptoms from latent Radiotherapy damage had gradually worsened over the last few months. I struggled with a severely weakened voice, and sleep was virtually non-existent. I had also started to suffer from neck spasms down the side which had had extensive treatment. They had become more severe and began to last longer.

Recently in the prison, I had needed to get kitted up in C&R gear in the seg for an incident at height. At one point, I'd taken my helmet off when I was having a spasm. Deep inside, I knew that I couldn't continue doing the job I loved. I wouldn't want to become a liability during an incident or cause a colleague to be injured.

I went to the doctor, who immediately signed me off for four weeks. I told my wife but said I would continue going to work because I needed to attend the meeting with the deputy director. I didn't tell anyone about my sick note and continued to attend work. Word had spread that I was going to the meeting and was going to tell all. A few staff gave me anonymous letters to hand to the director; one of them I saw before it was sealed, so I knew it backed up what I was going to say. Numerous staff came and asked me if I was really going to do what I described.

I came into work one morning and was setting up my class, ready for teaching. Munch had taken a phone call from Aaron Stowe, our POA branch's (pocketed) chairman. He told Munch to convince me not to attend the meeting as it wouldn't be in my best interest. I told Munch to ring him back and tell him to do one – "I'm going to the meeting."

I carried on teaching my lesson to the course.

Under the bus

Two days later and now just one week away from the meeting, I was in the classroom preparing my session when I heard the Governor outside the PE office next door asking if I was in. The other PEIs told her where I was, and she entered the classroom, closing the door behind her.

"Can I have a word?" she asked.

I replied, "Yes, sure." Being conscious of our last meeting, I made sure I kept a distance away until she approached me.

"I've heard you're going to put a vote of no confidence against me," she asked.

I replied, "Who to?"

To which she answered, "The POA."

I smiled and said, "What would be the point in me doing that? Everyone knows they're in your pocket." I added, "No, I'm going to the meeting with your boss, and I'm just going, to tell the truth."

With her familiar angry, contorted face, she angrily declared, "You're going to get thrown under the bus!"

"Bring the bus," I replied. The Governor left, slamming the door behind her. Once she'd gone, the other PE staff came and asked what had happened.

One last roll of the dice

Before the meeting, the Governor had one last throw of the dice to stop me from attending the meeting. I received a phone call from Governor and 'friend' John Barry. He asked me to come to his office for a chat. I went there and took a seat. I told him I had an idea what it was about. He said he'd been asked by the Governor to use whatever influence he had over me to stop me from attending the meeting. I told him it only needed to be a short conversation; I said, "Tell the Governor she can do one. I'm going to the meeting."

John tried to reason with me saying, "They will close ranks on you."

I simply replied, "I don't care; I'm going."

WHISTLEBLOWER

I said straight away, "With respect, Director, if you've come to hear the truth, I don't think you'll hear it if the Governor is present."

He asked, "Why not?"

I replied, "The Governor runs the prison through fear and is vindictive. We know there will be repercussions for anything we say." I told him: "I will speak out regardless, but I don't feel other people will."

He addressed the group and asked if anyone else felt the same. Tony was the only one who said he felt people would be wary of talking.

The DG said, "Well, if it's constructive, then we have to take it." He also pointed out that it wouldn't be a disciplinary hearing, and he wasn't a fan of them (oh, the irony).

Vince then addressed me and said he didn't really know me apart from the time I had treated him for a bad back, but the POA and the Governor had met with him before the meeting, and he'd been informed that I was a troublemaker.

I replied, "Have a look at my record; speak with both staff and prisoners and form a balanced view of me."

Vince replied, "It's also said that staff believe the POA are in the pocket of the Governor. I can tell you; this isn't true."

The meeting lasted for around 45 minutes, with the DG spending around half an hour trying to convince everyone that the troubles were mainly down to a change in clientele. On one of the few occasions I managed to speak, I pointed out that almost all prisoners involved in every incident had been at Long Lartin for many years or multiple times. I added the riots, and the problems, were down to a change of Governor, not prisoners. At that point, I knew I'd done the right thing packing my bag.

Officer Colin Clear tried to point out problems caused by the Governor turning children away on visits because of toeless footwear, but this again was ignored.

Next up was an officer called Sydney, son of an outstanding governor from years ago, a real staff man. He told how the Governor was very supportive in the seg, despite going through a difficult time. He thanked the Governor for her support of the staff. Those comments I found flabbergasting. I had worked down the seg numerous times, and I'm confident he was not speaking on behalf of the staff.

I later found out that Sydney wasn't even on the list to be at the meeting. I hope the CM position the Governor gave him a few weeks later was worth it.

The meeting ended, and I knew I was in my last minutes in Long Lartin. I returned to the Gym, collected my bag, said goodbye to the PE staff and left. On my way out, I saw a good friend Paul C; he asked if I was going training. I said no, I've just left and won't be back; he looked shocked and told me not to be too hasty.

Under Pressure

On day one, after walking out of the prison, I started to come under pressure from (CM) Grant, my line manager, and someone I had believed to be a friend.

The first thing was his phone call saying, "The governor wants to know when you'll be back at work."

I stated that I had a sick note running for another three weeks, but told him I wouldn't be coming back, so he could fill out an application form for me to apply for medical retirement.

On one of his first many visits to my home, he said the governor wanted to know if I regretted my actions. He looked surprised when I said to tell her no, I don't regret it, and I'm glad I did it, and I would do the same again.

He replied, "But I know how you love your job; you must regret it."

This was the first of many times I told him to "fuck off"!

The Prison Service, if you request medical retirement and you feel you have the grounds, are duty bound to fill out the necessary forms for your case to be heard by independent medical practitioners. They could recommend you're fit to return to work, in which case a governor like Governor C would automatically dismiss you on the grounds of medical inefficiency. This means being sacked and unable to claim any pension until retirement age.

Or, the medics recommend you're considered for medical retirement, of which there are two tiers. Tier one medical retirement is when you are deemed unwell enough not to be able to carry out any meaningful regular employment. So, you would get a higher figure in both pension and payout. But you're not allowed to carry out any paid work. Tier two means you get a lower monthly pension but can hold a paid job. Still, within the earnings you were getting before the medical retirement.

(CM) Grant informed the Governor of my intentions and rang me the following day, stating the Governor said you're not getting medical retirement, so you either return to work or she will dismiss you.

I told him, "Well, it's not her decision whether I get medical retirement; we'll let the medical experts decide."

The pressure continued daily. I received text messages from (CM) Grant with more instructions from the Governor. Eventually, he agreed to send off my paperwork and brought my sections to complete round to my home. He still said the Governor insisted that she would dismiss me and requested I attend a meeting with her in the prison. I declined. Just before leaving, he told me that he'd had to write on the report he'd submitted to the medical assessors that I had left work because of an altercation with the director. I said really, so why did you have to write that? The Governor had told him to, was his reply. I told him. "Fuck off out of my house," and added, "I never had an altercation with anyone. I never raised my voice in the meeting. I merely went and told the truth."

Weeks passed by, and the pressure continued, phone calls and a letter from the governor requesting I attend an ARM meeting with her.

"What's the point?" I asked the CM on the phone. "I've applied for medical retirement; let's await the outcome."

Again, he said the governor says she will dismiss you if you don't attend the meeting. He said, "I'll be in there with you."

I told him I didn't find that too reassuring.

My wife, who worked in admin in the prison at the time, was paid a visit at her place of work by the CM, where he told her he was advising her as my friend to attend the meeting, saying it would be for the best for me if I wanted medical retirement.

Sarah came home, and after lots of talking, she convinced me to attend. I no longer trusted my CM to have my best interest at heart; he was trying too hard to convince my wife and me. I certainly wasn't going to ask either of the pocketed two from the

POA. The only person with any fundamental POA knowledge that I knew and trusted was a man called Jerry. He was principled, and whilst we may not have always agreed about things over the years, I trusted him.

You've had cancer, get on with it

The day of the meeting arrived; I met Jerry at the gate. And (CM) Grant appeared. He informed us that he wouldn't be attending the meeting.

I asked, "Why? When you insisted that it was in my best interest."

He shrugged his shoulders and said, "The governor doesn't want me there."

I contemplated just walking out.

Jerry said, "Let's just see what she's got to say."

I reluctantly agreed, and we went to the meeting. We all sat down, and the Governor thanked me for attending. It went downhill from there. One of her first lines after saying she wanted me to return to work immediately on phased return was to say, "You're only off because you had an altercation with the DG."

I replied, "That's not the way I see it." I pointed out that I hardly got an opportunity to speak in the meeting, and if I had been disruptive, surely a DG would just request I leave the room. Again, I reiterated that it wasn't an altercation.

She said, "Well, he saw it that way." She then stated, "If you don't return to work, I will dismiss you."

Jerry rightly pointed out that I'd applied for medical retirement. I started to go through all my symptoms and reasons for applying for ill-health departure.

"You're not getting medical retirement," she declared, getting angry. And added in an annoyed tone, "You've had cancer, now get on with it."

I stood up; Jerry said we would take a few minutes out. We walked down the corridor, and Jerry said, "You're not coming back, are you? So, I'll just tell her the meeting is finished."

That was that. I did have many more phone calls and text messages with further threats passed on by the Governor. One day I had a knock at the door in the afternoon after I dropped my wife off at work; it was (CM) Grant.

He asked, "The Governor wants to know what you're doing driving if you're not fit to come to work."

Thankfully this coincided with my mother-in-law calling around; otherwise, it may have come to blows. I told him to leave and tell the Governor to do one.

On the advice of a good friend and retired SO called Steve Foxhall, I contacted a retired PO called Nick Dyer. Nick was an old-school PO, one that I knew would give me solid advice with my best interest at heart. I also knew he'd tell me if I was being an idiot or in the wrong. I met Nick and subsequently lodged a Grievance against the Governor. I will hand over to Nick to summarise the best he can how that procedure went; thankfully, to take the pressure off me and to protect my health, Nick took up all the paper trail for me, and I just attended the subsequent meetings.

Nick S Dyer, summary of grievance

As Phil indicated, I'm of a somewhat older generation. I joined the Prison Service in 1974. Over the years I have observed the crass system that has developed within the Service of promotion through cronyism, political correctness, improper 'positive' discrimination and sycophantism. This unprofessional set of trends has resulted in the decrease of excellent governors and an increase in overly ambitious, poor-quality managers.

Sadly, it came as little surprise when one of my ex-senior officers asked me to help Phil. To my amazement, even I was shocked by what I was told. So surprised in fact I offered to help unreservedly. It wasn't difficult to check Phil's story. I still had very reliable contacts within Long Lartin. Not only did I find everything he told me to be true, but I found enough evidence to file similar complaints for other staff, running into high double figures… had the POA done its job properly and other people not been too frightened for their livelihoods to complain.

I asked Phil what he wanted to achieve? Sadly, he had gone beyond any realistic wish for a return to work while Pearson was still in the prison and reluctantly wanted medical retirement.

It is a little long-winded, but it is worth examining this abridged version of Phil's allegations in order to grasp how serious they were:

That the Governor of HM Prison Long Lartin, Ms Clare Pearson, did victimise, bully and harass me, Officer Philip Currie, over a period of time extending from September 2017 to the present. By, among other acts:

- *Victimising and harassing me, by instigating an unreasonable investigation in September 2017 that, as yet, has not been concluded, in accordance with the instructions given in 'PSI Conduct & Discipline, or seen a notice of extension issued,' although I believe the investigating officers supplied with 'terms of reference' completed and submitted their findings last year.*
- *That on diverse occasions Ms Pearson has made groundless verbal allegations against me, which were conveyed by a third party*

in one instance, namely that I had intimidated her by sitting too close to her… and, that I had attempted to call a Prison Officers Association [POA] meeting in order to call for, "a vote of no confidence" in her. And, at a full staff briefing, Ms Pearson insinuated that I had bullied and intimidated her, during the course of an earlier meeting, with the Security Director.

- *Attempted to bully and intimidate me, with threats delivered by third parties, to not attend a meeting with the Security Director.*
- *That Ms Pearson did improperly threaten me with dismissal in order to stop me being medically retired [which is a documented recommendation made by doctors and a consultant] these threats were witnessed by my POA representative.*
- *That Ms Pearson has used abusive, threatening, inappropriate language to me, on diverse occasions, causing me stress so serious that it has had an extremely debilitating effect upon my already traumatised health.*
- *That Ms Pearson has completely failed in her duty of care towards me and has repeatedly, either by inconsiderate or contrived act, adversely affected my health.*

Further to the Formal Grievance submitted by me, Officer Philip Currie, on the 16th February 2018.

That the Governor of HM Prison Long Lartin, Ms Clare Pearson, my Line Manager Mr David Grant and my Manager's Manager Mr Simon Tilling have failed to properly implement the Attendance Management Policy [PSI 01/2017] and the Civil Service Management Code (CSMC) 2009, relating to me:

- *That the Governor, Ms Pearson, has taken an improper personal dislike to me – described to myself, my wife [an Administration Officer in HMP Long Lartin] on diverse occasions by my Line*

Manager and others – and has inappropriately subverted the line management chain and directly used PSI01/2017 as a tool to castigate me.

- *That on diverse occasions Ms Pearson has improperly attempted to influence decisions about my ability to drive a motor vehicle because of my medical condition. I have been informed that Ms Pearson considers I am unfit to drive.*
- *That Ms Pearson attempted to bully and intimidate me, with threats delivered by third parties, to report for duty within the prison [on gate duties] even though she knows that doctors and a specialist consultant have all stated that I can never work again and have recommended me for medical retirement.*
- *The threats were regarding dismissal, and accompanied with a further statement repeating Ms Pearson's personal dislike of me and, on another occasion, declaring that she would not recommend me for medical retirement but see me, "dismissed on reduced pay-out".*

It is quite certain that if even one of those allegations were proven, Pearson should have been reduced in rank and moved. An informal investigation conducted by Gareth Sands was biased, inappropriate and inadequate. He was junior in rank to Pearson and should not have been given the task at all.

I have no way of knowing what Sands' 'terms of reference were'; he should have stated them from the start. Clearly, he failed to interview witnesses or investigate each matter declared, and he showed an inappropriate bias in Pearson's favour. The concluding paragraphs of the response to Sands' official report about the allegations says it all:

Conclusion

During our interview, I found you to be a likeable, caring and decent man. However, I feel you were, perhaps, given a 'poison chalice' when asked to informally investigate so senior a governor as Clare Pearson. I also feel that such a task should have been dealt with by a more senior rank who would have perhaps been encouraged to conduct an in-depth and comprehensive investigation without the obvious omissions and bias.

Important witnesses have not been interviewed, prison rules have been noticeably disregarded and relevant written evidence remains unsourced.

You asked me what outcomes I wanted and I told you, during the interview, I was unsure. Having read your letter and had time to consider all that has happened I feel I must now inform you of my desired outcomes.

1. *That this matter is formally investigated taking all of the points I have made within this document into proper consideration.*
2. *Despite my disabilities, I harboured a hope to achieve successful employment for a few more years – had I enjoyed the correct management support and not been treated so improperly by Ms Pearson, which was the prime cause of my further deteriorating health – and I would ask that loss of earnings and the loss of my positive professional environment, which I miss so much, be given due consideration.*

Within a very short space of time, two things occurred. Phil was granted medical retirement at the higher level; what he wanted in other words, but of course it wasn't. What Phil really wanted was the job he loved to have continued for a few more months or maybe even a year or two. Many governors I knew in the past would have been more than content to have seen that happen. Someone like Phil Currie is an asset in any prison; a human 'safety valve' that can dispel tension where others cannot; that makes everyone that little bit safer.

So, we continued with the case and were granted an appeal hearing at head office in London. Before I summarise that protracted affair, it is worth mentioning a decision I made that haunts me to this day.

I believed I had just about enough evidence to institute Employment Tribunal proceedings against Pearson for constructive dismissal. Or in other words, Phil had been forced to resign by applying for medical retirement before he wanted to because of her improper actions. We had a mountain of evidence that, when viewed by an independent third party, would have surely proved Pearson's wrongdoing. I felt quite certain head office would have sought an out of court settlement before that much 'dirty washing' was aired in public. On the other hand, Phil had been granted what he applied for at the higher rate, which meant the highest qualified medical professionals were saying he should not be working at all then or ever.

Against my better judgement, because we could have lodged the Tribunal case and then withdrawn it with no consequences at a later date, I told Phil I thought we should stick with the internal appeal and see where that took us first. I believed we could not fail; and we didn't, but it was never the victory it should have been.

At the appeal hearing, we repeated the original grievances and embellished them with supporting statements from others. The amount of evidence was irrefutable. The deputy director, Ed Cornmell, heard us very sympathetically – an extremely personable gentleman – then he proceeded to lie through his teeth.

Cornmell asked for time above the usual ten days prescribed to deal with such matters under Service Rules. Of course, we agreed to this request; especially as Cornmell explained he wanted extra time to conduct a full investigation and consider "all" the evidence. However...

E Cornmell
Deputy Director
HM Prison Service
102 Petty France
London

27th September 2018
Copies to:
Nick S Dyer

Dear Mr Cornmell,

On the 27th June 2018, accompanied by Mr Nick Dyer, I attended an appeal hearing, chaired by you, regarding my complaints brought against the Governor of HMP Long Lartin, Clare Pearson, and the subsequent, inadequate investigation into those matters, conducted by Gareth Sands, Governor at HMP Hewell.

There are two points I wish to bring to your attention regarding the appeal. I completely understood why you requested more time above the specified ten days prescribed for delivering a response to the said appeal. And I thank you for your two letters regarding that response.

Whilst I considered it very realistic for more time to be judicious, I now believe those limits have been well and truly stretched beyond acceptable or reasonable boundaries. Surely you can understand when I say this matter should be concluded most expeditiously. Given the subject matter and accompanying on-going concerns, I would respectfully suggest that three months is far beyond realistic time limits.

The second point is, following a third application under the freedom of information act, it appears I am now in possession of the list which indisputably shows that Clare Pearson blatantly misled Gareth Sands. A fact, I feel, you should by now be fully aware of.

I consider it realistic to further submit that Ms Pearson has disregarded the core values of the civil service when it comes to honesty and integrity. Impartiality and objectivity also appear to be unheeded by her as well. Please bring a constructive and fair conclusion to this unhappy, debilitating matter.

Phil Currie.

To be clear about Phil's letter of 27th September '18, Pearson lied to Sands and he didn't bother to check the evidence. Both proving themselves to be disgraceful managers. Among the other paperwork we obtained there was a copy of an e-mail from Pearson to several people at head office.

Following that disclosure, I wrote directly to Cornmell.

Ed Cornmell Deputy Director High Security
HM Prison Service
102 Petty France 10th October 2018
London

Dear Mr Cornmell,

Last week I phoned your secretary and expressed my concerns about timescales concerning Phil Currie. Mr Currie also wrote to you on the 27th September 2018 regarding the same matter. His letter also explained that, following a third request under the Freedom of Information Act, we were about to take possession of the list, which clearly proves Clare Pearson undoubtedly misled Garth Sands. On this occasion, the application for disclosure was more than fulfilled and generated documentation that was not requested.

Among that documentation was a letter/e-mail dated 03 May 2018 10.57 from Clare Pearson to you. Had this communiqué been of a private nature, despite its contents, we may have been inclined to dismiss it. However, it was not; the letter was published to four other people. It is a contemptible document designed to deceive and that cannot go unchallenged or undeclared as possible evidence in any further proceedings.

The first paragraph glowingly describes Garth Sands' actions, which we submitted were wholly inaccurate and incomplete. Obviously, I am unaware if Mr Sands was issued with terms of reference, but being involved in such a serious matter, he should have at least checked the printed evidence and questioned all the relevant third parties that were mentioned by Mr Currie. His report shows he did neither. The time spent by Garth Sands was negligible and his report visibly shows his conclusions were inadequate and erroneous.

I am of the opinion that had it not been for the grievance that Mr Currie brought, Clare Pearson would have probably carried out the threat she had made, which was to 'sack' Mr Currie – I am persuaded she made such a threat and I do believe that threat was witnessed.

For Clare Pearson to insinuate that she enquired about Mr Currie's mental wellbeing with any degree of care is not only a deceit unworthy of her office, but then to declare an opinion that he is mentally unwell and fixated upon her shows a degree of ignorance I would not expect to find in a basic grade officer, leave alone the governing governor of a dispersal prison. Ms Pearson holds no medical qualifications to make such statements in, what is, an official document.

I started helping Mr Currie in March 2018. When he came to see me, he was nearly in tears and a shadow of the hardy individual I had come to always expect.

Despite my substantial age, a chronic heart condition and a complete lack of desire, I promised to place all my experience at his disposal. I utterly believed the sincerity he displayed and the documented evidence we were later able to amass, plus the testimony of other staff.

It was not Mr Currie's energy that was brought to focus as Ms Pearson suggests, but mine, as I'm sure you must by now realise.

There was never any intention to go before an Employment Tribunal. The reasons are obvious; Clare Pearson should know them in her position. Rather sadly, we achieved our target when Mr Currie received his medical retirement. While Mr Currie's treatment was disgraceful, it was certainly not unique and has no admissible substance for a claim of discrimination. Constructive dismissal could have been argued given the evidence that clearly shows Ms Pearson's inappropriate actions, but it would have been a churlish case to bring, after medical retirement was granted.

Compensation is reasonable under the circumstances, but it was never Mr Currie's first intention. Justice and an honourable conclusion to a long and worthwhile career have always been his goals. For Ms Pearson to insinuate that she needs protecting from such a man simply shows how naively unscrupulous, distorted and ludicrous her unevidenced comments are.

My last point is perhaps the most important.

Ms Pearson contradicts herself by implying that Mr Currie was fit for some duties within the jail; again, a pronouncement she is not qualified to make and in direct contradiction of medical experts. She never made any tangible effort to find out exactly what Phil's true health condition really was. Had she done so, to her eternal shame, she would have discovered that it was her bullying and harassment that was the final cause of him seeking medical retirement.

As I write this letter, Mr Currie has been taken into hospital again for the removal of a lump and other worrying tissue that has been identified in the same place as some of his original cancer. My concerns for this fine man's health have no doubt influenced my emotions, but I make no apologies for them.

Your protracted time boundaries do you no credit. If there has been an investigation, relevant witnesses appear to be remarkably ignorant of it. Both Mr Currie and I take pride in our long careers within HM Prison Service, a reflection that now appears to be old fashioned and somewhat disregarded. We both believe that the core Civil Service values have been wilfully ignored by Clare Pearson and we have relied upon you to provide justice and to uphold those core values…

Well, that didn't go down very well. There were a few more pages to my letter, but they are now largely irrelevant. Cornmell didn't address any of the issues raised and once more, very politely, 'lied though his teeth'!

Finally, after evermore pathetic and obvious excuses, we came to several speculative conclusions: Cornmell had a relationship with Pearson that went beyond the professional and was incapable of unbiased decision making. Or, Cornmell was having his 'strings pulled' by his superior Richard Vince who also appeared to have more than a professional interest in Pearson's career passage. Or, both Cornmell, Vince and the director general of the Prison Service, Phil Copple, are just a bunch of self-seeking, unscrupulous, dishonourable liars who do not give a damn for the very decent people who they are supposed to support and care for; you decide…

Phil Copple
Executive Director Prisons
102 Petty France
London 22nd November 2018

Dear Mr Copple,
Subject: Formal Grievance.

Please accept this paper as a formal complaint against Mr E Cornmell, Deputy Director of the High Security Estate.

On the 16th February this year I made a formal complaint/grievance, in accordance with Prison Service Rules, against Clare Pearson, the Governing Governor of HM Prison Long Lartin, where I was employed. The incident caused me to end my career prematurely, but the matter has still not been concluded.

An initial investigation took place, which was conducted by Gareth Sands, a Governor from HM Prison Hewell. His investigation was a farce and the following report no more than a placatory whitewash designed to cover up the grossly improper actions of Ms Pearson.

Following Mr Sands' abortive investigation, in accordance with Service Rules, in May this year, I appealed against his conclusions. After a delay owing to operational necessity, an appeal hearing was finally held in July 2018. The hearing was conducted by Ed Cornmell, the Deputy Director of the high security estate; it was held at head office [Petty France] and I was accompanied by Nick Dyer, a retired Principal Prison Officer.

At the hearing we produced evidence, or stated where evidence could be found and named witnesses that categorically proved Clare Pearson had lied, bullied me, abused her position as governing governor and, by so doing, brought the Prison Service and Civil Service into disrepute while repeatedly failing to uphold the Civil Service core values.

According to the rules governing such appeal hearings, Mr Cornmell should declare a decision within ten days. At the conclusion of the hearing, he asked for more time, stating there was a great deal of evidence to consider and that it would take more than ten days. Both Mr Dyer and I agreed his request was reasonable.

On the 15th August Mr Cornmell wrote to me stating, "... I am nearly able to finalise your appeal decision..." No decision was made. Following my further inquiry on the 11th September Mr Cornmell wrote, "... I will finalise your grievance appeal decision as soon as possible." And he apologised again.

Following communications from myself and Mr Dyer, on the 22nd October Mr Cornmell wrote to me again and apologised. It was a very polite and well-crafted communication as I have come to expect from such an intelligent and highly agreeable gentleman; however, it was really nothing more than excuses.

At the beginning of November, I wrote a final letter to Mr Cornmell [please find a copy attached] setting a deadline for when I would take this matter further. There are important points that must be made and should not be allowed to pass without some objective consideration.

It took me three requests under the Freedom of Information Act to access the document that categorically proved that Clare Pearson had acted improperly and told lies. Mr Cornmell could have sourced that communication in two minutes had he investigated appropriately.

Please also find attached the copies of two e-mails that shows it took Mr Cornmell an unreasonable time to question a witness, whose statement clearly proves that Clare Pearson acted improperly and perpetrated more deception.

Prison Service rules/orders have been flagrantly ignored by both Clare Pearson and Ed Cornmell. The rules are quite specific and not there to be disregarded by prison staff, some of whom appear to believe they have been promoted to a point where only lip service is necessary, or if it suits their own purpose.

Perhaps more importantly though, is the thought that the core values of the Civil Service have been entirely unheeded. To quote a famous Courts Martial summing up: "It is impossible to legislate for everything. Justice must be in the hearts of our officers or it does not exist at all."

It appears that, even given such comprehensive mandatory legislation, no justice dwells within the heart of Clare Pearson and sadly, for a clandestine agenda that one can only imagine, Ed Cornmell appears to be of a comparable persuasion.

Obviously, this case is far more complex than I have chronicled to you. At the risk of being dramatic, it does perhaps have Service wide implications. Although, it is more than enough to repeat that this matter caused a premature ending to my career, unnecessary financial loss for myself and the Prison Service, hours of heartache for my family, plus on-going concerns for Mr Dyer and his wife; she still works within Long Lartin.

Reluctantly, I have come to believe only intervention such as you are able to accomplish may result in a true and just conclusion ever emerging.

Yours sincerely,

Philip Currie, Prison Officer [PEI] retired.

Copple ignored the letter. We involved our local MP. He made the right noises and tried to expedite a conclusion from Cornmell. However, he was clearly 'got at,' the obvious clue was when he replied to something Phil or I said.

"You should know," the MP declared. "There are some people who think very highly of Governor Pearson."

Hmm, Cornmell, Vince and possibly Copple in varying degrees appear to have struck back behind the scenes.

We wrote to the then Prison's Minister; he didn't even have the decency to reply.

Finally, just in time for Christmas that year, on the 17th December we got a conclusion from Cornmell. Perhaps it was the result of pressure from the MP or maybe Copple kicked arses behind closed doors, who knows?

Six months to produce something that should be completed in ten days, but I guess maybe it takes that long to make a tin of whitewash. Because, that's what Cornmell's conclusion was, well written minimisations, disregarded facts and gross omissions. No proper inquiry was conducted, it was only ever a contrived time-wasting exercise hoping the stink would clear. And, to some extent, they were successful. Time had been wasted with some achievement. Phil was officially retired and because of that fact, the Civil Service Commission, though very sympathetic, couldn't do anything and neither could the Parliamentary System of Complaints.

Our victory, such as it was, came behind closed doors. I know what a pain in the backside we were and how many problems we caused senior managers. Good! Just a short time later, despite her seemingly influential connections, Pearson got demoted and moved; pretty sure I know how that came about. And, if you've managed to wade through this, believe it or not, brief summary, I hope you'll agree.

I want to record one more thing. There are very few men I've ever had complete respect for in my seventy-six years; I could probably count them on both hands. Phil Currie's certainly one of them. He doesn't purport to be perfect by any stretch of the imagination, then who of us are? Phil is a fine example to us all of courage, dignity, and good intent. The senior management of the Prison Service are not fit to clean his shoes. It has been, and continues to be, an absolute pleasure to help him in any way I can.

Nick S Dyer.

Out of the Blue

From nowhere, I was contacted by two female governors that said they had been asked to come and speak with me about how I'd been treated. I wondered if this was connected with the grievance I'd lodged against Pearson. They told me it was after a complaint from a prisoner from Long Lartin. He had told inspectors and visitors to the prison that someone needed to speak to me and that how I'd been treated was a disgrace.

I was surprised when hearing the prisoner's name; while he had been on the PE course, and I knew him and got on with him, I was still surprised he had taken the time to do such a thing. They had their own problems, just trying to stay clear of all the troubles in prison. I went through everything with them, thinking I had nothing to lose. They worked alongside Ed Cornmell in some capacity but I knew nothing more about them. After the meeting, I never heard from them, so I didn't find any results from their enquiry.

Medical retirement and the outcome

My wife and I received a date for my interview to assess whether I would be considered for medical retirement. Many people got really nervous about seeing the medical board; I've advised many people since not to be scared. They are medical professionals. You only have to fear if you're going to try pulling the wool over their eyes. If it's genuine and you're going to tell the truth, you have nothing to dread.

It was with that attitude I attended the meeting; I knew if their decision wasn't to recommend me, then the governor would have her day in the sunshine and get to dismiss me.

My wife and I attended the meeting. They already knew of all my medical history; I just told them about my recovery. The nurse congratulated me on returning to work and said it was remarkable that I had managed to work for five years in my job, what with the latent effects of chemotherapy and radiotherapy.

I hadn't really given it too much thought, but I think it had been a combination of just striving to get my life back to normal after the long battle with cancer and the recovery process from the harsh treatment. More importantly, it was to get back to doing a job that I loved with passion and still do. I could talk all day about the benefits of PE and the success stories, many of which I only became aware of after retirement.

A couple of weeks later, I received a letter with my reply. I had been recommended for medical retirement. My paperwork would now be submitted to the pensions group to assess whether it would be tier one or two. The pressure lifted, and Pearson knew she wouldn't get that day in the sun from this point.

The CM rang me, having received his copy of the letter he'd told the governor, who apparently was fuming; despite her attempts to sway the decision of the medical professionals, they had made their decision on medical grounds only. After the pensions contacted my consultant for clarification on a few details, I was awarded my pension at the highest tier. It meant I was unable to carry out any paid work. But more importantly, it freed me up to do some charity work I'd started for HANCUK. I began to do some mentoring work at Birmingham QE Hospital, helping others through the treatment process. If you go onto the HANCUK website, you will see my journey and others.

One last meeting

All the paperwork was back, and the governor, as a formality, now had to invite me back for an exit interview where she asked me if I accepted the offer of medical retirement. I was out walking my dog – I'd got it after receiving confirmation – when I received a call from the CM. He said the governor wants you to come in today to go through the paperwork and do your exit interview. I told him I was busy. He continued to press, saying she wanted to do it today.

Ultimately, I lost patience with him and said, "You might drop everything at the drop of a hat for her and run round for her, but I don't!" I told him to run back and tell her I'm not coming in today.

He rang back later, and we arranged for me to go in a couple of days afterwards.

I attended the meeting, and it was surreal. My wife asked me to go quietly and not make a scene. So, I promised her I wouldn't argue at the meeting or tell the Governor what I thought of her, which was my first inclination.

The Governor greeted me, asking in an almost friendly tone if she could get me a drink. She asked what my plans were in retirement and asked me about my dog. She then said, "You're obviously aware that you've been offered medical retirement, and I presume you're accepting it. So, I just need a signature."

After the signing ceremony, I got up to leave.

She said, "Oh and Phil, regarding your grievance, it's probably best for you and your health if you just leave it now and concentrate on enjoying retirement."

I smiled and replied, "That's not why I'm here today, but just to let you know, I will continue my grievance."

I smiled again and left with her face looking very similar to how it looked at the end of that first meeting I had had with her.

Many people, including my wife, didn't understand my insistence on carrying on my grievance beyond retirement. The way I looked at it was if I could prevent her from being able to destroy another prison and cause heartache to both staff, prisoners and families, I wasn't going to turn the opportunity down, at least in the same way I had in that meeting with the DG. I can hold my head up and say I did everything I could.

Broken jaw

I heard from colleagues at work that there had been yet another incident at Long Lartin. After I left, they continued at an alarming rate. So, it was no surprise when someone said there'd been another. However, this time I was told that a prisoner, David McKenzie, had attacked the governor whilst she was walking around the wing with the DG. McKenzie had punched the governor resulting in a broken jaw.

Even after all she had done, hearing the news brought me no pleasure. I will say it's extremely difficult to ignore the similarities between the governor's insistence on bringing China Walters back onto D-wing and ignoring the prisoner's words, 'Do they want someone to get killed?'. Richard Vince walked around with the Governor despite the numerous riots, 'the writing on the wall', and my attempt at telling him the real cause of the problems in Long Lartin.

Richard Vince may as well have landed that punch himself. His blind faith and the blinkered backing of a governor that had clearly been promoted way beyond her capability were quite frankly absurd. Scrutiny of her track record would tell you she should never have become the governor of Long Lartin. Only Richard Vince could answer questions like why.

Pearson was finally moved out of Long Lartin just after I was given the outcome of my Grievance by Ed Cornmell. She went on to have a negative influence on two more prisons afterwards. HMP Hewell and HMP Dovegate, where she was allegedly dismissed for bullying!

In a subsequent court hearing, David McKenzie was given ten years added to his sentence. My reaction had been an attempt to turn 'whistleblower'. I wonder if that court case delved deep enough to discover the answers to what resulted in such frustration that it manifested into violence.

We were taught very early on on our PE course, Newton's third law:

Newton's third law

'For every action, there is an equal and opposite reaction.'

I genuinely believe every prison officer should be taught to understand that law at college and every child in school from an early age.

For us as PEIs, it was to develop our coaching of gymnastics. But it applies to everything in life. From a simple argument in a school classroom to a knife crime. From insisting on putting China Walters back on the wing to almost losing the whole wing. From pots and pans confiscated to a full-scale riot. From the DG refusing to listen to staff to a broken jaw.

THE HARD MEN

Wherever I go, people always ask who were the most brutal men I have ever encountered. Again I could write a book just on this subject alone. The men I name here aren't an exhaustive list. There are many I know of but didn't meet, so I haven't included them. It is just the men I met in prison. I'll start in the South and work my way up the country.

The South

As I stated, the first man that comes to mind is Bill The Bomb, sometimes called Jango. I cannot look beyond him as the most fearsome man I have ever met.

Tony Argent, a man who reminded me of Bill The Bomb and was like a younger version when I met him, I got on really well with Tony; to use his own phrase, he was "staunch". Tony didn't care how big they were or about their reputation. What I liked about Tony was that despite being up there with the toughest men I had ever met, he never abused it, he wasn't a bully, and if anything, he would go and bully the bullies.

Two older men from rival gangs, the Krays and the Richardsons, deserve a mention: Eddie Richardson and Charlie Kray. You could also add Pat Purcell and Billy Tobin to these two. Four old-school criminals. Despite getting older as I met them, they still had that aura, and others feared and highly respected them.

Gary Nelson (Tyson). Gary never really did weights but was naturally strong. I've heard numerous stories about one of the all-time great prison fights between Gary and another Hard Man named Kev Lane. It was billed as King of the Blacks (Gary) against King of the Whites (Kev) (Lights Out Lane). The majority I have spoken to claim Gary was the winner, and a few claim that Kev was. What they all agreed on was it was an epic scrap. Kev was quick and could bang, and allegedly hit Gay first with a flurry of punches that Gary dusted off; most people would be gone, but Gary was a tough street fighter and, by all accounts, came back to get the better of Kev on the day.

One fight I witnessed the end of was Gary against a prisoner from Leicester and the toughest I'd come across from that area, Warren Slaney. The alarm bell had gone, and I responded, running to the wing. As I arrived on the wing, Gary was being held by staff, as was Warren. Gary was calmly talking towards Warren, saying, "You're a silly boy, Warren." Honestly, it didn't look like Gary had been in a fight; on the other hand, Warren looked shaken, like he had been in a car accident. It appeared Gary had bitten Warren. As I say, Gary is a streetfighter. That's not to say he can't do both. Warren would be among the most fearsome men behind bars, but this wasn't his day.

Charlie Bronson, who I've written about, would also have to come into the conversation. Charlie took some controlling once he lost his temper, especially in his younger years. The only thing questioned of Charlie was how he would have fared on normal location amongst many hard men.

Vic Dark, who I knew from Parkhurst and Long Lartin, would undoubtedly be at the top table of the Hardest Men I have ever met. He could box and had a martial arts background to go with it. Vic was also superfit and strong. He would definitely be a force to be reckoned with.

Roger Vincent, Roger was a terrific lad and completed a lot of Gym Courses with us, but you could just sense that he had that about him. You could see many of the other big hitters tread carefully around him. Similarly to Gary, I really got on with him, but you'd be a fool to underestimate him.

Lea Rusha. Lea was a kick boxer, extremely powerful and fit. Lea was our Gym orderly, and I witnessed him put it on numerous prisoners there. One was quite a notorious Muslim prisoner who could allegedly have a right row; he backed down from Lea, though.

Carl Burgess from Northampton is a professional rugby player and a man mountain of a man. Carl was built like a modern-day heavyweight champion. He was battle-hardened from his years playing rugby. A really polite, down-to-earth guy, but nobody would ever take Carl lightly.

Kenny Noye, Kenny had a bit of a fearsome record and, like his alleged associate Micky McAvoy, could have a real go.

John Onyemaechi, John was a huge imposing figure who didn't like the staff; he made a small exception for Gym Staff, although he was often still quite surly. After moving on from Long Lartin to Full Sutton, he went on a one-man rampage, attacking staff before setting fires and smashing the wing up. It took more than 100 C&R Staff to bring the incident to a close hours later.

King Of The Jungle

Yammy (Samson) was often called The King Of The Jungle. I knew Yammy very well from him attending the gym; him being a fellow Leeds fan, we often spoke about football and our beloved team.

We talked about both past and present teams. Yammy, pound for pound, was one of the strongest prisoners I'd met. What made it more astonishing was he often displayed these acts of strength whilst still doing drugs. On the wings, Yammy would switch sides working for anyone, which meant there would be a payday in the form of a package at the end of it. He always seemed to come up smelling of roses, even when the odds seemed severely against him. Astonishingly, Yammy, who had performed many hits for people in jail, managed to come through over 35 years in prison, living that life relatively unscathed, physically. I had watched many prisoners try to live that life over the years, and they all came to a sticky end, either murdered, seriously burned or maimed for life. I watched Yammy live that life for many years at Long Lartin. I recently met up with Yammy, a free man who is turning his life around. I appeared on his YouTube channel Yammy B TV.

Gloucestershire and Bristol

From this area, the standout characters and hard men are PJ McGuire, he was not only one of the strongest prisoners I have ever met, but he could really handle himself; I've known on several occasions that it took more than two C&R teams to move him. Jermaine Robotham from Gloucester would be a close second. From Bristol, it would have to be a lad called Luke Clayfield, a fiery character with a boxing background; Luke often knocked other prisoners out with one punch, and one time, he sparked out a big lad off the wing called Rodney Joseph, When Rodney came back to confront Luke, claiming he had caught him off-guard, Luke asked if he was ready now, and repeated his earlier punch with the same outcome.

Wales

This would have to be a lad called Luxy, who didn't fear anyone even if they were twice his size, and another lad called Tufty, who was getting on but still had the respect of all the Welsh lads.

Ireland

Tommy Mullen would have to be the pick, not the biggest, but he had an outstanding boxing record. At Long Lartin, he knocked out numerous prisoners up to three times his size and weight.

Nottingham

(Danger) Ezra Taylor, I already wrote about Ezra, also sometimes referred to as Danger. I witnessed Ezra that day on the CCTV footage in court, and it's not a pretty sight. Colin Gunn is one of the biggest names out of Nottingham; I always got on with Colin. I found him amiable, but he was feared just as much as the men mentioned above. Johno from Lincoln was also a prominent figure in Long Lartin, again a pleasant lad down the Gym who joined in Charity events. Still, he was a force to be reckoned with.

Birmingham

Birmingham was somewhat different from other regions; in recent years, it has become much more gang-related with the post-code wars, with numerous notorious gangs such as the Johnson Crew,

Burger Bar Boys, Frankley Killers,23 Drillas, The 61s and B515s, to name just a few. At Long Lartin, we had Gang members from most of these groups.

Liverpool

Over the years, I've met many hard men from Liverpool; one of the first I met was Tony Hennigan, who was shot after being released. Tony wasn't the biggest, but he didn't fear anyone. Then over the years, to name a few, there was Barry Williams, The Fitzgibbon brothers Jason and Ian, Joe Joe Collins, Curtis Warren, and the toughest I came across, Sam Cole. Sam was an excellent all-round sportsman and a commanding centre-half on the football pitch.

Manchester

Like Liverpool over the years at Long Lartin, we had many big hitters from Manchester, including Gary Shearer, The Noonans, Paul Massey, (Greggo) Jason Gregson, Franny Dixon, Ginge from Salford and many more. He is not as infamous to many, but from what I saw in prison and during his time at Long Lartin, John Gray was at the head of the Manchester firm and had the respect of all prisoners, not just those from Manchester.

Lancashire

Two men stand out from Lancashire, John Barber from Bolton, who was our Gym Orderly for a considerable period. John was a likeable character with a great sense of humour, but underneath it was a hard centre, and nobody crossed him. The second was Thomo, who had a real reputation for being able to "Bang". I witnessed one occasion down the Gym where Thomo displayed why he had this reputation despite being a hilarious guy. Thomo was down in the Gym with all the usual big characters; Thomo approached me and said, "Fancy a bum, Phil" – Thomo later explained it was a catchphrase from a TV show called Balls of Steel. We had a laugh then he proceeded to go and say it to other prisoners in the Gym; one of these included our Gym, Orderly Norman Shelbourne, around 5ft 9 and very stocky, who we nicknamed 20. The nickname came from whenever we asked him how many reps he was doing; it was always 20! Thomo said the catchphrase to 20 and moved on laughing. 20 hadn't seen the funny side of it, though, and thought they were all laughing at him. At the end of the session, as I cleared people out of the weights room into the sports hall, Thomo was walking around with a few others chatting. 20 saw his opportunity and approached Thomo from behind, delivering a punch to the side of his head from behind; Thomo didn't flinch, and after turning round, he delivered his reply, a thunderous punch of his own that ended with 20 asleep against the sports hall wall. I went in and spoke to Thomo; to be fair to him left it there, and Norman (20) wasn't interested in taking it further. I explained to Norman that it was off a TV show, not personal. Norman wasn't the sharpest of tools in the box, though.

Yorkshire

Two men spring to mind: Paul Sykes from Wakefield and Frank Burley from Leeds; Paul was from a boxing background and was a British Heavyweight Boxer; he was a fearsome character and similar to Bill the Bomb in that he liked a drink even in prison. Paul was regarded as a bully by many, but he was undoubtedly a feared character in jail. Frank wasn't as imposing physically but was feared among many in prison. Frank didn't get on with too many staff; however, I struck up a friendship with him over the years. I was saddened to hear of his death after his release; Frank was shot, and there's still a lot of mystery surrounding his death.

North East

Going back to the nineties at Long Lartin, the prominent figures from the North East were two associates called Bud Armstrong and Paul Ashton (Ashi). Ashi was a huge character and was a member of our powerlifting squad. Joe Hunt was another from the North East, a big hitter from that area.

Shane Taylor from Middlesbrough would be up there with the toughest I came across. Shane was fearless, and I saw him successfully challenge and beat much bigger men than himself. Brothers John and Stephen Sayers were the others I met at Long Lartin. They had a fearsome record both in and out of jail. Gary Vinter would also rank as someone feared by many and someone both prisoners and staff would be wary of. I know of many others, but they are not prisoners I came across.

The Bosses

I've met several bosses in jail, prisoners that run the wings they are on and sometimes the prison as a whole. One thing that most of these men had in common was they had big personalities and real characters, often getting along with staff. The first I met, as mentioned earlier in the book, was the Arif Family; Dennis, Dogon and Mehmet Arif filled the void on the streets of London left by the Krays and the Richardsons when they went to prison on long sentences. The Arifs arrived doing their own sentences and filled the void in the prison left by the Krays. History was to repeat in Parkhurst as the Krays were moved on; the Arif family took over the running of the wing and the jail.

Over the years, I met too many to mention that either ran the wing or the prison. Still, they all displayed similar personality traits to the Arif family. They would be charismatic with a good sense of humour; all the old-school figures I met also had that old moral code. Sometimes when one or two of these figures moved on, it could disrupt the wing or the whole prison, leaving behind a power struggle.

Return of the beast

I had enjoyed almost ten years of being cancer-free. If, when I was diagnosed back in 2012, someone told me to sign on the dotted line to be guaranteed ten years and then die peacefully, I'd have snapped their hands off. This was my primary focus: to live long enough for Dolly and my grandson Morgan to have a memory of me. I was now four years into retirement and enjoying walking my dog, Freddy, the labradoodle.

Exploring retirement with my Boy Freddy.

Jamaica, Runaway Bay.

We had a lovely family holiday in Jamaica. I trained five days a week, apart from Covid times when the gyms were closed.

I discovered the love of walking and exploring new places with Freddy, often walking more than ten miles at a time. I'd started to feel a strange pain at the top of my back and a tightening around my chest that sometimes would make walking a struggle. My wife eventually convinced me to ring 111. The result of this call was me being blue-lighted into the hospital; it came as a total shock; to be honest, I felt like I was wasting their time.

On arrival at the hospital, the specialist initially seemed convinced by my symptoms that I was having an aorta aneurysm. You can imagine my concern; I thought I must be the unluckiest bloke going, to battle cancer, only to die of an aneurysm when I didn't drink or smoke. After further checks and scans, I discovered I didn't have an aneurysm, but I did have several nodules on my lungs and rib.

After several failed biopsies and numerous scans, I was told that my cancer had either returned or I had a new cancer. They couldn't be sure which.

I was eventually diagnosed with stage four incurable cancer. I always believed it would come back at some point, but I never expected to be hit with stage four out of the blue. I now had to decide whether I would have treatment, meaning chemotherapy again – the same chemotherapy as last time, Cisplatin.

I always said I didn't think I could go through it all again, especially with no guarantee of it working. I was, and still am, very reluctant.

The decision was tough for my wife and family to understand at first. However, they're now on board. I've managed to go over two years without treatment and still make it to the gym most days.

In all honesty, I just can't bear to give up the quality of life I currently have for being sick in my bed and my loved ones watching me suffer. Treatment, at best, would only buy me an extra few months, and that would be in my bed.

I always said I would train till I drop, and if there is any justice, I will pass away while doing a chin-up; even better, if I've just finished one – I hate to fail a rep.

Charity event

Martin Beal (Bealey) and I

From work, my good friend Bealey organised a charity event for me, doing a triathlon in the prison outside gym. The response was amazing; so many of my distant and recent colleagues joined in on occasion. I can't possibly finish my book with a sad story, though.

My daughter Emma came up and did the event, and I managed to do a few miles myself. The target was to clock up enough distance over two days to travel to Cyprus, where Stomps and I got married and was a regular holiday spot for us. The miles were clocked up on running machines, rowers and bikes. HMP Hewell clocked up their miles too. We achieved the target over the two days.

Dave Williams is a good friend and colleague who organises a charity event every year for some great causes, many of which I had the pleasure of being involved with in the past. Those included cycling from London or Wales back to Evesham, where he would also organise a fundraising auction. This year I was one of the charities he raised money for. I'd like to pay a special thanks to him, not just from me but all the people Dave's helped over the years.

Proudest moment of my working life

We were invited into the prison and presented with a cheque from Martin (Bealey). Which we would use to have a nice family break, building some memories. Bealey made a lovely speech, and we were both struggling to hold it together. Bealey suddenly invited us to the classroom, making some excuses about being easier to hear. I never thought anything of it because I know the acoustics in the sports hall aren't the best.

I felt my legs wobble when we got to the classroom. Bealey unveiled a plaque outside the classroom (the magic room), renaming it 'THE PHIL CURRIE EDUCATION SUITE'.

It was the biggest honour I could ever imagine, and those who know me know how much that meant to me. I could again talk for hours about the magic room and the fond memories of teaching there. It was the foundation of many success stories I've written about. It was the proudest moment of my working life, and I will never be able to describe how proud I am.

A very proud day.

Copy of the plaque outside the magic room.

My Daughter Emma and Myself.

My Wife Sarah and I with my treasured Marching On For Phil Shirt.

Group photo after the hard work was complete.

The Mad Man

I couldn't finish the book without writing a couple of stories about the Mad Man, Brian Davis. Despite my constant wind-ups against him, I love the bloke to bits; he's got a heart of gold, and we've shared some great memories. If I live long enough, I might write a second book of similar stories.

It had become a bit of a custom to give the Mad Man his medication regularly. God knows how we conned him into taking it, but we did, and he did.

It started off with giving him a teaspoon of chilli sauce. As he got more accustomed to it, we found a stronger variety.

Eventually, we got some Dragon's Blood given to us that was three years out of date. I challenged him to take three tablespoons of it. After much deliberation, he agreed. Brian managed it, and to be honest, it didn't seem to affect him at all. Around half an hour later, he came running around the back saying, "you better get an ambulance".

He was in obvious pain, his forehead dripping with sweat. Brian looked like he'd been under a sunbed for three hours. I asked what was wrong with him; his stomach was cramping.

He replied, "Seriously, Phil, I'm in trouble."

I know it's not funny. Ok, I lie. I couldn't stop laughing. I then remembered I had a couple of Müller Rice Yoghurts in our fridge. I gave him one and said get this down, you; thankfully, he slowly recovered afterwards. Imagine having to explain calling an ambulance into the prison for him for that.

Great Balls of Fire

Two nights later, whilst on our tea break. I got the bottle of Dragon's Blood out and called out, "Medication time, Mad Man."

"Nhoooo, Phil, I'm not doing that again."

"No, don't be silly," I said. "I don't mean swallow it; I wouldn't do that to you again." I smiled. "We'll just put some on your bell end."

"No chance!" Brian replied.

With a bit of team pressure, you could see he'd started to warm to the idea; no pun intended.

"Ok then, but only a bit." Mad! He'd literally do anything for a dare.

I said, "It can't be as bad as swallowing three tablespoons of it."

We entered the kitchen, and he dropped his tracksuit bottoms and Y-fronts! I poured half a spoonful onto his helmet; he pulled away and said that's enough, I said you might as well finish the spoon off now; with that, he sighed. I got a prison tablespoon and filled it with Dragon's Blood.

Brian mumbled, "For fuck's sake."

I quickly rubbed it all over his 'japs eye' before he could pull away or change his mind. He stepped away and pulled up his tracksuit bottoms.

Just before Brian left the main gym to do his ED in the Hatton suite, the other smaller gym where Vinter used to train, it started to kick in. He ran to the toilet and had his little fella under the cold-water tap.

He said, "This is worse than drinking it! My knob's on fire!"

Brian and Munch left for the Hatton Suite.

After just getting the class in, our phone went, and it was Munch telling us Brian was in agony. I heard him in the background saying, "I might as well have just put it in the fucking fire."

I was crying with laughter; Munch said he'd shown it to him, and it looked like it was on fire. There was never a dull moment when the Mad Man was around.

As I finish this book I continue to kick the can down the road and make the most of every day. My three older children are all doing well and are very happy, with my two older daughters both working in a school setting and my older son Jack has secured several promotions at his place of work. Henry is waiting to go off to university and Dolly is 11 going on 21 and suffers no fools! My grandson Morgan is a budding YouTube star. All of them make me extremely proud. So that really is the end. However, I will leave you all with this prayer from my good friend, who I dearly miss.

WJKK WJKF my dear friends and family, I pray to the Almighty Lord that this message finds you and your loved ones in peace and happiness. I pray he keeps you all in good health and gives you everything you ask for. I pray that if you are going through a bad time, he gives you the strength to get through anything. I finally pray he keeps the ones we have lost peacefully in heaven until we meet again, have a wonderful day, God bless Rabh Rakha.

My friend, Jay Shoker.

Printed in Great Britain
by Amazon